Matej Santi, Elias Berner (eds.)
Music – Media – History

WITHDRAWN
UTSA LIBRARIES

Matej Santi studied violin and musicology. He obtained his PhD at the University for Music and Performing Arts in Vienna, focusing on central European history and cultural studies. Since 2017, he has been part of the "Telling Sounds Project" as a postdoctoral researcher, investigating the use of music and discourses about music in the media.
Elias Berner studied musicology at the University of Vienna and has been researcher (pre-doc) for the "Telling Sounds Project" since 2017. For his PhD project, he investigates identity constructions of perpetrators, victims and bystanders through music in films about National Socialism and the Shoah.

Matej Santi, Elias Berner (eds.)

Music – Media – History

Re-Thinking Musicology in an Age of Digital Media

[transcript]

The authors acknowledge the financial support by the Open Access Fund of the mdw – University of Music and Performing Arts Vienna for the digital book publication.

Bibliographic information published by the Deutsche Nationalbibliothek
The Deutsche Nationalbibliothek lists this publication in the Deutsche Nationalbibliografie; detailed bibliographic data are available in the Internet at http://dnb.d-nb.de

© 2021 transcript Verlag, Bielefeld

Cover layout: Maria Arndt, Bielefeld
Cover illustration: Astrid Sodomka
Proofread by Anthony Kroytor
Translated by Gavin Bruce (Hanns-Werner Heister's text)

Print-ISBN 978-3-8376-5145-4
PDF-ISBN 978-3-8394-5145-8
https://doi.org/10.14361/9783839451458

Contents

Editor's Note 7

An Introduction 9

"Living in a Material World," Contemplating the Immaterial One—Musings on What Sounds Can Actually Tell Us, or Not
Emile Wennekes (Utrecht University) 15

The (Re)Construction of Communicative Pasts in the Digital Age
Changes, Challenges, and Chances in Digital Transformation
Christian Schwarzenegger (University of Augsburg) 31

The Narratological Architecture of Musical *lieux de mémoire*
A Transmedial Perspective on Antonio Stradivari
Matej Santi (University of Music and Performing Arts Vienna) 51

Beethoven in 1970, Bernstein and the ORF: Cultural Memory and the Audiovisual
Cornelia Szabó-Knotik (University of Music and Performing Arts Vienna) 81

Women's Voices in Radio
Julia Jaklin (University of Music and Performing Arts Vienna) 107

'Real Sound,' Readymade, Handmade: Musical Material and the Medium Between Mechanization, Automation, and Digitalization as an Impression and Expression of Reality
An Implicit Call for Real Interdisciplinarity
Hanns-Werner Heister 119

Sonic Icons in *A Song Is Born* (1948): A Model for an Audio History of Film
Winfried Pauleit *(University of Bremen)* 151

The Production, Reception and Cultural Transfer of Operetta on Early Sound Film
Derek B. Scott *(University of Leeds)*.. 169

The Address of the Ear: Music and History in *Waltz with Bashir*
Rasmus Greiner *(University of Bremen)* 183

"I've never understood the passion for Schubert's sentimental Viennese shit"—Using Metadata to Capture the Contexts of Film Music
Elias Berner *(University of Music and Performing Arts Vienna)*........................197

Connecting Research: The Interdisciplinary Potential of Digital Analysis in the Context of A. Kluge's Televisual Corpus
Birgit Haberpeuntner and Klaus Illmayer *(University of Vienna and Austrian Academy of Science)* 217

Modelling in Digital Humanities: An Introduction to Methods and Practices of Knowledge Representation
Franziska Diehr *(Prussian Cultural Heritage Foundation)*........................... 241

Playing with a Web of Music: Connecting and Enriching Online Music Repositories
David M. Weigl and Werner Goebl *(University of Music and Performing Arts Vienna)* .. 263

A Few Notes on the Auditive Layer of the Film ★
Johann Lurf *(Artist and filmmaker)* 283

Afterword
John Corner *(University of Leeds)*... 287

List of Contributors 293

Editor's Note

This volume of *Music—Media—History* deals with a number of topics relating to digital humanities, more specifically to musicology, collecting contributions by a group of international experts from a variety of fields. Most of the chapters in this book were originally discussed at an interdisciplinary conference held at the University of Music and Performing Arts Vienna in early 2019 and organized by the *Telling Sounds* research project (www.mdw.ac.at/imi/tellingsounds), which was planned and financed as an enrichment of the university's infrastructure.

Using digitally available audiovisual material stored in various archives and collections and enriching their metadata by means of historical expertise and research, this project's main objective is to understand historicity as a socially and politically significant phenomenon in our society, a society in which it has become a part of everyday life to have immediate access to all manner of information as well as music and music repertoires of the most diverse origins and initial modes of distribution.

This research is ongoing; the present volume documents an important step in its development as well as representing the growing international academic community involved.

We want to thank all the individuals and institutions who have made this book possible in spite of the unforeseeable difficulties caused by the pandemic in Spring 2020 (in alphabetical order): Gavin Bruce (translation of Hanns-Werner Heister's text), Julia Jaklin (text formatting), Anthony Kroytor (proofreading), Astrid Sodomka (cover design) and Cornelia Szabó-Knotik (head of the *Telling Sounds* research project); the mdw and the Ministry of Science for their financial support and the publisher for their valuable cooperation.

Matej Santi and Elias Berner
(Editors)

An Introduction

to the subject

The thematic question common to all the articles in this volume is: How could audiovisual sources (radio broadcasts, newsreels, film, amateur recordings), now digitized and available on the internet, be evaluated and made into fruitful research opportunities?

Examined closely, each concept of the tripartite structure music–media–history is related to—and depends on—the others. Broadly speaking, media exert a significant influence on the storage and transmission of information and, consequently, on what is remembered and what is forgotten. Thus, history takes place through the interpretation of stored information, its communication by media, and its dissemination by means of media transmission. The same holds true for the history of music.

By taking a closer look at what falls under the umbrella term 'music history'—at least as reflected by those publications from the first decades of the 21st century which take an overview approach[1]—it becomes apparent that 'written music,' or music codified in signs on a physical carrier, is the primary object of study. Popular music or the musical practices of other cultures are relegated to the edge of this Eurocentric history of music. This is in part due to the problematic relation to the concept of 'musical work.'

At the beginning of its career as an academic discipline, historical musicology focused on finding out, analyzing and evaluating sources—such as

---

1   Cf. e.g. Heinemann, Michael. *Kleine Geschichte der Musik*. Stuttgart: Reclam 2004; Keil, Werner. *Musikgeschichte im Überblick*. München: Fink, 2012; Taruskin, Richard, and Christopher Howard Gibbs. *The Oxford History of Western Music: College Edition*. New York, Oxford: Oxford Univ. Press, 2013. An attempt to counteract this trend appeared in 2018: Strohm, Reinhard. *Studies on a Global History of Music: A Balzan Musicology Project*. New York: Routledge, 2018.

music manuscripts and biographic entries. Needless to say, this type of study could only be approached by attributing a privileged status to 'written' music—i.e. medialized information codified by a sign system and recorded on a physical carrier such as stone, parchment, and later paper. This is due to the fact that the technology of sound recording and reproduction, which is today ubiquitous, was in its first phases of development. The first fully functional phonograph was built in 1877 by Thomas Alva Edison, a few years before Guido Adler, Friedrich Chrysander and Philipp Spitta edited the first issue of the *Vierteljahrsschrift für Musikwissenschaft* ("Quarterly Journal of Musicology") in 1885.[2]

However, it is not only popular music or music from other cultures which function beyond the concept of 'work of art,' coded and mediatized by writing. It is needless to point out that this is the case for music from antiquity and from the Middle ages, passed down to us written on different media. Although the 'invention' of music printing in the early modern period enabled a previously unheard-of distribution of sheet music, which foreshadowed a standardization of performance practices, printed sources from the 19th century testify to a practice rich in ornamentation and improvisation over the written (and printed) musical score. But such sources are scarce, and performance practice is—if at all—ambiguously codified. There is additionally the fact that medialized information exerted influence on the development of music theory throughout the centuries, e.g. the medieval speculative doctrines on music and music theory would be unthinkable without the presence of texts from antiquity. And the history of opera wouldn't be the same without the (mis)interpretation of texts passed down from antiquity—the 'rebirth' of the antique drama is a *topos* that has accompanied every opera reform.

---

2   The potential of the new technology had been widely recognized: in 1899 the Phonogrammarchiv was founded in Vienna, and at the 3rd Congress of the International Musical Society in 1909 (Haydn's centenary celebration), organized by Guido Adler, the phonograph was considered an important instrument in the context of the work presented in Section II, Exotische Musik und Folklore (Exotic Music and Folklore). "The History of the Phonogrammarchiv." *Österreichische Akademie der Wissenschaften—Austrian Academy of Sciences*. https://www.oeaw.ac.at/en/phonogrammarchiv/phonogrammarchiv/history-of-the-pha/; *III. Kongreß der Internationalen Musikgesellschaft. Wien, 25. bis 29. Mai 1909. Bericht vorgelegt vom Wiener Kongreßausschuß*. Wien: Artaria and Co. / Leipzig: Breitkopf and Haertel, 1909. Cf. 9–10. https://archive.org/details/haydnzentenarfei00inte/page/8/mode/2up (last accessed 16 April 2020)

Not only did the invention of music printing in Venice and Paris and the resulting new 'medial environment' affect the concept and the practices of music and its historiography. The popularization of knowledge that happened at the turn of the 19th century—paired with the role of music in bourgeoise society—influenced both the musical practices of the time as well as writing on the subject of music. It is striking that in the majority of the overview publications, nearly half of a given work is dedicated to the history of the music after 1800. Research in Anno—Austrian Papers Online, reveals that the keywords 'Musik' ("music") and 'Zeitschrift' ("paper") yield 5353 publications between 1789 and 1833. In the time period, between 1838 to 1879, the total number rises to 40.435.[3] With all due caution, as the digitization of journals certainly does not reflect the total number of printed sources, it is obvious that the number of printed music-related magazines had increased exponentially. This general interest in music which characterized the 'long' 19th century, paired with the economic opportunity of (music) printing, had a deep and longstanding influence on music in Europe and beyond—music moved into the bourgeois public space.

At this point, an essential question arises: from the background of the briefly outlined development of different kinds of media—such as music writing, music printing, and journalism—and based on the understanding of music and on the imagination of its history, how could we deal with music and its history in the age of digital media?

First of all, digitization is a transversal phenomenon that may challenge established social structures and hierarchies. It concerns both storage and knowledge production. Manuscripts, old printed material, and many publications such as books, journals, and audiovisual sources are no longer only available in 'physical' archives: they can be accessed around the globe with the click of mouse. However, this shouldn't be unreflectively greeted as a democratization of information. The 'physical' archive has not dissolved in the cloud: (very material) servers consume resources. There is of course an additional problem that data could—in the best case—no longer be deciphered or, in the worst-case scenario, even be lost due to lack of maintenance. And all of this quite apart from the serious question of the formation of oligopolies which gain control over the flow of information.

---

3   "Musik, Zeitschrift." *Anno. Österreichische Nationalbibliothek—Austrian National Library*. http://anno.onb.ac.at/anno-suche#searchMode=simple&query=musik+zeitschrift (last accessed 16 April 2020)

On the positive side, digitalization stimulates confrontation with knowledge and its production. This is also the case regarding audiovisual archives. Historically relevant material that was long difficult to obtain for researchers is now available to the general public. In Austria the Österreichische Mediathek, the Phonogrammarchiv der Österreichischen Akademie der Wissenschaften, in England the British Pathé, in Italy the Archivio Luce—to only mention some collections referred to in the present publication and relevant to the topic—have digitized considerable parts of their historic collection and made them accessible on their websites. Some of them even took a further step and made their material available on the popular video portal YouTube.

Due to these circumstances, musicology, history, and of course other social sciences could tap into new kinds of sources. Music plays an essential role in film, newsreels, radio broadcasts, and amateur (video) recordings, to cite just a few examples. This material is a testament to a century of history. Considering the omnipresence of radio, the reception of film and newsreels in the cinemas around the globe, and of the television in the second half of the 20th century, it becomes apparent that audiovisual sources deserve more attention: the power of images paired with sound on the design of living world(s) can't be overestimated.

Now, over 140 years after Edison's invention of the phonograph, the sounds that one is confronted with are mostly mediatized. In this new sonic environment, music can no longer be exclusively interpreted as a 'work of art' or marked as incidental music. Music and sounds rather assume more the role of a meaning-carrier in the kaleidoscopic realm of medialized communication.

to this volume

Against that background, the *Music–Media–History* collection addresses the problem of the evaluation of audiovisual sources from several perspectives:

Cultural Memory: (Music) History Told by the Media

In this section the abilities and possibilities of interpreting the past with audiovisual sources in academia are debated. Part of this process is to reflect upon how this may affect the notion of 'cultural heritage.' As an extension of the introduction, the first two articles do this in a more general way, the first focusing on musicology, the second on the history of communication and the challenges of digitalization in the humanities. The following three articles are based on concrete case studies that aim to deconstruct hegemonic historic narratives. One case study examines the image of Stradivari projected by the Italian media of the time and shows continuities with the Mussolini era and post-war Italy. The other deals with the popularization and politization of Beethoven in Austrian Public Television in 1970, with Leonard Bernstein as a crucial stakeholder. The following article addressing this subject area investigates the advent of the female voice in Austrian Radio in the 1970s. As a counterpoint the last article considers the influence of media, especially the advent of sound recording, on the history of composition.

Film Music: Grasping Historicity in Film

The first two articles in this section ask how the invention of sound film interacted with music history and the development of genres. The first identifies a temporary trend in Hollywood of the late 1940s to deal with jazz music's history and aesthetics in a serious manner. The second compares how operettas from the beginning of the century were variously adapted for the screen in European, British, and American cinema. The remaining two articles are concerned with the role of music and sound in the construction of memory in films that deal with a traumatic past. One focuses on the function of film sound to trigger emotions and depict memorization processes in film. The other tries to identify conventions and stereotypes in the use of canonized musical works for the characterization of Nazi war criminals in order to explain their attitudes towards their crimes.

Digital Humanities: Models and Questions

In third section best practice models for digital humanities projects are presented, which may enable and support digital historiography of the kind presented in the previous sections. The first article in this section gives an excellent overview of the state of the art in data modeling in the humanities and presents a concept for designing a platform for an archive of Alexander Kluge's *Kulturmagazine* TV programs, a concept which facilitates and fosters interdisciplinary exchange with other research platforms. In combination with a case study analysis of a specific document, it addresses the main challenges of capturing analytical processes digitally and the need for interdisciplinary collaboration. The second article gives insights into the difficult and time-consuming task of designing a metadata model, which again relies on collaborative communication between humanities researchers, data modelers, and computer scientists. The last article in this section presents a digital humanities project that is designed to compare different interpretations of a musical work and therefore provides a useful support for both the theory and practice of music. Included is an excellent overview of metadata vocabularies and ontologies that can be used to describe music.

As an add-on before John Corner's afterword, we asked artist and film-maker Johann Lurf for a brief statement on his film ★, which was presented at the opening of our conference. Lurf's collection and montage of night sky panoramas throughout film history can be understood as an artistic version of the research methods and aims discussed in this volume. Therefore, we consider it an excellent example for artistic research and how the arts and science are interconnectable.

"Living in a Material World," Contemplating the Immaterial One—Musings on What Sounds Can Actually Tell Us, or Not

Emile Wennekes (Utrecht University)

Just as I have two titles for this contribution, I also have two beginnings; nevertheless, they are directly related, as I hope to clarify. Let me commence with the narrative behind the second title. Recently, an American colleague distributed a short clip, which he encountered on the website of the Franz Schreker Foundation. Members of the Suppressed Music mailing list, to which I subscribe, reacted with gratitude, stating that they were delighted to "finally" see some *unique* (italics EW) footage of a moving Schreker.[1] The MP4 file of only 32 seconds may not have a telling sound, yet the clip tells us a lot of other things.[2]

This is indeed a fascinating piece of home movie material in which we see Franz Schreker (1878–1934)—the one on the left, with his spouse Marie (née Binder, 1892–1979), a dog and some friends and colleagues, to whom I will return shortly. Of Jewish descent, Schreker moved to Vienna in 1888, studied at, and was later appointed to the Vienna Music Academy, presently known as the University of Music and Performing Arts Vienna, where the *Telling Sounds* project is hosted. So, Schreker could be of interest to the project. Short story short: Schreker was widely considered to be the future of German/Austrian opera before his music was banned by the Nazis. He died from a stroke two

---

1   Email message to The International Centre for Suppressed Music Mailing List on behalf of Lloyd Moore, 5 March 2019. The text is as follows: "Dear List, Buried deep on the Schreker Foundation website is this fascinating piece of home movie footage of Schreker, his wife Maria and some friends from what is likely sometime in the 1920s: http://www.schreker.org/neu/engl/works/Schreker.mp4. LM."

2   Cf. f.n. 1. "Movie (from the archive of Artur Rodzinski)." http://www.schreker.org/neu/engl/works/Schreker.mp4

days before his 56th birthday. These vicissitudes of his life are by now well-known.

The film is without a doubt a 'document humain,' compacted into only seconds of moving images. It indeed appears to be a 'unique' item. Yet, of course, it is not. In the first place, it is a digitally 're-mediated' piece of footage—not original source material. The genuine film reels are what may be considered as 'unique,' not this digital copy in its second life online, subsequently generating multiple copies on multiple computer screens.

Some of us may even already know that this footage, in better quality, has already circulated the Web since 2014 as part of a more extended clip which features the private materials of the Polish conductor Artur Rodziński (1892–1958).[3] The clip features many more well-known figures from the musical world, among them Richard Strauss, Vladimir Horowitz, Leopold Stokowski, Maurice Ravel, George Gershwin, and Karol Szymanowski, to mention only the most famous ones. A question that may then pop up is: does that make the recently disseminated Schreker clip useless as a source for research? Of course not. The silent shot clip offers us no audio track, so sound doesn't reveal anything; nevertheless, the clip does provide all sorts of germane information in the realm of 'Alltagsgeschichte,' the history of everyday life. We are presented with a peek into a private life where we encounter the relaxed 'off-stage doppelgänger' of a composer at the height of his fame; a personality in his social habitat who is still in our times (or perhaps better: once again) considered an important figure in music history. In its own right, the contemporary dissemination of the clip testifies to the fact that the Nazis failed in wiping Schreker off the face of history. This process is intimately related to recent Schreker reception: the restoration of his reputation and the reevaluation of his creative work. At the same time, we can deduce, at least partly, information about Schreker's social network due to the clip, and the network depicted in it had a strong American orientation. The person to the left of Mrs. Schreker is Richard Hageman (1888–1966), a pianist, composer, and conductor of Dutch descent who initially moved to the United States in 1906, where he won an Oscar in 1939 for his score for

---

3   "Archival Footage of Artur Rodzinski." https://youtu.be/kqQuKD8URFE

John Ford's *Stagecoach*.[4] The person on the right is Olin Downes (1886–1955), who was, at the time, music critic of the *New York Times*.[5]

Schreker may have been an important figure in the institution that later became the University of Music and Performing Arts Vienna, but his online presence in the Österreichische Mediathek, one of the two main archival sources for the *Telling Sounds* project, is limited to only thirteen audio sources dating from the mid-1970s on—therefore consisting of mostly fairly recent productions. All are surely posthumous. In the other main source of the project, the Phonogrammarchiv, Schreker is not present at all. That, however, can be duly explained—which leads me to my second opening.

In 1925, the British magazine *Gramophone* featured an article on "Archives in Sound."[6] In it, the Phonogrammarchiv in Vienna was lauded as the first of its kind, having been established as early as 1899. The sound archive in Vienna was, and is, an exemplary archive of cultural memory, although (modern) Western music was and is not documented there. *Gramophone* already stressed back then that it was, first and foremost, a treasure trove of "specimens of dialect and language, voices of famous people, and so on."[7] The archive did not so much exclude music in general, but the documented samples were of a typically ethnomusicological nature, with records of folkish performances, mostly from faraway places. Hence, the emphasis on sounds other than those of Western music was duly recognized in the *Gramophone* article. When one consults the archive today, the search term 'music' yields only some forty hits available online; none of these, indeed, features Western music.[8] This may come as a surprise in a city, which, within the musicological narrative, is not only hailed for one, but even two of the most influential 'schools' in music history. The absence of music is, of course, the consequence of rigid choices of collection criteria. Space, even digital space, is limited, and archives must focus, even specialize. It is subsequently unavoidable that archival collections reflect existential questions such as 'What is the main goal of our archive?' Related sub-questions are typically: 'What to acquire, and what not?' 'Which

4   Kathryn Kalinak, Nico de Villiers and Asing Walthaus are preparing a critical biography of the composer Richard Hageman (Peter Lang Publishers).

5   The film seems to originate not from the 1920s, as had been suggested by the members of the mailing list (see f.n. 1), but must date from the early 1930s, as a simple comparison of his photographs reveals.

6   Pollak, "Archives in Sound."

7   Symes, *Setting the Record Straight* 231.

8   "Phonogrammarchiv." https://www.oeaw.ac.at/phonogrammarchiv/

audio or audiovisual sources may have a surplus value or significance for our specific collection; what is relevant for the target audience?' And so on.

The most important yet subjective words here are surely 'value' and/or 'significance.' Despite being slippery, these are of the essence. The general information on the *Telling Sounds* project also refers to its task of "wissenschaftliche Auswertung:" scholarly (r)e-valuation.[9] In the 1920s *Gramophone* article, the Viennese archive was already considered exemplary as a national library of recordings and worthy of imitation. Nevertheless, it took until 1951—more than half a century—for the British Institute of Recorded Sound (BIRS) to, for instance, first open its doors. Subsequently, the British Museum, the Public Record Office, the BBC, a number of universities, and assorted other educational bodies principally joined forces in this particular UK endeavor.

120 years after the first, pioneering *Telling Sounds* initiative in Vienna, the current *Telling Sounds* research project can therefore boast of a long and established Austrian scientific tradition with international repercussions and reputation. However, simultaneously, we may stand at the crossroads of both contemporary challenges and future initiatives. In the paragraphs below, I will attempt to reflect on some basic concepts from the *Telling Sounds* project as now defined and to address the fluidity and overlap between those concepts. The first part will briefly address the issue of the materiality of audiovisual archives. I will subsequently concentrate on audiovisual documents as part of our cultural heritage; the abovementioned 'value' of archival documents is key. I will conclude with stressing the importance of documenting the 'cultural biography' of audiovisual sources.

The first general theme of the 2019 conference was: "AV Documents: Analysis in Context," with a subtitle in brackets: "close reading, materiality." Let me first share some thoughts on the second concept: materiality. When we discuss the materiality of these relevant 'objects,' we are basically dealing with the recording as the carrier of audiovisual information—incidentally studied in combination with the machine which is the necessary compliment to be able to replay the artefact for perceiving the information recorded. In more physical terms, we need the equipment to turn "sound waves into electrical charges into mechanical energy and back into sound waves."[10] Colin Symes coined the metaphor of the "transducer" for this process of converting musical information from one source of energy to the next. This is realized via a

---

9   "Telling Sounds." https://www.mdw.ac.at/imi/tellingsounds/?PageId=8
10   Symes, *Setting the Record Straight* 212.

"chain of transducers associated with the reproduction of sound: discs, record players, amplifiers, and loudspeakers."[11] But in terms of archiving such a complicated issue as 'cultural memory,' the materiality of the audiovisual artefact and its physical operation is of only limited importance. The history of technology is, of course, part of that larger realm of cultural history, yet the more fundamental cultural value of these artefacts is defined by what is 'registered on' them as the 'immaterial' complement of the audiovisual document. A CD or a DVD is essentially nothing more than a coaster, a shiny round object to rest a glass of wine on, or perhaps a mirror of only average quality, unless that is, you have a decoding tool which unveils an immaterial realm which is concealed—invisibly and inaudibly—inside the magical disc. An open door, surely. However, we need to continually keep the distinction between the two in the back of our minds.

This may be in line with how the Council of Europe (CoE) has defined the diverse manifestations of our cultural heritage, 'Kulturerbe' in German. "Cultural heritage shapes our identities and everyday lives," the CoE argues "[i]t surrounds us in Europe's towns and cities, natural landscapes and archaeological sites. It is not only found in literature, art and objects, but also in the crafts we learn from our ancestors, the stories we tell our children, the food we enjoy in company and the films we watch and recognize ourselves in."[12] A recent slogan stated: "Our heritage: where the past meets the future."[13] Isn't this an important aspect of the *Telling Sounds* project?

The Council of Europe has defined four types of cultural heritage useful for finding relevant methodological access to our material as well. In accordance with the first two categories, the artefact of the audiovisual document is (1) 'tangible,' however, it communicates (2) 'intangible' practices: knowledge, artistic expression and so on. For our research, both the tangible materiality and the intangible immateriality of AV documents can be sources of upmost importance. However, there is more. Dismissing for our purposes the (3) 'natural' category of the Council's cultural heritage concept (consisting of landscape, flora and fauna) the final category (4) addresses digital resources.

---

11   Ibid.
12   "European Year of Cultural Heritage." https://europa.eu/cultural-heritage/about_en.ht
      ml
13   "Our Heritage: Where the Past Meets the Future." https://www.interregeurope.eu/heri
      coast/events/event/1765/our-heritage-where-the-past-meets-the-future/

Even digital, or digitized documents are considered a cultural heritage category *sui generis* in the eyes of the Council. Rethinking the Franz Schreker MP4 clip as it was disseminated through the internet: it may not be unique, but it does display aspects of the composer's private habitat which overlap with his professional network, including various figures of cultural importance. Therefore, by situating audiovisual documents in even three of the four overall categories established by the Council, the societal and cultural importance of our research on audiovisual materials is both unmistakable and manifest. Nevertheless, this subsequently makes an unequivocal, unambiguous approach towards such sources a challenge. And there is, yet again, even more to it.

In his book on the material history of classical recording, *Setting the Record Straight*, Colin Symes stresses the significance of what he calls the "narrative architecture"[14] provided by the (often overlooked but nevertheless related) textual contexts and/or dimensions. He specifically refers to related cover/liner notes, magazines, advertisements, et cetera. These can all be relevant to and complementary sources for our research, be it as background information, as receptional evidence, for network or target group analyses, and for other contextual clues. Yet, these may be documented and included in collections other than phonographic or AV media archives. Once again, questions of definition and identification surface: why does a given archive collect certain types of sources? This leads to meta-questions, such as how archives containing different artefacts from perhaps different periods are (inter)connected. To address these issues, it is relevant to situate audiovisual documents in broader sociohistoric contexts, or cultural circumferences. Collections can become sterile and meaningless, unless preserved in context—and to apply this to our project here and now: preserved, yet also analyzed, researched, or contextualized; and ultimately, publicly disclosed, consciously shared. It is relevant, therefore, to define the different types of appraisals of the audiovisual documents to be researched.

But how to judge the value of an object? Every new generation may propose different arguments to define the slippery issue of value or significance. How to judge whether an (audio)visual source is worthy of collection, documentation and/or study? What arguments can be brought forward? In the Netherlands,[15] a four-letter level qualification was introduced around 2000.

---

14   Symes, *Setting the Record Straight* 212.

15   For this contribution, the volume Beirens, *Achter de muziek aan* has been a crucial inspiration.

This taxonomy ranged from A (denoting the artefact as unique/irreplaceable) to D (referring to objects that no longer fit in any given collection). Armed with this taxonomy, heritage collections were scanned. But despite giving administrators arguments to critically evaluate their archives, these rather managerial qualifications hardly provided the researcher with ammunition for scholarly analyzing or (re)contextualizing the content of their interest; a much desired "wissenschaftliche Auswertung" needs more tools and handles. Often, collecting has occurred rather intuitively, given the abundance of audiovisual sources surrounding us; well-argued and systematic criteria of how collections are to be established are increasingly needed. Such criteria also immediately raise more fundamental questions including: what to archive, what to study, and...why?

To answer these pertinent questions, archives frequently make use of the Australian *Significance 2.0* taxonomy. This method was developed by Roslyn Russell and Kylie Wink for the Collections Council of Australia. The idea was to "strive for more sustainable collections" and to stress "the potential that collections hold for further innovative thinking," according to the Chair of the Collections Council.[16] I will use their method as a springboard for more advanced reflections. The *Significance 2.0* taxonomy proposes four primary criteria for consideration: (1) historic significance, (2) artistic or aesthetic significance, (3) scientific or research significance, and/or (4) social or spiritual significance.[17] Briefly and to the point: if an object tests positive on at least one of these four criteria, it can be considered 'significant'—worthwhile to document, and subsequently: worthwhile for further study. *Significance 2.0* also incorporates four additional, comparative criteria for assessing archival importance: (a) provenance, (b) rarity or representativeness, (c) condition or completeness, and (d) interpretative capacity.[18]

Freely interpreting the primary criteria, we could argue that the historic significance is probably the most clear-cut category to grasp. In audiovisual terms, reference could be to a recording or a broadcast recording of a premiere of a musical piece which is considered important, or a piece by a composer considered significant, or a performance by an important performer, ensemble, orchestra, et cetera. Or, in more general terms: a recording of a

---

16   Russell, *Significance 2.0* v.
17   Ibid. 39.
18   Ibid. 39–40.

specific performance which relates directly to historic events. The rare news-reel footage of Furtwängler in Berlin in 1943 is illustrative for the position of music within a politicized context. Historic value can also probably be given to propaganda sound films. On the verge of losing the war, the Nazi propaganda machine released, for example, the film *Kolberg* (1943/44), directed by Veit Harlan and with music by Norbert Schulze, composer of the famous war song "Lili Marleen."[19] This tale of patriotic resistance stood in stark contrast to reality during the 'Totaler Krieg' which sacrificed even the youngest of German civilians while cities were being fiercely bombed (and movie theaters were closed) and turned into burning ruins. The movie holds historic significance yet only when narrated within an adequate context.

To skip the second category for the moment, and turning first to scientific or research significance, we can state that this criterium is also fairly easy to judge. In specific musicological terms, the object could be a manuscript of a composition deemed important. Consider what Dutch conductor Willem Mengelberg did with his scores with his precious performative notes in blue and red. In AV terms, scientific value would probably best refer to a recording which documents important information of a certain performance practice. For example, consider the typical use of violin portamento which we can see and hear in the early Mengelberg films, which were recorded in the Tobis Sonores studios in Épinay-sur-Seine near Paris in 1931. Previously, I have contextualized these recordings in the way they were produced, who was involved, etc., in concurrence with comparative performative information.[20]

With regard to audiovisual sources, the remaining categories of the *Significance 2.0* method are not always as straightforward to define relevant to our audiovisual sources. The artistic or aesthetic category is ambivalent or somewhat unarticulated as it may refer, for example, to the 'beauty' or the artistic quality of a performance, scoring high on those performative criteria a music critic might employ. Additionally, this criterium is convoluted in the sense that "no two critics [or for that matter: musicologists -EW] might ever agree in their concept of criticism, and different reviews by any one critic may vary in emphasis."[21] Moreover: issues of taste can change over time, both generally and personally. Transferring the aesthetical category to AV-registrations, we can also consider incorporating information distilled from the stage design of

19   Harlan, *Kolberg*. https://www.imdb.com/title/tt0036989/
20   Wennekes, "Mengelberg Conducts Oberon."
21   Schick, *Classical Music Criticism* 21.

a certain opera production. Both interpretations (the aesthetic value of a performance versus the aesthetic value of a stage design) can, of course, overlap with the previous two categories as well.

The most complicated feature of the Australian system, therefore, is the final category: social or spiritual significance. Here, I am again indebted to a Dutch/Flemish publication entitled (in translation): "Follow the music."[22] It addresses many relevant, even urgent challenges concerning cultural heritage.[23] When many volunteers are prepared to be involved in a certain project, social significance is generated. Maintaining mechanical instruments, for instance. The amazing amount of annual performances of the *St. Matthew Passion* in the Netherlands is included as one of the examples of this specific sound value category,[24] as is the specific tradition of performances of Gustav Mahler's symphonies, for which conductor Willem Mengelberg laid the foundation[25]—both traditions are listed by Ellen Kempers in the *Achter de muziek aan* publication.[26]

Or, to transfigure these local Dutch examples to Viennese music culture, we can grant the 'Neujahrskonzert' important social significance (23 online hits in the Mediathek) as well as the performance and composing practices of the Waltz within Vienna's cultural history (163 hits). Audiovisual recordings of all these examples are not only of historic, scientific, and/or aesthetic significance, they have a social impact, aiding in the identity of the specific Viennese musical culture. The *Significance 2.0* categories do not, however, provide the issue of cultural value exhaustive treatment. Reflecting on the criteria addressed above, and following Kempers's adaptation of *Significance 2.0*, objects can also be scrutinized in terms of their symbolic value, their 'calibration' value, their 'linking' value, as well as their rarity. Symbolic value relates to the aforementioned historic value and defines its relation to important national or historic events. The calibration value becomes apparent when there are many other objects which relate to the specific one under discussion.

The linking value, on the other hand, addresses an object's link to striking developments marking societal, scientific, or cultural change, or: in our case, an object's link to significant musical developments, for example: the early music revival. However, "Television [...] has contributed comparatively little to

---

22   See f.n. 15.
23   Kempers, "Waardering en selectie" 77–78.
24   See for instance: Wennekes, "Nachwelt im Nachbarland."
25   Zwart, *Conductor Willem Mengelberg* passim.
26   Kempers, "Waardering en selectie" 77–78.

the revival [....] television executives have understandably been wary of filling their screens with musicians wielding viols, crumhorns, and Baroque flutes, no matter how gifted or telegenic they may be."[27] We could, nevertheless, refer to Hindemith's adaptation of Monteverdi's opera *Orfeo*, which he presented in Vienna in 1954. This performance created momentum for Nikolaus Harnoncourt's innovative, revolutionary take on early music only a few years later. "This performance had the effect of a bolt of lightning on me," Harnoncourt reminisced: "I immediately began to occupy myself with the music of Monteverdi."[28] An audio recording of the *Orfeo* in this linking value performance is commercially available, as well as an audio fragment in which Hindemith explains his take on the opera.[29] It is not included in the two archives of the *Telling Sounds* project, but digitized and publicly accessible via YouTube.

The categories mentioned above are at least of some use for the 'Auswertung' of audiovisual sources. Having said that, the boundaries between all categories—the ones from *Significance 2.0* as well as those contextualizing these—are not always clear-cut or unambiguously detectable. Occasionally, they are even rather fluid. This is clear when we examine, for example, the *Austria Wochenschau* episode broadcast on 11 November 1955. It features the reopening of the Wiener Staatsoper a few days prior. The episode is digitized and available online via the portal of the Österreichische Mediathek.[30] Given the importance of the Staatsoper itself, and the significant reasons why it was closed in the first place, the narrated event shown in the *Wochenschau* episode is of historic as well as symbolic importance with, at the same time, an eminent linking relevance to an important turning point in Vienna's postwar music history. Fragments of the opening production of *Fidelio* conducted by Karl Böhm afford us aesthetic information on the specific performance practice of the time as well as the actual approach to stage production design (the 'Bühnenbild' was supervised by Clemens Holzmeister). Therefore, this specific audiovisual document also provides us with additional musicological and theatrical information. Additionally, the episode refers to the strong social significance of the role opera played/plays within Viennese society. The

27   Haskell, *The Early Music Revival* 123.
28   "New Changing Exhibition in the Hindemith Cabinet." https://www.hindemith.info/en/institute/publications/hindemith-forum/hf-39-2017/changing-exhibition/
29   "Hindemith Orfeo: Hindemith über seine Aufführung des Orfeo bei den Wiener Festwochen 1954." https://youtu.be/kwDq7KCgIPg
30   "Wiedereröffnung der Wiener Staatsoper." https://www.mediathek.at/atom/15BD3239-287-000CA-00000B28-15BC4BC7

audiovisual footage is rare since there are only incomplete audio recordings of this specific production in the archive (a complete audio recording can, however, be found on YouTube).[31] The online clip provides us with immaterial subtexts surrounding the unique event of the reopening of the Staatsoper. Yet the online clip is, in itself, not unique or even rare. Only the original television film would be a unique archival piece—in both its material and immaterial relevance.

This last category, the rarity of audiovisual artefacts, subsequently provides us with an interesting and multifaceted criterium, especially when it is relevant to visual reproduction in mass media. Is the archival object unique, or one of many? A one-off or a multi-millions-off? The questions raised in the *Significance 2.0* publication pose six relevant sub-questions: (1) "Does it have unusual qualities that distinguish it from other items in the class or category?" (2) "Is it unusual or a particularly fine example of its type?" (3) Is it singular, unique or endangered?" (4) "Is it a good example of its type or class?" (5) "Is it typical or characteristic?" and ultimately: (6) "Is it particularly well-documented for its class or group?"[32] Here, rarity directly encroaches upon the notion of originality. It is common among musicologists to search for the most authoritative source, that is, the one closest to the inception of a composition: a manuscript, an early print and so on—are there relevant concordances, et cetera? For gramophone recordings, the master is, in fact, the sole original. The rest are all reproductions. Nevertheless, sound archives of a cultural heritage nature seldom include masters.[33] Since audiovisual recordings have increasingly become 'editions' (consider the, on average, two to three hundred edits that German 'Tonmeister' Volker Strauss made in a single Mahler symphony conducted by Bernard Haitink on Philips),[34] this fact may stand at odds with both the scientific and aesthetic categories within the *Significance 2.0* method of qualification. A record is, consequently, not so much a testimony of a certain *performance* practice, but rather, first and foremost, of a *recording* practice. We should qualify these as recording aesthetics in line with the concept of "Perfecting Sound Forever," in reference to Greg Milner's eponymous book on the history of recorded music.

---

31   "Historic Reopening Wiener Staatsoper." https://youtu.be/tAEPTsBLvKs
32   Russell, *Significance 2.0* 40.
33   Television registrations were commonly broadcast live and, in most cases, never recorded. Compare with the paragraph on radio broadcasts below.
34   Bank, *De klank als handschrift* 153.

We have observed that the Council of Europe features a separate category for digital resources originally created in digital format or digitized later. In musical, musicological, and technological terms, however, there is an essential distinction between those two variants. In the case of 'born digital' material, no information or quality is lost—the reproduction is an exact copy of the original. This differs strikingly from a musical registration or recording which is subsequently digitized (or copied and/or registered in another format). From the single original master, copies are generated and multiplied for distribution. With each successive copy, information is lost, the sound quality reduced in a process defined as "generational loss."[35] Strictly speaking, in the latter case the reproduction is *not* an exact copy of the original. A later form of re-mediatization cannot intercept this process of (negatively) influencing the condition of the audio.

Radio broadcasts are a different kettle of fish and are a far more complex, less systematic type of source. Nevertheless, recordings of broadcasts do display a variety of manifestations. For a long time, since the early 20th century, broadcasts were live, one-time only events meant to be consumed directly via radio. Recordings of broadcasts were incidental and co-incidental; companies did not systematically record or archive their programs. The arrival of the tape recorder in households starting in the 1950s increased the possibility of preserving broadcast material. Due to the involvement of private collectors, such material has occasionally been included in sound archives. A parallel can be drawn with the introduction of the home video cassette recorder, which reached the mass market in the mid-1970s. Recording on tape is of a strikingly different ontology than recording on video disc because recording on the latter is definite and permanent; tapes, on the other hand, could be overwritten and re-used.[36] (This topic makes us drift too far from the topic of this chapter.) Nowadays, broadcast companies upload programs online in digitized formats, whereas shows were previously taped and stored, at times to be digitized at a later stage. Sound archives have at times taken up the collector's gauntlet by digitizing radio broadcasts. For example, a recent press release states: "The Archive of Recorded Sound at Stanford University, in collaboration with the Stanford Media Preservation Lab, recently completed the digitization and cataloging of 684 analog recordings of The Standard Hour radio

---

35   Hovinga, "Audiovisuele dragers" 148–9.
36   Milner, *Perfecting Sound Forever* 106–7.

broadcasts that occurred between 1938 and 1955. [...] These historically significant programs were the first broadcast radio series in the US devoted to symphonic music."[37] TV programs are comparable in the sense that, in the past, they were broadcast live; these days, we can replay and study them repeatedly via online sources. Although, as a rule, the recorded object is mass produced, it can still be unique in alternative fashions. Enter the so-called 'cultural biography'—or perhaps more in line with Symes's architectural metaphor: the biographical architecture.

The contextual information provided by the cultural biography can be of utmost importance because it offers the leverage necessary for any cultural (re)valuation of an artefact. The cultural biography provides contextual information on who the makers, the producers, performers, and the previous owners may have been. It is comparable with the provenance criterium of *Significance 2.0*. Even the special relationship of a certain object to a city can be of importance. By addressing questions of previous ownership, or chains of ownership, or even the reasoning behind production and dissemination, we exit the material realm of artefacts and reenter their immaterial world. This second domain extends beyond the contours of emotional and/or social content/context. Objects can acquire sentimental, i.e. 'priceless' value due to such contexts. Or, as Colin Symes formulates it: "They are thus retained irrespective of their material condition, which in some instances might be very decrepit. In the light of their special status they are sometimes even 'enshrined;' that is, they are withdrawn from circulation and framed in some way, such as being housed in special cabinets."[38] Symes was not aiming to define a sound archive. However, for me, this is exactly how his statement can be interpreted—doesn't the *Telling Sounds* project adhere to forming an 'enshrined' collection "withdrawn from circulation and framed as being housed in a special cabinet?" The cultural value is not only what the archive represents, collects or archives, 'in sum' it attains a cultural, symbolic significance in its own right. The archive withdraws (or should I say: rescues?) everyday objects from the biological circle of life and death, manufacture and decay. Research projects like *Telling Sounds* kiss their objects alive again.

To conclude: with the Viennese Phonogram Archive, one of Thomas Edison's dreams came true at the turn of the 20th century. He considered a record

---

37   Quoted from a message sent to the mailing list of IAML by Frank Ferko, "Sound Archives Metadata Librarian," *Archive of Recorded Sound*, Stanford University, 4 March 2019.
38   Symes, *Setting the Record Straight* 214.

library as a resource for scientific inquiry "one of the main cultural dividends of his invention."[39] The main goal of the British Institute of Recorded Sound (BIRS), now the British Library Sound Archive, was, as far as music was concerned, "to obtain copies of records as they are published and rescue as many of those [...] irrespective of their current value"[40] and preserve them under conditions that would make them available for study within the institute. Despite the fact that library use remains relevant, institutions have recently put a great deal of material online, allowing users to study re-mediatized material from a distance. Times have changed radically—as have technologies and methodologies, to no lesser extent.

Returning to the two titles of this chapter: we, as researchers, may indeed all live in a material world—albeit a slightly different one than that described by legendary pop star Madonna in her international hit. Nonetheless, after we have decided how to scrutinize the different material artefacts needed for our research, we must profoundly address the immaterial information enshrined in those objects. Our 'Auswertung' is a type of valuation of one object as opposed to another. More specifically: valuating one source of intangible information over another, in cross-referenced contexts. It is only then that we hear what sounds from the past are actually able to tell us—now and in the future.

Bibliography (last accessed 16 April 2020)

Bank, Jan, and Emile Wennekes. *De klank als handschrift: Bernard Haitink en het Concertgebouworkest*. Amsterdam: J.M. Meulenhoff, 2006.

Beirens, Maarten, Ellen Kempers and Heidi Moyson, eds. *Achter de muziek aan: Muzikaal erfgoed in Vlaanderen en Nederland* (trans.: Follow the music: musical heritage in Flanders and the Netherlands). Leuven, Den Haag: Acco, 2010.

Fisher, Trevor. "The British Institute of Recorded Sound: A National Collection." *Tempo: A Quarterly Review of Modern Music* 45 (Autumn 1957): 24–27.

Haskell, Harry. *The Early Music Revival: A History*. London: Thames and Hudson, 1988.

---

39   Ibid. 231.
40   Fisher, "The British Institute of Recorded Sound" 24.

Hovinga, Eerde. "Audiovisuele dragers." *Achter de muziek aan: Muzikaal erfgoed in Vlaanderen en Nederland*. Eds. Maarten Beirens, Ellen Kempers and Heidi Moyson. Leuven, Den Haag: Acco, 2010. 147–155.

Kempers, Ellen. "Waardering en selectie: Nederlands muzikaal erfgoed in perspectief." *Achter de muziek aan: Muzikaal erfgoed in Vlaanderen en Nederland*. Eds. Maarten Beirens, Ellen Kempers and Heidi Moyson. Leuven, Den Haag: Acco, 2010. 70–86.

Milner, Greg. *Perfecting Sound Forever: An Aural History of Recorded Music*. New York: Faber and Faber, 2009.

Pollak, Hans. "Archives in Sound: An Account of the Work of the 'Phonogram-Archives' in Vienna." *Gramophone* 2, 11 (1925): 415–18.

Russell, Roslyn, and Kylie Wink. *Significance 2.0: A Guide to Assessing the Significance of Collections*. Rundle Mall, SA: Collections Council of Australia, 2009. https://www.arts.gov.au/sites/default/files/significance-2.0.pdf

Schick, Robert D. *Classical Music Criticism*. New York, London: Garland, 1996.

Symes, Colin. *Setting the Record Straight: A Material History of Classical Recording*. Middletown, CT: Wesleyan Univ. Press, 2004.

Wennekes, Emile. "Mengelberg Conducts Oberon: The Conductor as Actor, Anno 1931." *Music in Art* 34, 1–2 (2009): 317–335.

Wennekes, Emile. "Nachwelt im Nachbarland. Aspekte der Bach-Pflege in den Niederlanden, ca. 1850–2000." *Tijdschrift van de Koninklijke Vereniging voor Nederlandse Muziekgeschiedenis* 50, 1–2 (2001): 110–130.

Zwart, Frits. *Conductor Willem Mengelberg, 1871–1951: Acclaimed and Accused*. 2 Vols. (trans. Cynthia Wilson). Amsterdam: Amsterdam Univ. Press, 2019.

Online Sources (last accessed 16 April 2020)

"European Year of Cultural Heritage." *European Union*. https://europa.eu/cultural-heritage/about_en.html

"New Changing Exhibition in the Hindemith Cabinet." *Hindemith Fondation*. https://www.hindemith.info/en/institute/publications/hindemith-forum/hf-39-2017/changing-exhibition/

"Our Heritage: Where the Past Meets the Future." *Hericoast: Interreg Europe*. https://www.interregeurope.eu/hericoast/events/event/1765/our-heritage-where-the-past-meets-the-future/

"Telling Sounds." *Universität für Musik und darstellende Kunst Wien*. https://www.
mdw.ac.at/imi/tellingsounds/?PageId=8

Audiovisual Sources (last accessed 16 April 2020)

"Archival Footage of Artur Rodzinski." *YouTube*. https://youtu.be/kqQuKD8U
RFE
Harlan, Veit (Director). *Kolberg* (1945). https://www.imdb.com/title/tt003698
9/
"Hindemith Orfeo: Hindemith über seine Aufführung des Orfeo bei den Wie-
ner Festwochen 1954." *YouTube*. https://youtu.be/kwDq7KCgIPg
"Historic Reopening Wiener Staatsoper." *YouTube*. https://youtu.be/tAEPTsB
LvKs
"Movie (from the archive of Artur Rodzinski)." *Franz Schreker Foundation*. http:
//www.schreker.org/neu/engl/works/Schreker.mp4
"Phonogrammarchiv." *Österreichische Akademie der Wissenschaften*. https://www
.oeaw.ac.at/phonogrammarchiv/
"Wiedereröffnung der Wiener Staatsoper." *Österreichische Mediathek*. https://
www.mediathek.at/atom/15BD3239-287-000CA-00000B28-15BC4BC7

The (Re)Construction of Communicative Pasts in the Digital Age
Changes, Challenges, and Chances in Digital Transformation

Christian Schwarzenegger (University of Augsburg)

> Everything not saved will be lost
> —Nintendo Quit Screen Message

Can contemporary history be written without pictures and sounds or without an adequate representation and incorporation of audio and visuals? Although this was a matter of debate only a couple of years ago, when historians were still engaged in a lively dispute about whether the history of the 20th and 21st centuries could be adequately written without properly taking into account the ubiquitous dissemination and reception of the mass media,[1] it already seems like the distant past. Meanwhile, we face a new period of transformation in the research into our communicative past, which makes it almost seem absurd that until rather recently the role of media was discussed predominantly with regard to their ambiguous value or validity as a source for historical work rather than as a crucial social and cultural factor playing a part in molding and shaping how historical processes developed.

Digital media have since had a massive impact on how we (can) do (media and communication) historiography on several levels. Digital media data or digitized analogue media as new sources that can be used and become relevant for the reconstruction of the past is only one of the levels affected. Against the background of digital change, many subjects of the arts and humanities as well as the social sciences are experiencing a radical structural

---

1   Classen, "Zeitgeschichte ohne Bild und Ton?"

change in their working routines and readiness to collaborate, their episte-mological and methodological bases as well as regarding their topics of in-quiry. Relatively new interdisciplinary formations like 'digital humanities' or computational social sciences' share the need for a reorientation and reeval-uation of research procedures and research interests in increasingly digital research contexts. Humanities and social sciences alike face the question of how, in the context of digitization, disciplinary knowledge, research inter-ests, and methods change and call for adaptation, as well as which specific problems (as well as opportunities) arise as part of these transformations.

In this chapter, I will try to contribute to this overall discussion by ad-dressing how these broader and more general developments affect a particu-lar field of inquiry, namely the area of media and communication studies. In doing so, I hope that the discussion of this particular subject matter will also provide valuable insights for research in other fields that engage with digital media. Therefore, I shall first provide an understanding of media and com-munication history from a media and communication studies perspective, and will argue why research into contemporary culture and society cannot be done without taking into account the particularities of digital media, which consequently also calls for expertise in the uses and analysis of digital media (communication).

I will then juxtapose how the impact of digitalization on (communica-tion) historiography is debated regarding its revolutionary potential with the rather little effective change it has spawned so far. Furthermore, I will con-tinue with a discussion (on the basis of examples) of how I think historical (re)construction is (and needs be) affected by digital change beyond revolu-tionary rhetoric. I conclude that the challenges and questions regarding the validity, reliability[2] and consistency of sources/data are not resolved by dig-ital means, nor merely transferred into new technological and cultural en-vironments. They pose genuinely new challenges and require new skills and literacies to be coped with.

---

2   Deacon, "Yesterday's Papers and Today's Technology."

Mediatization, Digitalization and the Expanse of Media and Communication Research

In media and communication studies, the so-called meta-process of mediatization[3] has become a relevant framework for the description of the profound and interrelated changes between society, culture, and the role played by the media and communication technologies and practices prevalent at the time. Just like other meta-processes such as individualization, commercialization or globalization, mediatization is not an empirical process that can be researched by considering the changes (or lack thereof) in a single phenomenon but must be understood by means of overall transformations. "By mediatization we mean the historical developments that took and take place as a result of change in (communication) media and the consequences of those changes. If we consider the history of communication through music or the art of writing, we can describe the history of human beings as a history of newly emerging media and at the same time changing forms of communication."[4] While the study of media and communication has long focused mostly on the public arenas of communication and communication mediated through the traditional institutions of mass communication, this limitation seems to no longer provide a feasible concept for the discipline.[5] With the advent and proliferation of digitalization and digitization, over the past several decades we also have witnessed a profound 'mediation of everything,'[6] i.e. an increasing qualitative and quantitative relevance and prevalence of mediated communication for processes of organization, coordination, and meaning-making in virtually all domains of society. Today, nearly all aspects of the social world are intermingled with and characterized by ubiquitous mobile media devices, digital communication, and data. This development has made inevitable the expansion of the field beyond 'journalism,' 'mass communication,' and 'public communication.' Since then, the very notion of mediated communication has become less clear and has expanded to nearly all areas of the human experience and encompasses a variety of technologies, tools, platforms, and intermediaries for communication.

---

3   Krotz, "Mediatization;" Hepp and Krotz, *Mediatized Worlds.*
4   Krotz, "Media Connectivity" 23.
5   Hepp, "Kommunikations- und Medienwissenschaft in datengetriebenen Zeiten."
6   Livingstone, "On the Mediation of Everything."

Unlike other disciplines, media and communication does not have stable boundaries but experiences rapid and constant change and reconfiguration. Issues of media and communication research and the shifting boundaries of the field together with the (changing) relationships of communication research with distant as well as closely related disciplines are hence recurrent topics in internal debates in the field and question what remains distinctive about the field if purportedly everything is characterized by media.[7] More recent approaches to the mediatization of culture and society describe the individual lifeworlds and social worlds which make up the everyday life of people as mediatized worlds, regard media as a world in which we live our lives, which have become media lives.[8] In all these varieties, social experience and the construction of social reality is seen as inseparable from the media we use. Some authors refer to the notion of 'deep mediatization' to describe the latest stage of mediatization, which is heavily driven by digitalization and is characterized by the (even deeper) entrenchment of digital media and data in everyday life.[9] But why does this roundup of recent developments in media and communication research matter for the issue I aim to consider here? In my view, it is important because it does not only change the face of the field in question and the areas of its inquiry at present but also affects the data, sources, and resources it requires for the long-term preservation of its knowledge and the historical reconstruction of its area of interest. If we do not incorporate the history and prehistory of the phenomena we study despite their having arrived late and only recently becoming part of our research interests, we are tempted to overlook continuities and persistences in the newly adopted fields, which happen to also have a history, and to overemphasize newness and change. An obsession or fascination with the new can be a temptation for a discipline always engaging with the latest technological devices in its vicinity.[10] Periods of transition in the phenomena a field investigates, following Lunt and Livingstone, calls for a "heightened historical awareness" which pushes us to go beyond a simplistic polarization of 'now' and 'before,' or 'old' and 'new' media, or the twenty-first century and 'the past' (a challenge of particular importance as analysis of 'the digital age' threatens to eclipse or

---

7   Livingstone, "If Everything is Mediated."

8   Hepp and Krotz, *Mediatized Worlds*; Bolin, "Institution, Technology, World;" Deuze, "Media Life."

9   Hepp, *Deep Mediatization*; Couldry and Hepp, *The Mediated Construction of Reality*.

10   Menke and Schwarzenegger, "On the Relativity of Old and New Media."

obscure a nuanced analysis of earlier periods).[11] In general, historically oriented communication research aims for the reconstruction of political and
sociocultural contexts, institutional forms, materialities, contents, and consequences of communication processes in the past—how they evolved over
time and are remembered in the present. Therefore, communication research
in a historical or long-term perspective asks what traces of media and communication can tell us about past events, past life, as well as changes and
continuities in social communication and the organization of society. Communication history builds on mediated communication but is not necessarily
media-centric. Relevant areas of interest include processes of communication
in history as well as the representation of history in current communication
and the communicative construction of memory in the present.

Historical media and communication research is dependent on finding,
accessing, and critically evaluating sources, which allow for the exploration
and understanding of the historical processes of social communication.[12]

Returning to the question raised at the beginning of this paper of whether
the writing of history or the chronicling of past times can be done properly without audio and visual material, this expansion of the field of media
and communication research also demands an expansion of the archives and
reservoirs of sources considered for research. When the scope of research extends to mass communication, it clearly cannot be enough to limit the reservoir of pictures and sounds used as sources or as material objects of inquiry
to the productions of traditional institutions of mass communication and the
treasures they collect in their archives.[13] Researchers then also need to think
about how to access the past of the private realms of communication they are
interested in, the cultural artefacts of digital communication and the digital
traces of interpersonal exchange, which are—at least until now—not systematically publicly recorded or stored and can only be partly covered by institutionalized public archiving initiatives. According to Balbi, "digitalization
also signifies a turning point in the way our culture is stored, recorded and
preserved, and this alters and will increasingly alter culture itself, making it
'digital dependent.'"[14] Such a change in culture, cultural forms, and cultural
expression will then of course have consequences for research into both of

11   Lunt and Livingstone, "Is 'Mediatization' the New Paradigm for Our Field?" 465.
12   Schwarzenegger, "Exploring Digital Yesterdays;" Schwarzenegger, "Herausforderungen
      des Digitalen Gestern."
13   Behmer, *Das Gedächtnis des Rundfunks.*
14   Balbi, "Doing Media History in 2050" 134.

these domains and require researchers—in media and communication research, fields in which I am able to closely observe this, and surely also in other disciplines and fields—to acquire new skills and literacies to cope with the new challenges, benefit from the positive potentials, but also be aware of the limitations and problematic implications of a changed research environment.[15] But what will this mean in particular?

Fast Hype but Slow Revolutions? The Digital Transformation of a Dedicated Few

So far I have argued that digitalization has the potential to cause change at all levels of the research process and tried to elaborate on this vague assumption regarding changes in the field of inquiry, i.e. regarding the formal and material objects of media and communication research as well as sources and data relevant for such investigations. Beyond that, the process of research as such and the working routines of scholars can also be affected and prompted to adapt or—phrased more positively—to embrace the new opportunities. Not only does the digital transformation of communication and culture which we observe in our research stimulate a shift in research practices and call for adaptation, but a digital transformation of the modes, methods, and possibilities of observation also has an impact on the research we can do and are doing. The increased availability of 'old communication' and analogue media in digitized form as well as digital tools of scrutinizing, reading, evaluating data, and distilling insight and patterns from these sources allow and call for new forms of academic engagement. Balbi summarizes:

> "Media historians, as well as all other historians, must be willing to accept significant changes in their profession: they will have to approach the digital heritage differently than the analogue one, because digital data are volatile, interconnected, unstable and abundant; they will seek new tools to manage this great mass of data; they will use technological systems [...]; they will interact with new institutions and they will learn new methods of access to sources; they will have to learn new methods to reconstruct the past from

15   Koenen et al., "Historische Kommunikations- und Medienforschung im digitalen Zeitalter;" Birkner and Schwarzenegger, "Konjunkturen, Kontexte, Kontinuitäten."

these digital sources; and, finally, they will face new difficulties, such as accessibility, ownership, fragility, originality, and contextualization of digital sources."[16]

Clearly, doing media historical work in the digital age comes with continuities and changes regarding historiographical practices, greeted with hype and revolutionary aspirations by some and indifference or composure by others.[17]

For instance, in 2012 the historian Toni Weller argued in his edited book *History in the Digital Age* that "[h]istory, as a field of inquiry, is standing at the edge of a conceptual precipice;"[18] and he is one among others who sees fundamental changes in the understanding of a practice or a profound paradigm shift in the wake of the digital revolution. Also, in German-speaking countries the challenges presented and chances offered by doing history in the digital age were debated;[19] there was a search for ways of mastering the digital instead of having researchers become overwhelmed by it, and the perils were addressed as well. Back in 2018, the Digitizing Communication History Initiative, cofounded in 2016 by Erik Koenen and myself, presented a conceptual paper in which we argued for the need for historical expertise in the study of digital media on the one hand as well as digital literacy and skills in the historical study of media and communication on the other.[20] We are currently editing a cooperative volume on digital communication and communication history to elaborate the potentials and perils of this endeavour in more depth. In the same year, when my colleagues and I organized a conference about media and communication history in the digital age for the *International Communication Association*, a leading academic society in the field of communication studies, an anonymous reviewer wrote that "If communication historians aren't addressing these issues, we will be left behind in the dust." So there seems to be wide agreement that changes are imminent and that they will indeed be profound, run deep, and maybe even revolutionize the field. But if we look more closely, it also becomes evident that these discussions are characterized by a strong emphasis on what historians are (allegedly) not yet doing and what they would have to become in order to compete and be

---

16   Balbi, "Doing Media History in 2050" 152.
17   Jensen, "Doing Media History in a Digital Age."
18   Weller, *History in the Digital Age* 1.
19   E.g. H–Soz–Kult, please note that there is a big difference between doing historical work in the digital age and being a digital historian.
20   Schwarzenegger et al., *Digitale Kommunikation und Kommunikationsgeschichte*.

viable in the digital age. But these debates do not appear to resonate strongly, aside from with a dedicated few, and are often relegated to special sections or niches within the respective fields. We can also observe that there is a divide between those who engage with digital technologies in their research in terms of topics, tools, and methods, and those who do not. These divides are only in part generational in nature; it is accordingly not necessarily the younger ones who are more open to the digital. This is partly also caused or sustained by a lack of attention to such issues in the current education of historians or media and communication scholars. In the case of media and communication research the limitations are twofold: there is a lack of institutionalized training in computational or digital methods and digital research literacy on the one hand and a lack of institutionalized training in historical research methodology and historical source criticism skills on the other. In this regard, a majority of (historically oriented) media and communication scholars seem ill-prepared for revolutionary ambitions. The absence of a revolution can however in some instances contribute to the widening of a gap. For instance, PhD students and early career scholars in media and communication studies today are very likely to engage with digital media communication as a field of inquiry. For historically oriented researchers within the field, not taking these topics into account, at least partially, may steer them away from the remainder of the field. However, if the revolutionary spark is confined to the circles of a dedicated few, does this mean that the projected revolutions will not take place? From my point of view, there will not be a sudden and broad upheaval, but change will instead likely come in the form of a slow and tedious process. If there will be a revolution, it is going to be a tiny but steady one.

Concepts—Sources—Literacies

But what are the areas that are likely to be most affected and where our understanding of media, memory, and history in its current state will be contested? In my perspective, digital transformation challenges historically oriented media and communication research (and broader inquiries into society and culture) on an epistemological level to revisit a number of fundamental concepts. However, reimagining concepts of media and communication is not an unusual exercise but occasionally necessary.[21] Media environments and

---

21   Filimowicz and Tzankova, *Reimagining Communication: Meaning*.

communication practices evolve over time and in relation to overall processes of social change, making media and communication 'moving targets' for research. In this sense, following the classic distinction proposed by Blumer, it is sensitizing rather than definite concepts that we are dealing with—concepts indicating general directions in which to look rather than telling us precisely what to see.[22] On the level of concepts, the digital transformation of research provokes us to rethink the temporality, translocality, and transmediality of media and communication.

Rethinking temporality suggests that through and in digital media the very sense of time or what we understand as 'the present,' 'a short while back,' or 'long ago' can change. Digital communication often appears to be accelerated, with an increase of communicative events in a given period of time—communication history hence moves closer to the present, and quite recent communication is dismissed from contemporary research, relegated to the long-term memory of communication history. In other words, the 'now' or the 'moment' of digital communication becomes shorter and the past starts earlier. This is also due to the fast pace of innovation in media and communication technology and, consequently, the high degree of technical instability and obsolescence in media technologies. Hickethier, back in 2003,[23] saw the continued existence of media history as such at risk because of the ephemeral character of the sources and communication's becoming ever more volatile. Paradoxically, while digital media are in fact somewhat elusive, there is a tendency in research to speak of digitalization as a still frame, as if once digital transformation began, digitalization in itself was a stable concept that did not change very much. In contrast, rethinking the temporality of digital media also requires one to think about the transformation of the digital over time and to acknowledge that digital media has referred to quite a lot of different things over the past few decades.[24]

Rethinking translocality in addition to this means that besides the temporal, the spatial or local dimension of media and communication needs to also be revaluated. As I have described elsewhere,[25] with the advent of digital communication the sense of space for media and communication research has been affected as well. Media and communication have previously mostly been

---

22   Blumer, "What is Wrong with Social Theory?"
23   Hickethier, *Einführung in die Medienwissenschaft* 358.
24   Histories of digital media are still scarce, one relevant exception: Balbi and Magaudda, *A History of Digital Media.*
25   Schwarzenegger, "Exploring Digital Yesterdays."

studied in relation to the nation-state, but it is quite obvious that digital communicative networks are less likely to be congruent with national boundaries. Instead, digital media platforms and the corporations behind communicative services are global in scope and decentralized and transnational in their organizational form. It is not by chance that the comprehensive *History of Digital Media* approaches the topic from a 'global perspective.'[26] On the level of topics, future communication history will need a sense of space to explore yesterday's questions concerning the mobility of people and devices, ubiquity, cross-border civic engagement, transnational community formation, and connectivity as well as a series of questions related to globalization and to the distribution, circulation, and appropriation of media contents and technologies. Besides the features of digital communication per se, the relationship between research and the local has changed as well. Digital archives allow access to data from afar and distant reading has become a feature for many different questions and research interests of media and communication scholars.[27] Rethinking locality is, however, far from implying that research collaboration or access to archives is no longer confined by space or local presence. To the contrary, researchers working with digital archives frequently report that physically being there can still be a decisive element in the success of archival work.[28]

Rethinking transmediality tempts us to question the very concept of research units, the multimodality of research material, and the interconnected character of data. We can only capture the consequences of mediatization if we do not focus exclusively on single media but rather on media environments and media ensembles of specific social domains and how they are entangled, interrelated with one another, and partly contesting or complementing each other. For instance, the radio broadcast is no longer limited to the audio transmitted via airwaves but embedded in a transmedia ensemble comprising, for instance, digital content, social media coverage, and audience interaction. Perhaps music recordings also pose prime examples of how we need to think in terms of transmediality instead of closed entities. A particular piece of recorded music available on a streaming portal can be embedded in a

26   Balbi and Magaudda, *A History of Digital Media.*

27   Koenen, "Digitale Perspektiven in der Kommunikations- und Mediengeschichte;" Ben-David, "What does the Web Remember of Its Deleted Past?"; Birkner et al., "A Century of Journalism."

28   Ben-David and Amran, "The Internet Archive;" Jensen, "Doing Media History in a Digital Age."

web of references, links, reactions, and recommendation systems or playlists as new cultural forms. An approach that would consider music in terms of single recordings or files would miss some of the particularities of its reception and proliferation within a specific media environment.

Besides the examples of concepts, we can also observe an important change with regard to the sources of research. This is however not specific to the digital age. Media and other histories have always been dependent on the archival material available for research purposes, testimonies, and relics which were collected with varying levels of completeness, integrity and reliability. Archives are agents of memory and historical preservation; they contribute to our understanding of the past and provide a sense of order and hierarchy of knowledge. But in doing so, they are not merely neutral institutions of preservation, but they are institutions of power and reflect power structures in societies, nations, or organizations. They keep a selective, curated, and by no means comprehensive record of past events, and in doing so each archive wields a "particular bundle of silences."[29] Archives possess "the power of the present to control what is, and will be, known about the past, about the power of remembering over forgetting...., it is essential to reconsider the relationship between archives and the societies that create and use them."[30] Archives are just as much about the preservation of records and relics as they are about forgetting, excluding, and silencing. Forgetting is the conjoined twin of all memory. The archive hence plays a crucial role in the construction of historical facts and the imagination of the past.[31] In other contexts, together with my colleagues I have discussed the challenges of building a research corpus based on digital archives, hence I do not want to go into much detail regarding the detailed work with digital archives. In line with other authors,[32] however, we conclude that the actual work with digital archives, due to legal, institutional and technological hindrances is still tedious and does not necessarily allow us to fully benefit from the advantages and potentials they theoretically harbour.

A further promise of digital communication in many areas was the purported democratization of access and participation. In the sense of digital media, the very notion and idea of the archive has also been affected by such

29   Ankerson, "Writing Web Histories" 389.
30   Schwartz and Cook, "Archives, Records, and Power."
31   Birkner et al., "A Century of Journalism."
32   Keute and Birkner, "Digital Wiedergeboren?"

aspirations in terms of the web and of digital and social media as the biggest archive the world has ever seen—albeit one that lacks most of the features of a professional archive. Nevertheless, we find numerous accounts that nothing is ever forgotten on the web. At least allegedly, this is true. Over the past several decades it has become sort of an—albeit errant—commonplace that whatever something may be, once it exists in digital form, will forever remain available for everyone to access and for no one to hide. Archiving, this instrument of power, is allegedly made more democratic, allowing for a polyphony of voices to take part in the communicative reconstruction and evocation of the past.[33] Making collections available online and curating them as a collaborative process is seen as an "unparalleled opportunity to allow more varied perspectives in the historical record than ever before. Networked information technology can allow ordinary people and marginalized constituencies not only a larger presence in an online archive, but also generally a more important role in the dialogue of history."[34] Similar statements were made more than a decade later and until very recently, with regard to social media, which—like Twitter in this example—provide "a platform for people who might traditionally be excluded from public discourse to have a voice in representing themselves as well as their perceptions of the world around them."[35] Media historians Myers and Hamilton have accordingly argued that the history of our current times cannot be written in the future without taking into account the many voices and testaments of social media as one complementary source.[36] It may be true that "[o]ne of the important implications of our current digital society is that so much more of our political and social lives are captured and stored through media technologies."[37] The consequences for research however are ambiguous. The question for many aspects of the historical reconstruction of communicative pasts is hence pushed away from whether we want to take audio and visuals into consideration with regard to questions of how we can access the data which would be relevant for analysis. We may produce more data and records about past communication than ever before, but in this post-scarcity culture,[38] the sheer volume of material makes it hard to comprehend what

---

33   Schwarzenegger and Lohmeier, "Reimagining Memory."
34   Cohen, "The Future of Preserving the Past."
35   Humphreys, "Historicizing New Media" 414–15.
36   Myers and Hamilton, "Social Media as Primary Source."
37   Humphreys, "Historicizing New Media."
38   Hoskins, "The Right to be Forgotten in Post-Scarcity Culture."

is relevant and what isn't, and the ability to separate treasure from trash becomes an important skill. In this "age of abundance"[39] or "age of profusion"[40] for digitally available sources, questions regarding the availability, accessibility, and usability of this data for research purposes are more pressing than ever before.[41]

However, it remains arguable whether a history which relies heavily on digital media and traces of digital communication as sources will truly be more comprehensive or democratic. In their current state, we cannot even say that all the myriad data produced by digital media will be available at all. Due to the lack of public archiving or proper publicly accessible repositories as well as technological obsolescence, we might instead be on the brink of the Digital Dark Ages, as some gloomy prophecies maintain. Historical information could then, as a result of being outdated and unreadable, of corrupt software, updated systems, or unavailable, scarce, or inaccessible hardware and technologies, be beyond our reach. Rather than remembering everything, future media historians may face inaccessible sources locked away in unreadable software or on obsolete physical storage devices like floppy disks or, increasingly, CD-ROMs or DVDs. Researchers have further demonstrated that the web has in fact only limited recollection of its own deleted past;[42] with regard to the durability of records and archived information, it can at times be easier to find a film from 1924 than a webpage from 1994.[43] In place of the idea that nothing is ever forgotten on the web, when it comes to digital archiving I therefore prefer the Nintendo Entertainment System quit screen message: "everything not saved will be lost," which seems to be more accurate. If everything not saved will be lost, however, it becomes evident that questions about what is saved, who decides what is to be saved, and who shall do the saving become paramount.

The rhetoric surrounding studies of and with digital media suggests not only an increased equality among the voices represented, but also a heightened level of authenticity for digitally preserved data, for attainable completeness of data collection, and an increased immediacy of the data, i.e., the proximity of the data to the actual event it is meant to represent. In research,

39   Fickers, "Towards a New Digital Historicism?"
40   Birkner et al., "A Century of Journalism."
41   Ibid.
42   Ben-David, "What does the Web Remember of Its Deleted Past?"
43   Ankerson, "Writing Web Histories."

notions and metaphors (like digital traces), which become resources for research and are allegedly left behind like a trail of breadcrumbs through the mere use of our digital devices (and which will then become 'found data') suggest improved genuineness. Digital data is imagined to be something simply left behind that researchers will be able to pick up just as it was, as real as it ever was—in digital humanities and computational social sciences, rhetoric data is collected, stored, mined, and harvested from the web just as it was when the crop (so to speak) was grown.

However, it is an important lesson to learn that digital archives and preserved digital data do not allow us to access the digital past as it was. Data is never raw, but always cooked; it changes fluidly and collaboratively over time[44] ("Raw data is both an oxymoron and a bad idea"[45]). Data has always been produced and gathered with a particular purpose and aim, or as Nicholson puts it, digital reborn data[46] is not composed of preservations or simple representations of digital or analogue material in digital form, but remediations—sources are remediated and not just reproduced. The data we find in digital archives are not preservations or simple representations but become unique originals through the process of being archived, coming to have particular features which characterize their value as a source.[47] The nature of data is dynamically linked to the process of its collection and is subject to change and inconsistencies through this process. Search engines and filtering processes generate data as custom-made products and provide only very little insight into how the data were gathered.[48] Similar concerns were raised about the lack of transparency regarding the data which is made accessible through collaboration with digital media providers and corporations: the integrity, completeness, the logic of its composition and the blind spots of the materials remain non-transparent.[49] All in all, digital media

"provide a complex source of historical insight that represents many dichotomies. These sources are authored by individuals, but regulated by elites; they are used for political articulation, but are part of a larger movement; social media use a new form of communication, yet rely on standard

---

44   Gitelman, 'Raw Data' Is an Oxymoron.
45   Gitelman and Jackson, "Introduction."
46   Nicholson, "THE DIGITAL TURN."
47   Brügger, "When the Present Web is Later the Past."
48   Andrejevic, "Cultural Studies of Data Mining."
49   Pfaffenberger, "What you tweet is what we get?" 61.

communication practices; social media are new media, but retain old media qualities."[50]

For researchers doing media historical work, dealing with the peculiarities and affordances of their sources as well as the contexts of their initial collection or recording are a usual exercise. In digital media environments, the usual skills in source criticism need to be complemented by data literacy. In my view, it is also essential for researchers, even if they do not plan to follow the path of computational methods or digital humanities, to have this kind of literacy. Being able to reflect on the peculiar challenges of digital media as an object of research, or source for interpretation, or regarding the tools they provide is vital even if digital media remain rather peripheral in a researcher's working routine. In addition to literacy, I would also argue that 'doing data' and doing digital becomes important, i.e., that researchers have at least some kind of experience in navigating digital research environments in order to really internalize the requirements.

Conclusion

I have discussed some of the challenges, opportunities, and changes digital media bring for engaging with history, especially the history of media and their contents. It is partly a challenge, a chance, and a consequence presented by pending change, that through digitalization new questions, new perspectives, and insights are made possible. Digital media help us think anew about the old, to address the established media and the traditional questions we asked about them using new tools and means and thus to broaden or deepen the scope and understanding of the past and the present.

Among the challenges we are about to face, we can see that methodological debates (e.g., digital methods vs. traditional approaches and their genuine limitations or potentials) can be revitalized or take on new, nuanced features. Digital humanities approaches and computational methods will however continue to benefit from being complemented by qualitative analysis, hermeneutics, close reading, and special in-depth scrutiny of particular sources.

Additionally, research is likely to demand new interdisciplinary configurations. For instance, computer scientists may become collaborators with

---

50   Myers and Hamilton, "Social Media as Primary Source" 450.

scholars in fields where the solitary mind is still considered the academic ideal or norm. Furthermore, media and communication scholars are beginning to share their knowledge with scholars from other fields, e.g. musicology, and since the field of communication has expanded, they also need to rely on the expertise of others. Another challenge, which affects the social form of the academy (i.e., scholars and researchers), is to prevent new digital divides among scholars to be drawn or existing gaps to be widened. Adapting to changes in the course of digital transformation will call for skills and competencies in dealing with innovations. But equally important will be the acceptance of innovations as something that can help us do better research or address some questions in more suitable or convenient ways. Therefore, it will be necessary to (re-)establish required skills and literacies in the teaching and training of scholars as well as making them accessible for more senior scholars. Digital archives and digital sources create new challenges and perpetuate others, as I have argued, so a familiarity with the potentials and problems that digital research environments may bring does not only enable dialogue between digitally savvy and digitally averse scholars but also helps prevent embellished expectations. I mentioned interdisciplinary configurations and new grounds for cooperation. And I do indeed believe that working routines and typical workflows could be affected the most. Historical research in general as well as in cultural studies or media and communication research in particular has been characterized by individualized researchers. The historian Jon Olsen argued[51] that digital history is dependent on team effort rather than individual talent. One major impact of the digital age could hence be that media historians also become increasingly dependent on and open to collaboration with those who can add particular competencies to the blend of skills required for engaging with digital research situations.

Bibliography (last accessed 16 April 2020)

Andrejevic, Mark, Alison Hearn and Helen Kennedy. "Cultural Studies of Data Mining: Introduction." *European Journal of Cultural Studies* 18, 4–5 (June 2015): 379–94. DOI: 10.1177/1367549415577395

---

51   Olsen, "Digital History als Mannschaftssport."

Ankerson, Megan Sapnar. "Writing Web Histories with an Eye on the Analog Past." *New Media & Society* 14, 3 (May 2012): 384–400. DOI: 10.1177/1461444 811414834

Balbi, Gabriele. "Doing Media History in 2050." *Westminster Papers in Communication and Culture* 8, 2 (October 2011): 133–57. DOI: 10.16997/wpcc.188

Balbi, Gabriele, and Paolo Magaudda. *A History of Digital Media: An Intermedia and Global Perspective*. London: Taylor and Francis, 2018.

Behmer, Markus, et al., eds. *Das Gedächtnis des Rundfunks: Die Archive der öffentlich-rechtlichen Sender und ihre Bedeutung für die Forschung*. Wiesbaden: Springer, 2014.

Ben-David, Anat. "What does the Web Remember of Its Deleted Past? An Archival Reconstruction of the Former Yugoslav Top-Level Domain." *New Media & Society* 18, 7 (August 2016): 1103–19. DOI: 10.1177/1461444816643790

Ben-David, Anat, and Adam Amram. "The Internet Archive and the Socio-Technical Construction of Historical Facts." *Internet Histories: Digital Technology, Culture and Society* 2, 1–2 (April 2018): 179–201. DOI: 10.1080/24701 475.2018.1455412

Birkner, Thomas, et al. "A Century of Journalism History as Challenge: Digital Archives, Sources, and Methods." *Digital Journalism* 6, 9 (October 2018): 1121–35. DOI: 10.1080/21670811.2018.1514271

Birkner, Thomas, and Christian Schwarzenegger. "Konjunkturen, Kontexte, Kontinuitäten: eine Programmatik für die Kommunikationsgeschichte im digitalen Zeitalter." *medien & zeit* 31, 3 (Januar 2020): 5–16. https://medienundzeit.at/thomas-birkner-christian-schwarzenegger-konjunkturen-kontexte-kontinuitaeten/

Blumer, Herbert. "What is Wrong with Social Theory?" *American Sociological Review* 19, 1 (February 1954): 3–10. DOI: 10.2307/2088165

Bolin, Göran. "Institution, Technology, World: Relationships between the Media, Culture, and Society." *Mediatization of Communication*. Ed. Knut Lundby. Berlin: De Gruyter, 2014. 175–98.

Brügger, Niels. "When the Present Web is Later the Past: Web Historiography, Digital History, and Internet Studies." *Historical Social Research* 37, 4 (2012): 102–17. DOI: 10.12759/hsr.37.2012.4.102-117

Classen, Christoph, et al. "Zeitgeschichte ohne Bild und Ton? Probleme der Rundfunk-Überlieferung und die Initiative 'Audiovisuelles Erbe.'" *Zeithistorische Forschungen: Studies in Contemporary History* 8, 1 (May 2011): 130–40. DOI: 10.14765/zzf.dok-1668

Cohen, Daniel J. "The Future of Preserving the Past." *CRM: The Journal of Heritage Stewardship* 2, 2 (Summer 2005): 6–19.

Couldry, Nick, and Andreas Hepp. *The Mediated Construction of Reality*. Cambridge, UK: Polity, 2017.

Deacon, David. "Yesterday's Papers and Today's Technology: Digital Newspaper Archives and 'Push Button' Content Analysis." *European Journal of Communication* 22, 1 (March 2007): 5–25. DOI: 10.1177/0267323107073743

Deuze, Mark. "Media Life." *Media, Culture & Society* 33, 1 (January 2011): 137–148. DOI: 10.1177/0163443710386518

Filimowicz, Michael, and Veronika Tzankova, eds. *Reimagining Communication: Meaning*. London, New York: Routledge, 2020.

Fickers, Andreas. "Towards a New Digital Historicism? Doing History in the Age of Abundance." *Journal of European Television History and Culture* 1, 1 (February 2012): 19–26.

Gitelman, Lisa, ed. *'Raw Data' Is an Oxymoron*. Cambridge, MA: MIT Press, 2013.

Gitelman, Lisa, and Virgina Jackson. "Introduction." *'Raw Data' Is an Oxymoron*. Ed. Lisa Gitelman. Cambridge, MA: MIT Press, 2013. 1–14.

Hepp, Andreas, and Friedrich Krotz, eds. *Mediatized Worlds: Culture and Society in a Media Age*. Basingstoke, Hants: Palgrave Macmillan, 2014.

Hepp, Andreas. "Kommunikations- und Medienwissenschaft in datengetriebenen Zeiten." *Publizistik* 61, 3 (July 2016): 225–46. DOI: 10.1007/s11616-016-0263-y

Hepp, Andreas. *Deep Mediatization: Key Ideas in Media & Cultural Studies*. London, New York: Routledge, 2020.

Hickethier, Knut. *Einführung in die Medienwissenschaft*. Stuttgart, Weimar: J. B. Metzler, 2010.

Hoskins, Andrew. "The Right to be Forgotten in Post-Scarcity Culture." *The Ethics of Memory in a Digital Age*. Eds. Alessia Ghezzi et al. Basingstoke, Hants: Palgrave Macmillan, 2014. 50–64. DOI: 10.1057/9781137428455_4

Humphreys, Lee, et al. "Historicizing New Media: A Content Analysis of Twitter." *Journal of Communication* 63, 3 (June 2013): 413–31. DOI: 10.1111/jcom.12030

Jensen, Helle Strandgaard. "Doing Media History in a Digital Age: Change and Continuity in Historiographical Practices." *Media, Culture & Society* 38, 1 (November 2015): 119–28. DOI: 10.1177/0163443715607846

Keute, Annika, and Thomas Birkner. "Digital Wiedergeboren? Die Bedeutung von digitalen Archiven für die Journalismusforschung." *Digitale Kommu-*

nikation und Kommunikationsgeschichte: Perspektiven, Potentiale, Problemfelder.
Eds. Christian Schwarzenegger et al. [forthcoming]

Koenen, Erik. "Digitale Perspektiven in der Kommunikations- und Medien-geschichte: Erkenntnispotentiale und Forschungsszenarien für die historische Presseforschung." *Publizistik* 63, 4 (October 2018): 535–56. DOI: 10.1007/s11616-018-0459-4

Koenen, Erik, et al. "Historische Kommunikations- und Medienforschung im digitalen Zeitalter. Ein Kollektivbeitrag der Initiative 'Kommunikationsgeschichte digitalisieren' zu Konturen, Problemen und Potentialen kommunikations- und medienhistorischer Forschung in digitalen Kontexten." *Medien & Zeit* 33, 2 (2018): 4–19. https://medienundzeit.at/erik-koenen-christian-schwarzenegger-lisa-bolz-peter-gentzel-leif-kramp-christian-pentzold-christina-sanko-historische-kommunikations-und-medienforschung-im-digitalen-zeitalter/

Krotz, Friedrich. "Media Connectivity: Concepts, Conditions and Consequences." *Connectivity, Networks and Flows: Conceptualizing Contemporary Communications.* Eds. Andreas Hepp et al. Cresskill, NJ: Hampton, 2008. 13–31.

Krotz, Friedrich. "Mediatization: A Concept with Which to Grasp Media and Social Change." *Mediatization: Concept, Changes, Consequences.* Ed. Knut Lundby. New York: Peter Lang, 2009. 21–40.

Livingstone, Sonia. "On the Mediation of Everything: ICA Presidential Address 2008." *Journal of Communication* 59, 1 (March 2009): 1–18. DOI: 10.1111/j.1460-2466.2008.01401.x

Livingstone, Sonia. "If Everything is Mediated, What is Distinctive About the Field of Communication?" *International Journal of Communication* 5 (2011): 1472–75.

Lunt, Peter, and Sonia Livingstone. "Is 'Mediatization' the New Paradigm for Our Field? A Commentary on Deacon and Stanyer (2014, 2015) and Hepp, Hjarvard and Lundby (2015)." *Media, Culture & Society* 38, 3 (April 2016): 462–70. DOI: 10.1177/0163443716631288

Menke, Manuel, and Christian Schwarzenegger. "On the Relativity of Old and New Media: A Lifeworld Perspective." *Convergence: The International Journal of Research into New Media Technologies* 25, 4 (March 2019): 657–72. DOI: 10.1177/1354856519834480

Myers, Cayce, and James F. Hamilton. "Social Media as Primary Source: The Narrativization of Twenty-First-Century Social Movements." *Media History* 20, 4 (October 2014): 431–44. DOI: 10.1080/13688804.2014.950639

Nicholson, Bob. "THE DIGITAL TURN: Exploring the Methodological Possibilities of Digital Newspaper Archives." *Media History* 19, 1 (January 2013): 59–73. DOI: 10.1080/13688804.2012.752963

Olsen, Jon. "Digital History als Mannschaftssport." *H–Soz–Kult*, 23.11.2015. https://www.hsozkult.de/debate/id/diskussionen-2894

Pfaffenberger, Fabian. "What you tweet is what we get? Zum wissenschaftlichen Nutzen von Twitter-Daten." *Publizistik* 63, 1 (February 2018): 53–72.

Schwartz, Joan M., and Terry Cook. "Archives, Records, and Power: The Making of Modern Memory." *Archival Science* 2, 1–2 (March 2002): 1–19. DOI: 10.1007/BF02435628

Schwarzenegger, Christian. "Exploring Digital Yesterdays: Reflections on New Media and the Future of Communication History." *Historical Social Research* 37, 4 (2012): 118–33. DOI: 10.12759/hsr.37.2012.4.118-133

Schwarzenegger, Christian. "Herausforderungen des digitalen Gestern: Kommunikationsgeschichte und die Quellen einer gegenwärtigen Zukunft." *Das Gedächtnis des Rundfunks: Die Archive der öffentlich-rechtlichen Sender und ihre Bedeutung für die Forschung.* Eds. Markus Behmer et al. Wiesbaden: Springer, 2014. 403–15.

Schwarzenegger, Christian, and Lohmeier Christine. "Reimagining Memory." *Reimagining Communication: Meaning.* Eds. Michael Filimowicz and Veronika Tzankova. London, New York: Routledge, 2020.

Schwarzenegger, Christian, et al., eds. *Digitale Kommunikation und Kommunikationsgeschichte: Perspektiven, Potentiale, Problemfelder.* [forthcoming]

Weller, Toni. *History in the Digital Age.* London, New York: Routledge, 2012.

The Narratological Architecture of Musical *lieux de mémoire*
A Transmedial Perspective on Antonio Stradivari

Matej Santi (University of Music and Performing Arts Vienna)

This paper investigates the narrative of Antonio Stradivari (c. 1644–1737) and the *topoi* related to his persona in audiovisual media from a historical and transmedial perspective.

The chosen sources are available online and are part of the historical collection of the Archivio storico Istituto Luce in Rome.[1] Despite having its own digital archive, the institution has, since 2010, made some documents available on the popular video sharing portal YouTube. This is a clear sign of how digitalization and social media have brought historical sources, which can no longer be ignored by research, into everyday life. This concerns not only the history of music but also the humanities more generally, bringing with it several questions. How and why should these sources be evaluated? What does it mean for (music) historiography if music-related audiovisual sources—material that has long been difficult to access—becomes available worldwide with a simple mouse click? What does it mean for (music) historians, trained to mainly deal with written sources? How can the Internet affect the established way of thinking about history and presenting it? These evident questions are only the tip of the iceberg.

These questions can hardly be answered in this short contribution. Nevertheless, the present article will attempt, on the basis of a case study, to demonstrate the added value of audiovisual sources for understanding the impact of medialized discourses on the shaping of Antonio Stradivari as a

---

1   In 2013, the Newsreels and Photographs Collection of the Istituto Luce was included in the UNESCO Memory of the World Register. "Chi siamo, Archivio storico Luce." www.archivioluce.com/chi-siamo/

musical *lieu de mémoire*—or 'site of memory'—in the 20th century and address the meanings related to this process.

The Myth of Stradivari

Nearly everyone, that is, people without any specific knowledge in the field of 'classical music,' has heard of Stradivari. His name has pervaded society, not least because of the narrative of his apparently lost 'secrets.'[2] We are often greeted with newspaper articles about how someone discovered them. And yet another respectable subgenre are the reports of fraudulent instruments, where Stradivari counts as *pars pro toto*.[3]

But why is the violin so fascinating? With the exception of singing, human beings express their musical creativity with the help of musical instruments. An instrument, as the word itself explains, enables the performer to overcome the natural limitations of the body and, in this specific case, the voice. With the use of an appropriate instrument the timbre and register of the voice are no longer the only means of artistic expression. For this reason, of all the musical instruments, the violin seems to have a special status; in his exhaustive monograph David Schoenbaum defines the violin in the subtitle as "the world's most versatile instrument."[4]

Remarkably, ever since its appearance in Europe in the 16th century, the violin hasn't changed significantly in its design.[5] Only minor changes in the length and inclination of the neck as well as innovations in the setup have taken place over the centuries. It is no coincidence that the first composer who earned his fame exclusively with his instrumental music, Arcangelo Corelli (1653–1713), was a violinist.[6] Since then the violin has occupied a central place in the orchestra, gaining the status of the quintessential embodiment of instrumental virtuosity. Because of the consistency of its design over the cen-

---

2   One of the most influential treatises on violin making from the 20th century is Simone Fernando Sacconi's *I 'segreti' di Stradivari*. With the title, the author signals his intention to disclose the alleged 'secrets.' Sacconi, *I 'segreti.'*

3   The violinmaker and restorer Roger Hargrave warns of the dangers of the highly speculative market for instruments made on the Italian Peninsula during the 17th and 18th centuries. Hargrave, "Pry Before You Buy."

4   Schoenbaum, *The violin.*

5   Dilworth, "Violins" 97.

6   Talbot, "Corelli" 457.

turies and its special status within the orchestra (and as a solo instrument), the violin—and more generally string instruments—have become objects of market speculation.

Present day media often report the exorbitant prices paid for instruments made by Antonio Stradivari in Cremona. For instance, the Nippon Music Foundation sold the virtually unblemished 1721 'Lady Blunt' Stradivari for charity after the tsunami and the Fukushima Daiichi nuclear disaster for close to 16 million US dollars.[7]

The myth that made the instruments constructed in Stradivari's workshop so valuable most likely developed in the 19th century. In German-speaking areas, instruments built south of the Alps, on the territory of modern-day Italy, were highly prized, as the catalogs of string instruments available on the market at the end of the 18th century testify.[8] However, in the *Dizionario delle arti e de' mestieri*, printed in Venice 1770, Stradivari is not described as the most sought-after violinmaker; this position was granted to Jacob Stainer (1617–83), who worked in Absam in Tyrol.[9] Interestingly, the Guarneri dynasty—the instruments attributed to Bartolomeo Giuseppe Guarneri 'del Gesù' (1698–1744) are highly valued today—isn't even mentioned in this source. Possibly due to the flat arching enabling a more powerful sound, a common feature of the instruments from Stradivari's and Guarneri del Gesù's workshops, the sound-ideal associated with higher arching, typical of the instruments made by the Amati dynasty and Jacob Stainer, went out of fashion. Due to a lack of sources, this gradual process of change is hard to reconstruct. The same is true for the evolution of the Stradivari myth in the 19th century. It is commonly known that Giovanni Battista Viotti (1755–1822), who became highly regarded as a soloist and composer in Paris and London, probably played a violin made by Antonio Stradivari.[10] Even if no sources prove this unequivocally—for instance, Count Cozio di Salabue (1755–1840) remarks that Viotti played instruments made by Gioffredo Cappa (1644–1717), although this evidence isn't reliable[11]—the *Stradivari* brand became synonymous with quality in both craftmanship and tone.

---

7   The 'Lady Blunt' Stradivarius was offered by the Tarisio auction house. "Notable sales: 'Lady Blunt' Stradivarius of 1721." https://tarisio.com/auctions/notable-sales/lady-blunt-stradivarius-of-1721/

8   *Musikalische Realzeitung*, 7 September 1791. http://anno.onb.ac.at/cgi-content/anno?aid =muz&datum=17910907&seite=3

9   Griselini, "Liutiere" 198. https://books.google.at/books?id=wXCVfiJvb3lC&pg=PA196

10   Lister, *Amico* 79.

11   Ibid. 80.

This ascription of meaning is today more powerful than ever: to play a 'Strad,' as the instruments made by Stradivari are nicknamed, is perceived to be both a prestigious privilege and a sign of top-level professionalism.

In recent years, blind tests have shown that tonal differences between violins made by Stradivari and modern instruments are difficult to recognize for both performing musicians and for the public.[12] Such attempts, undertaken to deconstruct the myths surrounding string instruments from the 17th and 18th centuries, don't seem to be effective—quite the opposite. Only two months after news of the research project, which had taken place in Paris in 2017, appeared in *The Strad*, the violinist Frank Almond explained in a column in the very same magazine that only old Italian violins develop synergistically with the player. This characteristic, besides the tonal character of the instrument, is difficult to find in a newly built instrument—at least in the opinion of Almond.[13] The result of such explanations in the media is clear: the myth of Stradivari and Italian string instruments lives on.

Stradivari as a *lieu de mémoire*

Due the ubiquitous presence of Stradivari in print media and, with the popularization of film, on screen, the question of whether Stradivari and the violin could be understood as a *lieu de mémoire* becomes relevant. In his *Realms of Memory*, Pierre Nora defines *lieux de mémoire* as: "[...] any significant entity, whether material or nonmaterial in nature, which by dint of human will or the work of time has become a symbolic element of the memorial heritage of any community [...]."[14] Pessimistically, Nora also states that the mass media, in a process that he calls "mediatisation," undermine the ability to differentiate between relevant and less relevant collective memories. But we should not disregard the fact that that audiovisual documents distributed by the media shape collective memory. They make use of this abovementioned "symbolic element of the memorial heritage" in order to forge a shared identity. This happens, obviously, through the use of narratives and their transformation,

---

12   Fritz et al., "Soloist Evaluations;" Fritz et al., "Listener Evaluations;" Curtin, "Paris Projection."
13   Almond, "Sound Legacies."
14   Nora, "Realms of Memory" XVII.

adaptation, and realization in the light of new social situations, a view supported by many scholars: "Media can be understood as forms which do not simply represent the content of the narratives but indeed construct them in different ways."[15]

Therefore, it becomes relevant to analyze narrative strategies that shape *lieux de mémoire* in the media. One of the criticisms levelled against Nora is that the term itself is quite vague. The historian Patrick Schmidt noted in this regard that Nora, when using the term, doesn't differentiate between the media of memory on the one hand, and national myths, *topoi*, as well as institutions on the other. He simply subsumes these entities under the umbrella term *lieux de mémoire*.[16] This is *per se* not an unintended weakness: the broadness of the term is ultimately due to its vagueness, which enables various (re)interpretations.

However, this paper tries to negotiate a model which relates *topoi* to narratives in media. In doing so, different layers involved in the architecture of a *lieu de mémoire* become manifest: in fact, a 'site of memory' consists of an entity (person, place, or idea) related to *topoi* by narratives spread through different media in different times. This is also the case for Antonio Stradivari.

Stradivari and the Violin Making School

The early documents stored in the Archivio storico Luce in Rome are a product of fascist Italy. L'Unione Cinematografica Educativa (L. U. C. E., an acronym that means 'light'), was founded in 1924. The relevance of audiovisual material for the purpose of propaganda was however only recognized in 1933 when a diplomat, Giacomo Paulucci di Calboli (1887–1961), took over management of the institute.[17] At that time, Luce basically produced two kinds of material to be shown in cinemas around Italy: the *Giornale Luce* und the *Rivista Luce*. The *Giornale Luce* presented brief films on current affairs, while the *Rivista Luce* produced longer films with clear pedagogical objectives.[18] Aware of the need for the distribution of audiovisual material in the countryside (where cinemas didn't exist), the regime decided to reach the audience by organizing traveling cinemas.

---

15   Müller-Funk, *The Architecture of Modern Culture* 43.
16   Schmidt, "Zwischen Medien und Topoi" 35.
17   Dalla Pria, *Dittatura e immagine* 58.
18   Ibid. 63–64.

The popularization of what was once an elite culture grew out of the need for social cohesion, and as part of an attempt to develop industry to enable Italy's total economic autonomy, the use of propaganda and educational material in cinema was on the agenda. Reaching back to the past in order to define a shared, albeit invented, cultural heritage, such as the culture of ancient Rome, the medieval guilds, and the Renaissance, was an ongoing process. For instance, evoking medieval guilds and mixing them with the artistic achievements of the Renaissance, the regime tried to establish Florence as a significant European manufacturing center.[19] Furthermore, prominent musicians and individuals associated with high culture entered the repertoire of that imagined past. In the Lombard city of Cremona, both the opera composer Amilcare Ponchielli (1834–86) and the violinmaker Antonio Stradivari were used to promote large international events that included concerts and exhibitions.[20] The celebration of the 100-year anniversary of Ponchielli's birth took place in 1934 and served as a trial run for the *Bicentenario stradivariano*, the huge celebration of the 200-year anniversary of Stradivari's death between May and October 1937. According to estimates, during the *Bicentenario stradivariano* 100,000 people from all over the world visited Cremona. Interest in the event was also bolstered by the prominence of the invited guests. An exhibition of old Cremonese instruments, which took place in the Palazzo Cittanova, was curated by leading experts in the field, such as Simone Fernando Sacconi (1895–1974), Fridolin Hamma (1881–1969), Max Möller Jr. (1915–85), Paul Deschamp, and Leandro Bisiach Sr. (1864–1946).[21]

The promoter of the *Bicentenario* was the fascist politician Roberto Farinacci (1892–1945) who was also the founder of the newspaper *Il Regime fascista*, the party's chief mouthpiece.[22] As is apparent from archival materials, the organizing committee decided to open a violin making school instead of erecting a statue of Stradivari.[23] The reason for the foundation of the school in 1938 was pragmatic in nature. Based on the brands of Stradivari and Cremona, the school would be an attempt to bring contemporary instruments to the mar-

---

19   Palla, *Firenze nel regime fascista* 234.
20   Santoro, "Le grandi mostre del 1937" 14–15.
21   Ibid. 17.
22   Moglia, *La stampa quotidiana nella Repubblica Sociale Italiana.* http://www.larchivio.com/xoom/paolomoglia.htm
23   Bellomi, "Celebrazione del Bicentenario Stradivariano: Verbale di seduta del Comitato" 53.

ket. Convinced of the power of the medium, the committee also planned the production of a film about Stradivari's life. However, the plan failed.[24]

Before closely examining a newsreel from 1941 about the newly founded violin making school, it may be of interest to consider some core aspects of audiovisual material. An audiovisual source represents a network of meaning conveyed by two different layers. The (a) audio layer conveys spoken words, music, and noises—as, for instance, background noise. These need not only be sounds that have been deliberately recorded by the producers to add a particular meaning to their presentation. In older sources, sounds resulting from the original recording technique are present, and in the later sources they may be the result of dubbing. Interestingly, these sounds represent *per se* a kind of medial *topos*—e.g., the sound of a movie projector implies a whole world of meanings. The (b) visual layer conveys iconography. Also, in this case, optical effects—the most obvious being filming in black-and-white—create associations. Both (a) the audio and (b) the video layer are subject to historical changes and both reflect and reproduce the use of iconographic and auditory impressions common at the time of their production. In this manner, they consolidate inherited cultural themes, or *topoi*. The *topoi* from the audiovisual productions of the past—specific stereotypical sound and iconographic motifs—would be used in later times for purposes of nostalgia or with the goal of recreating visual and sonic environments with specific historical references. Of course, these kinds of references could only be detected by an audience aware of and previously socialized with their historical dimension. Even if both layers make sense separately, in combination they create a new, much more sophisticated, and deeper meaning. Without the spoken word, a film would hardly convey the same meaning, and the same is true if the audio layer were presented without images.[25]

The question arises: which ideas and *topoi*—in the sense of literary motifs—are conveyed by the different layers of the abovementioned film and which narratives—in the sense of an organized use of words or of film iconography—are used to convey them?

The relatively short newsreel about the violin making school, which will be presently discussed, was produced in 1941, in the third year of the institu-

---

24　Loffi, "Agosto 1935, il primo grande film su Stradivari." http://cremonamisteriosa.blogs pot.com/2015/11/era-il-novembre-del-1936-quando.html

25　See also: Cook, *Analysing Musical Multimedia* 20–23.

tion's existence, and is called a *Cinegiornale Luce*.[26] The format was produced between 1940 and 1945 for propaganda purposes; its main novelty was the participation of directors in both shooting and editing.[27] A year earlier, in June 1940, Italy had declared war on France and England, so the film may be considered not only as propaganda material meant to increase awareness of the craft tradition in Italy, but also as an attempt to feign normality in everyday life.

At this point, a few scenes will be discussed.[28] The film's opening shows the hard work of conceiving the design of the instrument in a classroom (00:04–00:14). The instructor demonstrates on the board how the outline of the instrument should be drawn (00:04–00:08). At least two or three dozen well-dressed students in suits and ties—as the dress code of the time demanded—carefully listen to the teacher's explanation. The following scenes (00:15–00:31) show students, now wearing work coats, working on their instruments in the workshop while the head of the workshop, Carlo Schiavi (1908–43), gives them instructions. The audio layer conveys an additional message: the second movement of J. S. Bach's *Brandenburg Concerto* No. 6 refers to the achievements of 18th-century music, in this manner alluding to the time period in which Stradivari worked.[29]

It should be noted that interest in the music of the past was growing fast at that time. For instance, Alfredo Casella (1883–1947) set a precedent for the reception of Antonio Vivaldi's (1678–1741) music. He was one of the promoters of a music festival that took place for the first time in Siena in 1939 (*Settimana Musicale Senese*), just two years before the production of the newsreel.[30] The

---

26   Gemmiti, *Cremona: Una visita alla scuola di liuteria*. https://patrimonio.archivioluce.com/luce-web/detail/IL5000014203/2/cremona-visita-alla-scuola-liuteria.html

27   "Cinegiornale Luce C (1940–1945)." https://www.archivioluce.com/giornale-luce-c/

28   Due to length restrictions, the transcription will not be printed; only the most important statements—in the opinion of the author—will be recounted.

29   Music by German composers is strongly represented in the audiovisual sources of the Archivio Luce. For example, Beethoven's Symphony No. 3 and 5 serve as soundtrack in a documentary film about Gabriele D'Annunzio, the 'poeta vate' strongly mythologized by the regime (01:54–06:00). Unsurprisingly, the music is associated with D'Annunzio's alleged 'heroism.' The second movement of the Concerto for 2 violins RV 522 by Vivaldi was used as the opening theme; the same piece is also heard as D'Annunzio's 'sala della musica' (musicroom) is shown; the camera turns to Beethoven's and Liszt's death masks decorating the room (11:50–12:39). Cerchio, *Ritorno al Vittoriale*. https://patrimonio.archivioluce.com/luce-web/detail/IL3000090705/1/ritorno-al-vittoriale.html

30   Talbot, *The Vivaldi Compendium* 41.

event made the newly discovered musical works from the past accessible to a wide audience as well as fashionable. At the same time, fresh interest in the well-known works of the past was aroused.

At the very beginning of the film, the narrator's voice explains that Cremona is the birthplace of the most prominent violinmakers. As the camera turns to a single artisan (00:23–00:24, medium shot), the narrator explains how a real violinmaker should have "l'anima del liutaio" (the soul of a violinmaker); for this reason, at least as stated in the newsreel, only a few selected craftsmen are suited for apprenticeship and then the profession. After showing the construction process of the violin, Carlo Schiavi tunes an instrument made by a student. As he does so, the background music stops playing; the sound of the newly built violin comes to the sonic foreground (00:32–00:46). Then, Bach's music begins to play again while the production of varnish in a modern laboratory and the varnishing process is displayed (00:46–00:57). The next few scenes are filmed in a huge room with hundreds of instruments hanging from the roof—a common practice to let the varnish dry (00:58–01:04). The technically advanced approach in analyzing sound quality is conveyed by the image of a violinist playing the Ciaccona—a core piece of the repertoire, for a long time erroneously attributed to Tommaso Antonio Vitali (1663–1745)—in front of a microphone (01:05–01:12).[31] Accompanied by the Ciaccona, the molds used by Stradivari are shown in the next scene (01:13–01:20). Stradivari's manuscript (01:21–01:25) and a painting (01:26) of him by Edouard Jean Conrad Hamman (1819-88) close the newsreel.[32]

As mentioned, in 1941 the school was in its third year of existence. A total of 8 students, separated into three classes, were studying there (the total duration of the course was four years).[33] Due to this very small number, it may safely be assumed that the newsreel is largely staged—the classroom and the workshop at the beginning of the film are full. The impression was created that two or three dozen apprentices were studying and working there. Also, the huge amount of instruments hanging from the roof couldn't have accurately represented the amount of instruments built by relatively few students within the short period of three years. Even though the school is most likely

---

31   Suess, "Vitali, Tomaso Antonio" 799. The piece became very popular after Ferdinand
       David (1810–73) published it in his *Hohe Schule des Violinspiels* (*Advanced School of Violin
       Playing*) Vol. 2.
32   Hamman, *Stradivarius*. https://gallica.bnf.fr/ark:/12148/btv1b8425075w
33   Nicolini, *The International School of Cremona* 31.

not accurately depicted, the creation of an 'invented tradition' through the new technology of film can be seen. Under the illusion of reproducing 'objective reality,' the sounds and images transmitted by film mediate a constructed utopia in this case.

Working Alone

An image of Stradivari working alone at night under the starry sky, derived from Hamman's rendition, seen at the end of the short newsreel about the violin making school, was used as advertising material for the *Bicentenario* in 1937, and was reproduced on a large-format poster.[34] It was created by Giulio Cisari (1892–1979), a prolific engraver and illustrator who was particularly active in the interwar period.[35] The iconography certainly resembles that of the long-haired Ludwig van Beethoven (1770–1827), who, since the 1830s, embodied the quintessence of the romantic artist.[36] The narrative of his talent and will, which enabled him to rebel against social and artistic norms as well as fate itself—he became deaf—to produce great achievements in the field of music, was pervasive. In accordance with this idea of the creative genius who is not content to follow in the footsteps of his predecessors, the Stradivari on Cisari's poster is pondering his work, sitting in his solitary shop. Behind him—he is presumably sitting in front of a large window—is the Cremonese cathedral with its *torrazzo*, one of the tallest brick towers in Europe, and the baptistery shines a bluish light that emphasizes the surreal atmosphere of the night. The picture also refers to the *topos* of Stardivari's 'lost secrets.' On Stradivari's right-hand side, we see a small bottle laid on the window ledge. It reminds us of his much-admired and highly regarded varnish. However, considering that the output of his workshop was about 600 instruments, it is hard to believe that he worked alone. As Steward Pollens suggests, he and his assistants spent, on average, between 2 to 3 weeks on a single instrument.[37] So time spent pondering was reduced to a minimum. And even though he may have had a good look at the final product, he certainly did not do so at night because the light would have been too dim.

---

34   Cisari, *Bicentenario Stradivariano Cremona.* http://www.collezionesalce.beniculturali.it/?
      q=scheda&id=11256
35   Pallottino, "Cisari, Giulio." http://www.treccani.it/enciclopedia/giulio-cisari_(Dizionario
      -Biografico)/
36   Jungmann, *Sozialgeschichte der klassischen Musik* 91.
37   Pollens, *Stradivari* 38–41.

The iconographic rendition on Cisari's poster—Stradivari working in front of Cremona's cathedral—can be read as a sign of the times. In 1929 the Lateran Treaty between the fascist regime and the pope was signed. Thereby the conflict between the church and the Italian national state that had lasted for over six decades, since the middle of the 19th century, was resolved. Italy recognized the sovereignty of the Vatican and the Vatican recognized the national state of Italy.[38] The state permitted religious instruction in primary and secondary school. Correspondingly, religious instruction also took place at the violin making school in Cremona. The development of Stradivari's iconography from Hamman to Cisari, from a dark and chaotic workshop to an open, public space—in fact an Agora in front of the church—also reflects the changed function of music and culture in fascist-era society: a formerly elite culture was popularized and thus stylized as an important part of everyday public life.

As may be expected, the new historical circumstances are also present in film. The media representation of violin making is put in relation to the Lateran Treaty, as is seen in a documentary film stored in the Archivio Luce. The film *La bottega della melodia* (*The workshop of melodies*) was released in 1942, one year after the newsreel about the violin making school.[39] The film is part of the collection of *Documentari INCOM* (*Industria Corti Metraggi*), whose general director was Sandro Pallavicini (1908–66). *Documentari INCOM* produced shorts between 1938 and 1965. It was a private enterprise, which at its inception followed the regime's propaganda directives. The short films stand out in their tendency to recreate short stories about their subjects. Documentaries about the Spanish Civil War, Italian industry, art, and the development of mass media were the main subjects of *Documentari INCOM* during the regime. Additionally, directors like Roberto Rossellini (1906–77) worked there. The collection was later bought by the Archivio Luce.[40] Unlike with the short newsreel, the credits of this documentary film are known. Michele Gandin (1914–94), was a prolific director of documentaries who—according to IMDb—was still active in the 1980s.[41] Gandin also worked with Vittorio De Sica (1901–74), the director and actor associated with Italian neorealism. Even though it seems

---

38   Ray, "Lateran Treaty." https://www.britannica.com/event/Lateran-Treaty
39   Gandin, *La bottega della melodia*. https://patrimonio.archivioluce.com/luce-web/detail/
      IL3000051047/1/la-bottega-della-melodia.html
40   "Documentari Incom (1938–1965)." https://www.archivioluce.com/documentari-incom/
41   "Gandin, Michele." *IMDb*. https://www.imdb.com/name/nm0304170/

that the music was explicitly produced for the documentary film, the composer remains unknown. In comparison to the newsreel about the violin making school, which was shaped by music of the past, the documentary film is characterized by the aesthetic of neorealism—even on the musical level. If the short newsreel showed (as previously demonstrated) a largely constructed version of the activities in the newly founded violin making school, Gandin's film seems to pursue the pedagogical aim of explaining—and making tangible and visible—the circumstances in which Stradivari worked. But in doing so, the contemporary imagination of history paired with elements of ideological propaganda was, as I will show, projected into the past. And how could it be otherwise, considering that the circumstances under which Stradivari ran his workshop are completely unknown, and regarding the fact that every narrative structure is *per se* embedded in the time in which it is conceived?

At the opening of *La bottega della melodia*, the references to Christianity are immediately evident. At the very beginning, an expressive orchestral introduction evokes tension. The musical idiom is close to a late romantic aesthetic. On an iconographic level, that is, on the visual layer of the film, a crucifix with the sky in the background appears (00:46–00:52) as the music changes into a solo violin melody with an ascending flourish at its beginning. It conveys a feeling of transcendence. The spotlight expands and shows us that the crucifix is the one held by an angel standing atop the baptistry (the same building seen on Cisari's poster); it is the archangel Gabriel (00:53–00:58). Then, other angels appear on screen, this time painted ones (00:59–01:16). While a painting with angels playing rebecs and violins is shown, the narrator declares that divine inspiration, the reason why the violin was brought into being, is also the reason why artists of the past chose to paint angels playing these instruments. As the scholar Steward Pollens noted, one of the earliest representations of the violin is found in a painting by Gaudenzio Ferrari (1477/78–1546) in Vercelli's San Cristoforo Church, *La Madonna degli aranci* (*The Madonna of the Orange Tree*), where an angel plays a violin with three strings.[42] Particularly during the 17th century, the violin had become increasingly used in the iconography associated with revelation of the divine.[43] Then, the narrator's voice tells us of a legend: it was an angel that revealed the secrets of violin making to the violinmakers of Cremona (00:19–00:52). The link to the bibli-

---

42   Pollens, *Stradivari* 5–6.

43   Carter and Butt, *The Cambridge History of Seventeenth-Century Music* 506.

cal story is evident: like the virgin Mary, violinmakers had conceived by the archangel.

In the next series of scenes, an old man is seen in his workshop at the end of a winding corridor (01:53–02:23). A crucifix dominates the wall of the workshop. The narrator's voice then explains that the luthier's trade stopped for a long time. Later on, the violinmaker is shown working behind a barred window (02:24–02:35). The *topos* of the prison as a place of enlightenment is very common in the life of the saints. For instance, Saint Francis of Assisi (1181/82–1226) prayed in the hermitage *Eremo delle Carceri*. The solitary prayer of Francis was increasingly practiced by members of the Franciscan order in Italian convents during the 17th century.[44] As a development of these ideas, working in solitary confinement to reach lofty artistic goals became a *topos* during the 19th century, as we see in the legends of Niccolò Paganini (1782–1840) practicing violin and of Bartolomeo Giuseppe Guarneri 'del Gesù' making violins in prison.[45] The devoted artisan working alone behind bars—as a security measure a rather common architectural feature of ground-floor workshops even today—embodies the link between angelic music and the music played by human beings. On the musical level, the melodic theme played by the solo violin at the beginning (00:45–01:00) is later developed by the orchestra. Several instruments adopt the theme. The thematic development of the solo violin melody with its ascending flourish could be interpreted as a musical symbol for the angel from whom everything in the narration develops.

Related to each other, the text, the music, and the iconography of the briefly analyzed initial sections of the documentary suggest that violin making in Cremona developed because of an angel, that is, because of religion. In the following scenes (02:36–03:15) the idea is conveyed that after Stradivari—in the 19th century, the era of the Italian *Risorgimento* (a term which ironically means resurrection)—violin making perished because of religion's absence. To emphasize this idea on an iconographic level, the camera draws back from the crucifix (03:04–03:11). In the further course of the film, the idea is implicitly conveyed that now, with the treaty with the Vatican and the

---

44   Mertens, *Solitudo seraphica* 148–150.
45   See also the 1830 lithograph by Boulanger (1806–67). Boulanger, *Niccolo Paganini en prison*. https://gallica.bnf.fr/ark:/12148/btv1b8423316f. As described by Lütgendorff, Count Cozio di Salabue, the author of the most valuable source for violin making in 18th century—his *Carteggio*—made the story about Guarneri working in prison well known. Lütgendorff, "Guarneri, (Bartolomeo) Giuseppe 'del Gesù'" 221.

foundation of the violin making school, the holy spirit will help Cremona once again, just as it helped Stradivari in the 18th century.

Stradivari after the World War—Continuities and Discontinuities

World War II didn't give the violin making school of Cremona the chance to expand and evolve as its founders had intended. Nevertheless, despite wartime circumstances the school continued to function, even if (presumably) not as presented in the audiovisual source from 1941. After the war, in order to adapt to the new situation and to possibly achieve the missed targets of previous years, a celebration of the 300-year anniversary of Stradivari's birth took place in Cremona in 1949.[46] At that time, the idea that Stradivari was born in 1648 and not in 1644 was under discussion; the exact year of his birth remains unknown even today. As part of this celebration, an exhibition of instruments built after 1880 was organized. As in 1937, the aim was to attract an international audience in order to bolster economic exchange.

To give the event visibility on a national level, a short newsreel was produced by *Settimana INCOM*, which was founded by Sandro Pallavicini in 1946 and remained active until 1965. Although Luce still produced newsreels (e. g. *Notiziario Nuova Luce*), the institution gradually turned into an archive.[47] *Settimana INCOM* focused on current affairs—the presence of politicians belonging to the Democrazia Cristiana (Christian Democracy) such as Alcide De Gasperi (1881-1954) and Giulio Andreotti (1919–2013), is striking—as well as fashion and sports.[48]

As the audiovisual documents produced by *Settimana INCOM* testify,[49] the celebration of Stradivari's birth was to be understood as a sign of both continuity and discontinuity with the past. Cremona was a key cultural center in fascist Italy: the nationally distributed newspaper *Il Regime fascista* was printed there and its director Roberto Farinacci, the organizer of the *Bicentenario stradivariano*, was a party official with connections to Mussolini and German officials. Due to the massive promotion of handicrafts and art in fascist Italy—not only violin making—the art contest *Premio Cremona* was held

---

46   Santoro, "La mostra di liuteria del maggio 1949."
47   Hüningen, "Luce." https://filmlexikon.uni-kiel.de/index.php?action=lexikon&tag=det&id=2410
48   "La Settimana INCOM (1946-1965)." https://www.archivioluce.com/la-settimana-incom/
49   *Cremona: Mostra concorso di liuteria.* https://patrimonio.archivioluce.com/luce-web/detail/IL5000013285/2/cremona-ostra-concorso-liuteria.html

in Cremona between 1939 and 1941.[50] It is therefore not surprising that in the search for a new identity after the horror of war, the same topics relevant to the cultural identity of the small city in the fascist era were to be reinterpreted in the new post-war context.

In the newsreel, the cultural heritage of the city comes to the fore, as expected. The film opens with a series of views of the *torrazzo* from ground level (00:08–00:13). While Antonio Vivaldi's *The Spring* from the *Four Seasons* serves as the soundtrack, a voice exclaims: "Bella questa Cremona" (beautiful this Cremona). On the visual layer, the buildings from the past, like the cathedral with the *torrazzo* and the baptistry are presented as the most important physical monument of the small Lombard city. By contrast, as stated by the narrator, Stradivari—"maestro della nobile e quasi magica arte della liuteria" (master of the noble and almost magical art of violin making)—embodies its most meaningful immaterial heritage (00:19–00:25).

After showing Cremona's buildings, the newsreel focuses on the exhibition of musical instruments. Many elements here share similarities with the already mentioned sources. In the second part of the newsreel, for instance, the violinist Marco Brasi (1905–58) tries out—accompanied by a harp, which can be seen in the frame—an instrument built by violinmakers who participated in the violin making contest (00:53–01:07). His posture and movements resemble those seen in the 1941 newsreel about the violin making school (a violinist playing the Ciaccona in front of a microphone). The musician's gestures and the position of his hands seem to be unusual: in this manner, audiovisual documents from the past are an important source for the study of performance practice during the 20th century. In the last part of the newsreel (01:36–01:43), the narrator refers to angels playing violins in paintings of the past—a *topos* with a long history, as mentioned above. In this last scene, the image of a violin is distorted by a kaleidoscopic camera effect.

The 1949 Cremona exhibition was important in the fight against speculation with instruments made on the Italian Peninsula in the 17th and 18th centuries. Giovanni Iviglia, who at that time worked in Switzerland, was chosen to preside over the event. In 1948 he launched a campaign against the forgery of old instruments. He claimed that many instruments attributed to

---

50   A critical examination of the art of that time took place in Cremona in 2018. An exhibition of the paintings was organized, and a publication was printed. Sgarbi, *Il regime dell'arte*.

Stradivari, Amati, and other violinmakers were, in fact, the work of other artisans. In the 1950s he took the most important instrument dealers of the time—Fridolin Hamma (1881–1969), Emil Hermann (1888–1968), and Albert Philips Hill (1883–1981)—to court.[51] The whole process clearly had economic motivations: from that point on the Italian Chamber of Commerce could defend the quality and authenticity of products, past and present, made in Italy. However, in the 1949 newsreel, Iviglia's name is only briefly mentioned without reference to his campaign. Later on, Iviglia published a critical essay on the subject.[52] Even if the reception of a given audiovisual document is difficult to reconstruct, the newsreel's aim was undoubtedly to sensitize the general public to cultural heritage issues.

Stradivari in the '60s

The use of Vivaldi's music seems to have been common in post-war Italy in the context of lutherie, at least from the few sources available online: *The Autumn* was also used as a soundtrack at the beginning of the newsreel about the exhibition of Stradivari's instruments on the Isola Bella on the Lago Maggiore in 1963.[53]

This source is, like *La bottega della melodia* from 1942, part of the *Documentari INCOM* collection.[54] It opens with an orchestral theme on the audio level, and, on the visual level, with a headshot of Michelangelo's David (00:08–00:14), not unlike the 1942 film. This isn't the only reference to the Renaissance. As Vivaldi's music plays, images of the Lago Maggiore are shown while the narrator explains the crucial role played by industrialists, "uomini d'affari che hanno l'animo dei signori del Rinascimento" (businessmen with the souls of Renaissance lords) in organizing the event in the

51   Catani, "La guerra dei violini." https://www.larivista.ch/la-guerra-dei-violini-1948-1955-la-lotta-della-ccis-contro-le-falsificazioni/

52   Iviglia, *Cremona, wie es nicht sein soll.*

53   Orengo, *Antonio Stradivari una eccezionale rievocazione.* https://patrimonio.archivioluce.com/luce-web/detail/IL3000053122/1/antonio-stradivari-eccezionale-rievocazione.html

54   The same footage was also used for two shorter newsreels: *Mostra di Stradivari nell'isola Bella sul lago Maggiore: Il maestro Sandor Vegh dirigerà un concerto; i musicisti, allievi della scuola di Zermatt, suoneranno degli autentici Stradivari.* https://patrimonio.archivioluce.com/luce-web/detail/IL5000039233/2/mostra-stradivari-nell-isola-bella-sul-lago-maggiore-maestro-sandor-vegh-dirigera-concerto-i-musicisti-allievi-della-scuola.html; *Italia: Quarantadue Stradivari a Stresa.* https://patrimonio.archivioluce.com/luce-web/detail/IL5000049798/2/italia-quarantadue-stradivari-stresa.html

Palazzo Borromeo (00:57–01:00). Forty-five instruments made by Cremonese violinmakers were exhibited there. They were insured for 1.3 billion Italian lire (03:40–03:49). This would be worth about 15 million euros today (with inflation taken into account)[55]—less than the amount paid in 2011 for just one Stradivari violin (albeit a particularly special one), the 'Lady Blunt' from 1721.

Besides the sum involved, the impression of elitism is striking. As the audiovisual document unfolds, the lawyer Italo Trentinaglia de Daverio, the founder of the 1962 *Stresa Festival*,[56] explains while sitting in a salon how Prince Vitaliano Borromeo (1892–1982) permitted the exhibition and a series of concerts in the Salone degli Arazzi in the Palazzo Borromeo (01:26–02:09).

While we see visitors arriving at Isola Bella on a small ship on the video layer of the film, the narrator explains how Stradivari merged the characteristics of the Brescian and Cremonese violin making schools—quite a bold theory (02:43–02:51). Before an interview with Sándor Végh (1912–97), who was in charge of conducting the festival's chamber orchestra, a rehearsal of the second movement of W. A. Mozart's Divertimeno KV 137 is shown. The members of the orchestra were pupils of the Sommer school in Zermatt and were allowed to play Stradivari instruments for the occasion. In the interview, Végh mentioned that it was the first time since the *Bicentenario stradivariano* in 1937 that a whole orchestra played instruments made by the Cremonese violinmaler (05:49–06:00).

In order to show the tonal qualities of the exhibited instruments, Végh plays two excerpts from the Ciaccona by J. S. Bach on his 1724 Stradivari, nicknamed 'Paganini,' which was also part of the exhibition, and on a 1715 Stradivari, the 'Cremonese' (07:43–08:18). This instrument, which belonged—among others—to the violinist Joseph Joachim (1831–1907), was acquired by the Provincial Tourism Board of Cremona in 1961 and is today considered one of the most historically interesting pieces in the collection of the Museo del Violino in Cremona.[57]

As expected, in this film the *topos* of Stradivari's 'secrets' comes into play. While the instruments are shown behind glass, the narrator mentions a few

55   "Inflationhistory." https://inflationhistory.com/
56   "La storia." http://www.stresafestival.eu/festival/storia/
57   "Antonio Stradivari 1715 'Cremonese.'" https://artsandculture.google.com/asset/antonio
      -stradivari-1715-cremonese-violin-front/xwF8x4QbRZOmwg

theories (09:16–09:52). But in the end he concludes that "il segreto era nelle mani dell'artista" (the secret was in the hands of the artist).

Domenico Fantin—a Link to the Present

The most recent document about violin making—besides some behind-the-scenes material about Giacomo Battiato's (1943–) 1988 film *Stradivari*—presently available online in the Archivio Luce dates from 1970.[58] It is a black-and-white newsreel presenting the work of the violinmaker Domenico Fantin, born in Varese in 1928. Fantin continues to work today, as his online presence shows.[59] The newsreel was produced by *Radar Cinematografica*, which was active between 1965 and 1982, and whose collection has been recently bought by the Archivio Luce. The focus of *Radar* was politics and current affairs as well as fashion and art.[60]

The 1960s were prosperous years in which the Italian 'economic miracle' reached its peak.[61] But even though the Cremonese violin making school became recognized internationally, craftmanship was regarded as a remnant of the past, and the poor artist *topos* remains unaffected in this source. The staging of the newsreel about Fantin is based on this idea. At the very beginning, the sounds of a synthesizer—sounds today recognized as typical of the 1970s—play the program's theme melody (00:00–00:12). The difference between the synthesized sound and the sound of the cembalo that serves as the soundtrack for the first part of the newsreel couldn't be clearer. On an iconographic level, the violinmaker, wearing a work coat, is working on a piece of wood; he is tracing the outline of the back of a violin (00:12–00:25). His hunched-over position closely resembles Stradivari's in the 19th-century Hamman painting, which also served as a model for the *Bicentenario stradivariano* poster. In a mood of cultural pessimism, the narrator explains that the 500-year-old art of violin making is a legacy which is known to few people; in his opinion it is today "un'arte che scompare" (a dying art). He refers to the poor poet *topos* by associating violinmakers with poets (00:24–00:27) and defines

---

58   *Italia: Un liutaio varesino fabbrica violini come Stradivari.* https://patrimonio.archivioluce. com/luce-web/detail/IL5000041014/2/italia-liutaio-varesino-fabbrica-violini-come-stradivari.html

59   Homepage: http://www.domenicofantin.com/en/Home.html

60   "Radar (1965–1982)." https://www.archivioluce.com/radar/

61   Sapelli, "Le basi del 'miracolo economico'" 143.

violin making as "un'arte che non da pane, o ne da poco" (an art that doesn't make bread, or a little bread).

The most popular rendition of the idea of the poor poet is Carl Spitzweg's (1808–85) 1839 painting *Der arme Poet* (*The poor poet*), displayed at the Neue Pinakothek in Munich.[62] It shows an author occupied with his work, lying on a mattress, covered with a white blanket. The open umbrella hanging from the ceiling leads the viewer to suspect a leaky roof. Books are stacked next to his mattress. On the wall, on the right side of the painting, a gold medal hangs from a nail in the wall—the poor poet had earned an award. This romanticized picture of an artist working apart from 'productive civil society' seem to be a warning to aspiring artists; it is needless to point out that writers of that time often belonged to the more affluent social classes.[63] It isn't difficult to show that the idea of the 'poor artist' does not necessarily correspond to historical circumstances, at least not in the field of lutherie—if one is inclined to call violin making an art rather than a craft. The Amati and Stradivari dynasties became very wealthy. And as the letter written by the acclaimed virtuoso Yehudi Menuhin (1916–99) shows, Fantin was already well known in 1969, a year before the footage was shot.[64] That he wasn't financially well-off is hard to imagine—Menuhin bought an instrument from him and made him famous in the blink of an eye. But the *topos* of the poor artist seems to be much more powerful—and fascinating—than historical evidence shows (although clearly not every violinmaker in the history of violin making was financially successful).

As the film develops, the claim of inspiration received in a dream is revealed. The narrator explains that Fantin learned how to build exquisite violins by this means (00:34–00:38). As is later explained (02:07–02:11), Stradivari appeared to Fantin as the 'euangelos'—the 'good messenger.' The dream *topos* is closely associated with artistic activity. It is often the artists themselves who report their inspirational dreams; one of the earliest known examples is

---

62 Spitzweg, *Der arme Poet*. www.pinakothek.de/kunst/meisterwerk/carl-spitzweg/der-ar me-poet

63 Gustave Flaubert is here one of the many examples. Hauser, *Sozialgeschichte der Kunst und Literatur* 832.

64 Menuhin's letter, full of compliments on Fantin's work, is viewable on Fantin's home-page. http://www.domenicofantin.com/en/Clients.html

Albrecht Dürer's (1471–1528) 1525 watercolor *Traumgesicht* (*Dream face*).[65] The most popular such story in the field of violin music is likely Giuseppe Tartini's (1692–1770) dream. The devil himself is said to have inspired him to write the *Devil's Trill Sonata*, the only one of his sonatas which remains in the canonized repertoire and is therefore well known to a relatively large audience. A popular rendition of Tartini's dream is the 1824 *Le songe de Tartini* by Louis-Léopold Boilly (1761–1845).[66] As the film continues, the narrator explains how a violin is made. Even though research has shown that the origins of the instrument are obscure, the narrator's voice states that Gasparo Bertolotti da Salò (1540–1609) 'invented' the form of the violin (00:46–00:51).[67] The iconographic motif seen in the 1941 film *La bottega della melodia*—the artisan working in his workshop behind a barred window—is repeated in this film (01:29–01:43). At the end, after discussing the importance of the varnish and its 'secrets,' (02:41–02:57) Fantin plays the Gavotte from the Sonata No. 10, Op. 5 by Corelli on his violin—the same Gavotte serves as the theme for the 50 variations by Tartini, *L'arte dell'arco* (02:58–03:41). The narrator reports that Fantin worked on his violins for years by night, instruments which he later destroyed because they didn't have the proper sound; only after Stradivari told him 'the secret' in his dream was he able to build his excellent instruments (03:18–03:25). His work embodies, as stated by the narrator, that Italian art which spread throughout the whole world. At the same time, on the iconographic level, the image of Fantin playing the violin is distorted and multiplied as if seen through a kaleidoscope (03:21–03:41); the kaleidoscopic effect was already seen at the end of the newsreel about the celebration of the 300-year anniversary of Stradivari's birth.

Fantin remains active today. The musicians who play his instruments post their recordings on video portals.[68] On the title page of Fantin's website, an image of him in front of his tools working on a violin takes center stage. He wears a work coat very similar to the one seen in the 1970 film. On the left, a cello and two violins are stored in a display cabinet ornamented with baroque elements; in the middle of the photograph we see a picture of Antonio Vivaldi,

---

65   Schneider, "Zum Verhältnis von Traum und künstlerischer Aktivität" 14. A reproduction is available online: Dürer, *Traumgesicht*. https://www.wikiart.org/en/albrecht-durer/tra umgesicht-d%C3%BCrer-dokumentiert-einen-seiner-albtr%C3%A4ume-1525
66   Boilly, *Le songe de Tartini*. https://gallica.bnf.fr/ark:/12148/btv1b8426664g/
67   Pollens, *Stradivari* 5–8.
68   The young musicians Caroline Adomeit and Christian Kim posted recordings of themselves playing Fantin's instruments on YouTube.

a crucifix, and a violin hanging from the ceiling. Although it is a color photo, the impression of a yellowish patina, which suggests a longstanding tradition, is present.

Closing Remarks

By means of reaching back to 17th and 18th century violin making, the process of popularizing an imagined national heritage took place in Italy through the media of cinema and later, in the second half of the 20th century, television. This process obviously did not take place overnight and should be understood as the continuation of a discourse that had begun in the late 18th century.[69] Because of this longstanding process of popularization, the name 'Stradivari' (paired with the image of the violin) became pervasive. This results in a paradox: on the one hand, his presence attests to his position as a *lieu de mémoire* and, on the other, reinforces it.

In the above-analyzed audiovisual sources different *topoi*, designed and transported by different narratives, came to the fore. For instance, the *topos* of the genius—and sometimes poor—artist appears in both the audio layer (via verbal narration) and on the visual, iconographic level.

In the film about the violin making school, the narrator refers to "l'anima del liutaio," which is a narrative expressing the *topos* of the genius artist. In the film *La bottega della melodia* the idea is suggested that only a violin-maker 'with the right soul' will be touched by an angel at night, an angel who will reveal secrets to him. Working in solitude behind barred windows—like a monk—enables the artisan to achieve the loftiest artistic goals. The irony is that the fascist regime tried to establish a huge manufacturing center in Cremona that by definition couldn't have been run by a single, or even a few, 'genius' artisans.

---

69   In the print media of the 19th century we find an increasing interest in Stradivari. For instance, the term 'Stradivari' in the search engine of the Austrian National Library's print media digitization project *Anno* shows that there are 25 matches between 1791 and 1832, 231 between 1833 and 1874, and 595 between 1875 and 1917. This result represents only a random sampling. Presumably only a small number of the originally published sources have been digitized. Also, due to the nature of the institution, sources in German are predominant. "Stradivari." http://anno.onb.ac.at/anno-suche#searchMode=simple&query=Stradivari&from=1

On a visual level, the iconography of Hamman's rendition of Stradivari is recurrent; it is obviously based on the concept of the creative genius working in the darkness of his workshop apart from the 'normal' bourgeoise life that permeated the 19th century. Interestingly, as part of the general fascination with magic and horror stories, violin virtuosos were associated with the dark power of the devil. Giuseppe Tartini's *Devil's trill Sonata* was published in France only in 1803,[70] and the famous painting by Louis-Léopold Boilly depicting Tartini in bed while the devil teaches him was painted in 1824, six years after Niccolò Paganini's *24 Capricci* (1818),[71] the pinnacle of violin virtuosity, had been published in Milan by Ricordi. Hence, the *topoi* and their narratives, expressed through different media (such as literature and painting) are obviously to be understood as a part of a "[t]ransmedia storytelling," that is, "narratives in different media types working together to form a larger whole," as Lars Elleström suggests in his recent work on transmedial narration.[72]

Music from the 17th century—performed in the fashion of the mid-20th century—came to be regarded as the quintessence of the 'sonic' atmosphere of 18th century North Italy. Seen in this light, the music of Stradivari's contemporaries best evoked the 'zeitgeist' of the (imagined) past. Thus, the music from the 17th and 18th centuries, which served as soundtracks, became a *topos* itself. From a historical point of view, this music was involved in the rise of instrumental music and brought with it the importance of the violin. All of this conveyed the image of a glorious Italian (imagined) past. But the Italian national state didn't yet exist in the 18th century, and Italy was a geographical rather than a political concept.

As the photo on Fantin's homepage shows, *topoi* conveyed through the different layers of audiovisual media are powerful entities that influence the present. Scenery similar to that of Fantin's photo, except in black-and-white, had already appeared in the earlier audiovisual sources stored in the Archivio Luce. It is hard to imagine that Fantin staged himself in this manner with explicit knowledge of these audiovisual sources. It should rather be assumed that he was inspired by the idea of the violin and violin making, an idea which

---

70   Tartini, "Le Trille du Diable." http://digital.onb.ac.at/RepViewer/viewer.faces?doc=DTL_2880719

71   Paganini, *24 Capricci*. https://archive.org/details/24capriccipervio00paga/page/n3/mode/2up

72   Elleström, *Transmedial Narration* 6.

was also (re)produced and (re)interpreted by the abovementioned audiovisual sources. Recently, the documentary *El Complex de Stradivarius*, the subject of which is the Catalan luthier David Bagué i Soler, makes use of a similar iconography: Bagué i Soler is, for instance, shown working behind the barred window of his workshop (27:06–27:18).[73] Remarkably, the color of the workshop walls and the lighting evoke the yellowish hue that characterizes Fantin's homepage photo.

It is readily apparent that *topoi* developed at different times in different media through the use of different narratives. Due to their constant revival and reinterpretation, *topoi* become part of the collective imagination. These 'imagined' entities, reinterpreted through narratives specific to their era and put in relation to places, sounds and historical figures—like Stradivari—play a decisive role in shaping *lieux de mémoire*. Their function in society is to convey the idea of a longstanding tradition and to legitimize the present and give it credibility. But, as has been shown, the staged traditions possibly never existed, at least not in the form presented by print and audiovisual media.

To, as it were, draw the bow back to our starting point, it is worth noting that the Stradivari example is only a case study. But when various case studies based on digitized audiovisual sources marked with standardized metadata are put in relation to each other on a digital platform, deeper insights into the role of *topoi* and narratives and the resulting *lieux de mémoire* in the media will be possible. As shown in this case study, the relationship between music, iconography, and voice narration are a product of historical circumstances and exert a notable influence on contemporary culture. This kind of analysis isn't focused on a simply chronological historiography, but rather on continuity and the achronological reappearance of similar, reinterpreted, phenomena.

Postscript: In light of what has been said, it becomes questionable whether written historiography remains an appropriate means of showing the intricate web of meanings found in the print and audiovisual sources available today. Considering that the analysis of written sources produces written historiography, the next logical step would be the use of new media in the anal-

---

73   Padró, *El complex de Stradivarius*. https://www.ccma.cat/tv3/alacarta/el-documental/el-complex-de-stradivarius/video/4584351/

ysis of audiovisual sources—my writing is certainly not a good example of this.[74]

Bibliography (last accessed 16 April 2020)

Almond, Frank. "Sound Legacies." *The Strad* 128, 1528 (August 2017): 24.

Bellomi, Tullo. "Celebrazione del Bicentenario Stradivariano: Verbale di seduta del Comitato." *Le celebrazioni stradivariane a Cremona 1937–1949.* Ed. Elia Santoro. Cremona: Turris, 1996. 51–54.

Carter, Tim, and John Butt, eds. *The Cambridge History of Seventeenth-Century Music.* Cambridge: Cambridge Univ. Press, 2014

Cook, Nicholas. *Analysing Musical Multimedia.* New York, Oxford: Oxford Univ. Press, 1998.

Cook, Nicholas. "Theorizing Musical Meaning." *Music Theory Spectrum* 23, 2 (Fall 2001): 170–95. DOI: 10.1525/mts.2001.23.2.170

Cozio di Salabue, Ignazio Alessandro. *Carteggio.* Ed. Renzo Bacchetta. Milano: Antonio Cordani, 1950.

Curtin, Joseph. "Paris Projection." *The Strad* 128, 1526 (June 2017): 36–43.

Dalla Pria, Federica. *Dittatura e immagine: Mussolini e Hitler nei Cinegiornali.* Roma: Edizioni di Storia e Letteratura, 2012.

Dilworth, John, and Carlo Chiesa. "Violins." *Musical Instruments in the Ashmolean Museum: The Complete Collection.* Ed. John Milnes. Oxford: Oxford Musical Instrument Publishing, 2011. 97–100.

Elleström, Lars. *Transmedial Narration: Narratives and Stories in Different Media.* Cham: Palgrave Macmillan, 2019. DOI: 10.1007/978-3-030-01294-6

Fritz, Claudia, Joseph Curtin, Jacques Poitevineau, Hugues Borsarello, Indiana Wollman, Fan-Chia Tao and Thierry Ghasarossian. "Soloist Evaluations of Six Old Italian and Six New Violins." *Proceedings of the National Academy of Sciences of the United States of America – PNAS*, Durham NC, USA (April 2014). DOI: 10.1073/pnas.1323367111

Fritz, Claudia, Joseph Curtin, Jacques Poitevineau and Fan-Chia Tao. "Listener Evaluations of New and Old Italian Violins." *Proceedings of the National Academy of Sciences of the United States of America – PNAS*, Durham NC, USA (May 2017). DOI: 10.1073/pnas.1619443114

---

74   An attempt to synthesize all the problems and possibilities of the ongoing process of digitization for historiography was made by the historian Siegfried Mattl in 2015. Mattl, "What's next: Digital History?"

Griselini, Francesco. "Liutiere, o fabbricator di violini, ed altri stromenti." *Dizionario delle arti e de' mestieri*. Vol. 8. Venezia: Modesto Fenzo, 1770. 196–99. https://books.google.at/books?id=wXCVfiJvb3IC&pg=PA196

Hauser, Arnold. *Sozialgeschichte der Kunst und Literatur*. München: Beck, 2018 (1967).

Hargrave, Roger. "Pry Before You Buy." *The Strad* 122, 1460 (December 2011): 33–38.

Iviglia, Giovanni. *Cremona, wie es nicht sein soll: ein kritisches Essay nebst Buchbesprechung zur Berichtigung romantischer und anderer Fehler vieler 'Geigengeschichten.'* Bellinzona-Lugano: Instituto Editoriale Ticinese, 1957.

Jungmann, Irmgard. *Sozialgeschichte der klassischen Musik: bildungsbürgerliche Musikanschauung im 19. und 20. Jahrhundert*. Stuttgart: Metzler, 2008.

Lister, Warwick. *Amico: The Life of Giovanni Battista Viotti*. New York, Oxford: Oxford Univ. Press, 2009.

Lütgendorff, Willibald Leo. "Guarneri, (Bartolomeo) Giuseppe 'del Gesù.'" *Die Geigen- und Lautenmacher vom Mittelalter bis zur Gegenwart*. Rev. ed. Thomas Drescher. Tutzing: Hans Schneider, 1990. 220–21.

Mattl, Siegfried. "What's next: Digital History?" *Bananen, Cola, Zeitgeschichte: Oliver Rathkolb und das lange 20. Jahrhundert*. Vol. 2. Eds. Lucile Dreidemy, Richard Hufschmied, Agnes Meisinger et al. Köln, Wien: Böhlau, 2015. 1041–1052.

Mertens, Benedikt H. *Solitudo seraphica: Studien zur Geschichte der Exerzitien im Franziskanerorden der Frühzeit (ca. 1600–1750)*. Kevelaer: Butzon and Bercker, 2008.

Mostra di Antonio Stradivari. Ed. Settimane musicali di Stresa. Cremona: Turris, 1996 (1963).

Müller-Funk, Wolfgang. *The Architecture of Modern Culture: Towards a Narrative Cultural Theory*. Berlin: De Gruyter, 2012.

Nicolini, Gualtiero. *The International School of Cremona: Two Score Years of Violin-Making*. Trans. Helen Palmer. Cremona: Edizioni Stradivari, 1979.

Nora, Pierre. "Realms of Memory: Rethinking the French Past." *Conflicts and Divisions*. Vol. 1. Ed. Lawrence D. Kritzman. New York: Columbia Univ. Press, 1996. XV–XXIV.

Paganini, Niccolò. *24 Capricci*. Milano: Ricordi, 1818. https://archive.org/details/24capriccipervio00paga/page/n3/mode/2up

Palla, Marco. *Firenze nel regime fascista*. Firenze: Olschki, 1978.

Pollens, Stewart. *Stradivari: Musical Performance and Reception*. Cambridge: Cambridge Univ. Press, 2010.

Sacconi, Simone Fernando. *I 'segreti' di Stradivari, con il catalogo dei cimeli stradivariani del Museo Civico 'Ala Ponzone' di Cremona*. Cremona: Libreria del Convegno, 1972.

Santoro, Elia. "Le grandi mostre del 1937—The Great Violin Making Exhibitions of 1937." *Le celebrazioni stradivariane a Cremona 1937–1949*. Ed. Elia Santoro. Cremona: Turris, 1996. 11–40.

Santoro, Elia. "La mostra di liuteria del maggio 1949—The Violin Making Exhibition in May 1949." *Le celebrazioni stradivariane a Cremona 1937–1949*. Ed. Elia Santoro. Cremona: Turris, 1996. 199–206.

Sapelli, Giulio. "Le basi del 'miracolo economico.'" *Storia della società italiana: Il miracolo economico e il centro-sinistra*. Parte quinta. Vol. XXIV. Eds. Ugo Ascoli et al. Milano: Teti, 1990. 133–151.

Schmidt, Patrick. "Zwischen Medien und Topoi: Die Lieux de mémoire und die Medialität des kulturellen Gedächtnisses." *Medien des kollektiven Gedächtnisses: Konstruktivität – Historizität – Kulturspezifität*. Eds. Astrid Erll and Ansgar Nünning. Berlin: De Gruyter, 2004. 25–43.

Schneider, Marlen. "Zum Verhältnis von Traum und künstlerischer Aktivität." *Traum und Inspiration: Transformationen eines Topos in Literatur, Kunst und Musik*. Eds. Marlen Schneider and Christiane Solte-Gresser. Paderborn: Wilhelm Fink, 2018. 11–29.

Schoenbaum, David. *The Violin: A Social History of the World's Most Versatile Instrument*. New York: Norton, 2013.

Sgarbi, Vittorio, and Rodolfo Bona, eds. *Il regime dell'arte: Premio Cremona 1939–1941*. [Place of publication not identified]: Contemplazioni, 2018.

Suess, John G. "Vitali, Tomaso Antonio." *The New Grove: Dictionary of Music and Musicians, Second Edition*. Vol. 26. Eds. Stanley Sadie and John Tyrrell. London: Macmillan, 2001. 798–99.

Talbot, Michael. "Corelli, Arcangelo." *The New Grove: Dictionary of Music and Musicians, Second Edition*. Vol. 6. Eds. Stanley Sadie and John Tyrrell. London: Macmillan, 2001. 457–63.

Talbot, Michael. *The Vivaldi Compendium*. Woodbridge: Boydell, 2011.

Tartini, Giuseppe. "Le Trille du Diable." *L'art du Violon: ou Division des Écoles choisies dans les Sonates Italienne, Françoise et Allemande, Précédée d'un abrégé de principes pour cet Instrument. Dédié au Conservatoire de Musique qui en a favorablement accueilli l'hommage. Troisième Edition. Revue et Corrigée*. Ed. Jean-Baptiste Cartier. Paris: Janet et Cotelle, 1803. 307–13. http://digital.onb.a c.at/RepViewer/viewer.faces?doc=DTL_2880719

Online Sources (last accessed 16 April 2020)

Istituto Luce – Cinecittà. www.archivioluce.com

Boilly, Louis-Léopold. *Le songe de Tartini.* Bibliothèque national de France. htt ps://gallica.bnf.fr/ark:/12148/btv1b8426664g/

Boulanger, Louis. *Niccolo Paganini en prison.* Bibliothèque national de France. https://gallica.bnf.fr/ark:/12148/btv1b8423316f

"Cinegiornale Luce C (1940–1945)." *Archivio storico Istituto Luce.* https://www. archivioluce.com/giornale-luce-c/

Cisari, Giulio. *Bicentenario Stradivariano Cremona.* Museo Nazionale – Polo Museale del Veneto – Collezione Salce. http://www.collezionesalce.benicultu rali.it/?q=scheda&id=11256

"Documentari Incom (1938–1965)." *Archivio storico Istituto Luce.* https://www.ar chivioluce.com/documentari-incom/

Dürer, Albrecht. *Traumgesicht.* WikiArt. Visual Art Encyclopedia. https:// www.wikiart.org/en/albrecht-durer/traumgesicht-d%C3%BCrer-dokum entiert-einen-seiner-albtr%C3%A4ume-1525

"Fantin, Domenico." *Homepage.* http://www.domenicofantin.com/en/Home. html

"Gandin, Michele." *IMDb.* https://www.imdb.com/name/nm0304170/

Gatani, Tindaro. "La guerra dei violini (1948–1955): la lotta della CCIS contro le falsificazioni." *larivista.ch.* https://www.larivista.ch/la-guerra-dei-violini-1948-1955-la-lotta-della-ccis-contro-le-falsificazioni/

Hamman, Edouard. *Stradivarius.* Bibliothèque national de France. https://gal lica.bnf.fr/ark:/12148/btv1b8425075w

Hüningen, James zu, and Irmbert Schenk. "Luce." *Lexikon der Filmbegriffe.* Universität Kiel. https://filmlexikon.uni-kiel.de/index.php?action=lexikon&t ag=det&id=2410

"Inflationhistory." *ISTAT—Istituto Nazionale die Statistica.* https://inflationhisto ry.com/

Loffi, Fabrizio. "Agosto 1935, il primo grande film su Stradivari." *Cremona Misteriosa*, 3 November 2015. http://cremonamisteriosa.blogspot.com/2015/11/ era-il-novembre-del-1936-quando.html

Moglia, Paolo. *La stampa quotidiana nella Repubblica Sociale Italiana – Il Regime fascista – il giornale proprietà di Roberto Farinacci.* Master thesis, Sapienza Univ. of Rome, s.a. http://www.larchivio.com/xoom/paolomoglia.htm

Musikalische Realzeitung, 7 September 1791: 285–87. http://anno.onb.ac.at/cgi-content/anno?aid=muz&datum=17910907&seite=3

"Notable sales: 'Lady Blunt' Stradivarius of 1721." *Tarisio*. https://tarisio.com/auctions/notable-sales/lady-blunt-stradivarius-of-1721/

Pallottino, Paola. "Cisari, Giulio." *Dizionario Biografico degli Italiani*. Vol. 34 (1988). http://www.treccani.it/enciclopedia/giulio-cisari_(Dizionario-Bio grafico)/

"Radar (1965–1982)." *Archivio storico Istituto Luce*. https://www.archivioluce.co m/radar/

Spitzweg, Carl. *Der arme Poet*. Neue Pinakothek München. https://www.pina kothek.de/kunst/meisterwerk/carl-spitzweg/der-arme-poet

Ray, Michael. "Lateran Treaty." *Encyclopaedia Britannica*. https://www.britanni ca.com/event/Lateran-Treaty

"La Settimana INCOM (1946–1965)." *Archivio storico Istituto Luce*. https://www. archivioluce.com/la-settimana-incom/

"La storia." *Stresa Festival*. http://www.stresafestival.eu/festival/storia/

"Stradivari." *Anno*. Österreichische Nationalbibliothek. http://anno.onb.ac.at/anno-suche#searchMode=simple&query=Stradivari&from=1

"Stradivari, Antonio 1715 'Cremonese.'" *Museo del Violino*. https://artsandcul ture.google.com/asset/antonio-stradivari-1715-cremonese-violin-front/xwF8x4QbRZOmwg

Audiovisual Sources (last accessed 16 April 2020)

Archivio storico Luce

Cerchio, Fernando. *Ritorno al Vittoriale*. Istituto Nazionale Luce (1942). 00:16:12. Code: D048707. https://patrimonio.archivioluce.com/luce-web/detail/IL3 000090705/1/ritorno-al-vittoriale.html

Cremona: Mostra concorso di liuteria. La Settimana Incom/00295 (27/05/1949). 00:01:36. Code: I029503. https://patrimonio.archivioluce.com/luce-web/d etail/IL5000013285/2/cremona-ostra-concorso-liuteria.html

Gandin, Michele. *La bottega della melodia*. Documentari Incom (1942). 00:08:10. Code: D025003. https://patrimonio.archivioluce.com/luce-web/detail/IL3 000051047/1/la-bottega-della-melodia.html

Gemmiti, Arturo. *Cremona: Una visita alla scuola di liuteria*. Giornale Luce C/C0113 (27/01/1941). 00:01:24. Code: C011305. https://patrimonio.archiv

ioluce.com/luce-web/detail/IL5000014203/2/cremona-visita-alla-scuola-liuteria.html

Italia: Quarantadue Stradivari a Stresa. Cronache del mondo/CM398 (21/09/1963). 00:01:33. Code: CM039805. https://patrimonio.archiviol uce.com/luce-web/detail/IL5000049798/2/italia-quarantadue-stradivari-stresa.html

Italia: Un liutaio varesino fabbrica violini come Stradivari. Radar/R0398 (10/12/1970). 00:03:29. Code: R039801. https://patrimonio.archivioluc e.com/luce-web/detail/IL5000041014/2/italia-liutaio-varesino-fabbrica-violini-come-stradivari.html

Mostra di Stradivari nell'isola Bella sul lago Maggiore: Il maestro Sandor Vegh dirigerà un concerto; i musicisti, allievi della scuola di Zermatt, suoneranno degli autentici Stradivari. La Settimana Incom/02404 (20/09/1963). 00:07:04. Code: I240401. https://patrimonio.archivioluce.com/luce-web/detail/ IL5000039233/2/mostra-stradivari-nell-isola-bella-sul-lago-maggiore-maestro-sandor-vegh-dirigera-concerto-i-musicisti-allievi-della-scuola. html

Orengo, Vladi. *Antonio Stradivari una eccezionale rievocazione.* Documentari Incom (1963). 00:14:00. Code: D029705. https://patrimonio.archivioluce. com/luce-web/detail/IL3000053122/1/antonio-stradivari-eccezionale-rievocazione.html

Corporació Catalana de Mitjans Audiovisuals, SA

Padró, Josep. *El complex de Stradivarius* (2013). 00:52:00. https://www.ccma.ca t/tv3/alacarta/el-documental/el-complex-de-stradivarius/video/4584351/

Beethoven in 1970, Bernstein and the ORF: Cultural Memory and the Audiovisual

Cornelia Szabó-Knotik (University of Music and Performing Arts Vienna)

The material for the following case study of the 200th anniversary of Beethoven's birth, which was celebrated in Vienna in 1970, is taken from the broadcasts of the ORF (the Austrian Broadcasting Corporation). It is undertaken with the aim of drafting a working method in the context of (music) history informed by audiovisual media.[1] This case study strives to define those aspects and contexts of Beethoven's popularized image which would otherwise be hardly recognizable or differently apprehended. Beethoven's 1970 bicentenary, celebrated in Vienna, was accompanied by a rather heavy media presence. Under the auspices of mass media's growing spread and importance,[2] the city of Vienna organized a special exhibition, *Die Flamme lodert* (The Flame Blazes), which featured, for the first time at such an event, a 'music program' of Beethoven's works, consisting of 15 compilationst[3] on audiotape, taken from LP stereo recordings on the Decca, Deutsche Grammophon, and Philips labels. The program was accompanied by introductions

---

1   Such an approach is only possible because the amount of video material available online has reached critical mass; it is based not so much on the reading (of texts), as is traditional in academia, but is meant to involve hearing and seeing instead. Cf. the research project *Telling Sounds*' agenda (www.mdw.ac.at/imi/tellingsounds), which inspired the publication of this book.

2   TV sets entered households and tape recorders became popular (as did CDs, at the end of the following decade). In 1969, VCRs and video cameras became available, with VHS becoming a widely accepted standard towards the end of the following decade. Perné, "Eine kleine Geschichte der Schallaufzeichnung." https://www.mediathek.at/unterrichtsmaterialien/eine-kleine-geschichte-der-schallaufzeichnung/

3   Split into segments of 5 recordings for each of the three chronologically defined periods "early (up to 1802) [...] middle (1803–1815) [and] late (until 1815)." Racek, *Die Flamme lodert* 145.

written by Fritz Racek and narrated by the then popular newsreader, presenter, and radio play announcer Wolfgang Riemerschmid. The program
was played at three listening stations, following a schedule published in the
exhibition's catalogue.[4] In an essay for the *Vienna Festival Almanac*, Fritz Racek
calls the use of "the modern media of video and sound projection" one of
the exhibition's more important features.[5] Also, he makes reference to the
"smash hit" that was the 1927 commemoration of the 100th anniversary of
Beethoven's death, which, he claims, could easily have been "resurrected"
because "in effect the stock of historical documents has remained essentially
unchanged."[6] He continues to point out that this approach was nevertheless
avoided because of the public's changed attitude; informative, 'educational'
material became at that time preferred to a collection of valuable objects;
media were included in the exhibition.[7] In contrast to the anniversary celebrations of composers that were held both in earlier and later years, neither a
biopic nor a documentary was produced in Austria in 1970, which was typical
of the country's contemporary film industry. International films (mainly
US-produced) dominated in cinemas, which in turn had conceded their
traditional popularity as places of mass entertainment to home TV sets.[8] A
glance in the most popular program guide of the time, *Hör Zu*, [9] followed by
a database search of the ORF media archive provided the necessary information (table 1 in appendix). The resulting network of AV material with different

---

4   The Volkshalle of the Vienna City Hall, Tue 26.05.—Sun 30. 08.1970. Racek, *Die Flamme
     lodert* 145–48.

5   Racek, "Zur Wiener Beethoven-Ausstellung" 101–02.

6   "[…] wäre es nicht eine reizvolle Aufgabe gewesen, für sie die erfolgreiche Monster-
     schau von 1927 nochmals erstehen zu lassen? Nun, diese Möglichkeit hätte durchaus
     bestanden; tatsächlich ist ja, […] der Effektivbestand an dokumentarischen Erinne-
     rungsobjekten in der Hauptsache derselbe geblieben." Racek, "Zur Wiener Beethoven-
     Ausstellung" 102.

7   In fact, this is in a sense also true for the 1927 centenary—not regarding the exhibits
     themselves, as tape was not yet available and records were still pressed on shel-
     lac—but regarding radio broadcasts. For its contemporary effect on the Early Mu-
     sic movement in Austria: Szabó-Knotik, "Zwischen Rückbesinnung und Aneignung"
     199–208.

8   Walter Fritz devotes a considerable part of the last of his three volumes on Austrian
     film history to the detailed description of this situation. Fritz, *Kino in Österreich* 93–162.

9   The Dokumentationsarchiv Funk keeps all volumes of this periodical in full-text-
     searchable pdfs on its site: http://www.dokufunk.org/upload/periodika_digitalisiert_20
     200117(1).pdf. My thanks to Herbert Hayduck and Michael Liensberger for their support
     of this and other studies in the frame-work of the abovementioned project research.

production contexts together with additional detailed analyses of images (including facial expressions and gestures) and sound (including tone of voice and articulation) is meant to convey insights into the interrelationship of meanings in the communication and popularization of (music) historical content. This, however, is not done here with regard to the music repertoire performed, but to the dissemination of the 1970 Beethoven celebration's ideas and meanings to the consumers of mass media.[10] In short, we are concerned with the question of which images were transmitted on that occasion. A comparison between the anniversary celebration's numerous events and their coverage on TV reveals, unsurprisingly, a focus on the festival in Vienna and, in turn, on the contributions of Leonard Bernstein. His concert with the Vienna Philharmonic as well as his new staging of *Fidelio*[11] were the subjects of a wide variety of programs throughout the year,[12] among which we find a politically significant performance at the Social Democratic Party's convention, and Bernstein in the role of presenter for a documentary coproduced by CBS and ORF (table 2 in appendix). The latter two are good examples of the different strata of distribution typical of the essentially achronological construction that such video material has. They were therefore chosen as the main examples for this case study.

Bernstein's 'Beethoven Moment'

The German-language version of the documentary film *Beethoven's Birthday* (80 minutes in length), coproduced by CBS and ORF, was shown on TV; it was subtitled "a music festival in Vienna with Leonard Bernstein." Inserts divide it into three parts, beginning with a general introduction to the celebrations

---

10   Television had a largely monopolistic position in Austria at the time; there were two Austrian TV channels, it was only possible to tune in to others near the border, and private television did not yet exist. The restriction of broadcasting times and the gradual spread of TV sets also contributed to television's becoming considered a leisure activity. "Geschichte des Fernsehens in Österreich." https://de.wikipedia.org/w/index.php?title= Geschichte_des_Fernsehens_in_%C3%96sterreich&oldid=194523170

11   Note that *Fidelio*—not in Bernstein's staging—is also the subject of an episode of *Opernführer* (with Marcel Prawy, 22.11.) and of a broadcast from the Berlin Opera of the production, conducted by Karl Böhm (13.12.). Cf. table 1.

12   Thus, nothing is reported about the *Beethoven Symposium* (01.06.–05.06.), and there is only one broadcast about the already mentioned Vienna *Beethoven Exhibition* (*Kultur aktuell*, 30.05.).

in Vienna and Bernstein's role in them, then focusing on two major events in turn: the new production of *Fidelio*—in itself an important Austrian *lieu de mémoire*[13]—and the performance of Beethoven's Symphony No. 9.[14] The use of color film was, besides the presenter's celebrity status, one of the features emphasized in announcements for the film. Another, as mentioned in one of Bernstein's on-screen statements, was the film's careful use of historical documents and landscape paintings, many of which were used as illustrations and mentioned in the credits as having been taken from H.C. Robbins Landon's biography of the composer[15] and from "Beethoven, Pall Mall Press."[16] Producer and director Humphrey Burton had already by that time had experience with classical music productions for both TV and radio.[17] The film promptly earned him an Emmy (1972) together with James Krayer (awarded as executive producer) and Leonard Bernstein (awarded as the star)[18] and was initially distributed on VHS (1992), then on DVD (2006)[19]—proof of the continuing popularity of both big Bs. The film opens with Bernstein conducting the Vienna Philharmonic performing the second movement of Beethoven's Symphony No. 9 and a bird's eye view of the Ringstrasse and the Opera House ("Before us is Vienna, B's adopted country [...]"). Bernstein continues speaking off-camera, mentioning the three events he has taken part in, namely the performance of Beethoven's Symphony No. 9, the staging of *Fidelio*, and the performance of Beethoven's Piano Concerto No. 1, Op. 15. At the word "Fidelio," we are shown an excerpt from the performance: Pizzarro (Theo Adam) is

---

13   This is documented and reinforced by performances right after the end of World War II, when the first opera season at Theater an der Wien opened with this work (06.10.1945) as well as by the spectacular re-opening of the rebuilt State Opera house a decade later (05.11.1955). Cf. Marcel Prawy's recollection of this in Prawy, *Die Wiener Oper* 323. As a matter of fact, *Fidelio* is also a cornerstone of the 2020 Vienna Beethoven Celebration; all three versions are staged (1805, 1806, 1814). "Viennese Beethoven Events in 2020." https://musik2020.wien.info/en-us/beethoven-events-2020

14   "Zweiter Teil *FIDELIO*" (13:21) with two inserts listing the staging's main performers (13:46); "Dritter Teil *9. SYMPHONIE*" (53:38) begins with Bernstein's statement on the importance of Beethoven's music (to 57:20). See below in this text.

15   Landon, *Beethoven: sein Leben*.

16   Most probably the edition of a book (re)issued several times: Schmidt-Görg, *Ludwig van Beethoven*.

17   "Humphrey Burton." https://en.wikipedia.org/w/index.php?title=Humphrey_Burton&oldid=946250094

18   Outstanding Single Program—Variety or Musical—Classical Music. "Primetime Emmy Awards." https://www.imdb.com/event/ev0000223/1972/1

19   Wulff, *Ludwig van Beethoven im Film* 6.

singing the vigorous motif of the famous aria "Ha, welch ein Augenblick,"[20] which itself acts as an allusion to Bernstein's emotional state. Following the chronology just laid out, Bernstein is subsequently seen performing the Piano Concerto No. 1, which is repeatedly heard in the film's next section, starting (at 02:25) with the *topos* of 'Vienna, the city of music' and dedicated to a description of Beethoven's biography blended with what seems to be Bernstein's personal assessment of the composer's character and personality. The following segment, on *Fidelio* (13:21–53:34), opens with the end of the final choir; the curtain closing to fervent applause; this is followed by excerpts from rehearsals (including some spoken instructions and gestures from director Otto Schenk) and some behind-the-scenes shots.[21] Bernstein's energetic conducting gestures and his intense facial expressions during a choir's piano rehearsal, repeatedly shown in close-up (15:23–16:33), captivate the singers as well as the film's viewers. By contrast, a short sequence (33:16) documents the performers' exhausted and subdued mood after an evening rehearsal. At the end of that sequence (34:08–35:55), Bernstein is shown alone in the venue, in a long shot, standing in the orchestra pit, the seating in the background empty, the conductor's baton twirling in his hands. He tells us in English (dubbed over in German[22]) that at that very moment he is experiencing "Beethoven's spirit" and is thus overwhelmed by a sense of identification with the composer, who had conducted from the very same spot. He describes this moment of identification as creating an intense empathy with what Beethoven must have felt when, due to hearing loss, he could not understand the performers' questions and also when—and here Bernstein's face is shown in close-up—he intensely felt the boredom and resentment of the audience, then consisting not of the usual sympathetic Viennese but of French officers, present because Napoleon had occupied Vienna that very week. Beethoven must have felt their stares drilling right into his back. In terms of the effect created, this narrative is very moving and impressive. However, it strays from the known historical facts, as Beethoven conducted neither the opera's first and indeed unsuccessful performance in 1805, which Bernstein alludes to, nor one of the following premieres

---

20   "Ah! the moment has arriv'd." "Ludwig van Beethoven, Beethoven's Opera Fidelio. German Text, with an English Translation [1805]." https://oll.libertyfund.org/titles/beethov en-beethovens-opera-fidelio-german-text-with-an-english-translation

21   Similar material was used to make a special feature, broadcast on 19.07. Cf. table 2.

22   Because of the asynchronous dubbing (we hear both the original English and the German voiceover) and Bernstein's impassioned facial expressions, a distinct feeling of irritation is caused.

(in 1806 and 1814) of the work's revised versions.[23] Nevertheless, there is the remarkable fact that Bernstein's story about his identification with Beethoven forms a narrative pattern which recurs, almost word-for-word, in a recording produced that year in Vienna, under rather different circumstances and meant for another purpose. In a so-called voice portrait (02:47) stored in the Phonogrammarchiv of the Austrian Academy of Sciences,[24] Bernstein begins with the phrase, "I've had an extraordinary experience this week, these last two weeks in fact, conducting *Fidelio* in Vienna." He goes on to mention that he stood "on the same podium" as Beethoven and that he also studied the latter's remaining documents and work while working on a film about the bicentenary celebration in Vienna for American audiences. What follows is a repetition of the same narrative pattern about his moment of intense identification, while standing on the podium, with Beethoven at the opera's first premiere. But this time the tale is more personal: "I felt that this was *my* opera I had just written—I was very worried about it—and as I went through it—I kept feeling 'oh no, I should've used the other overture, I, why did I end that piano instead of forte, I meant to let that aria out, I meant to correct that bar, the audience isn't getting it [...]" (01:04—01:25). And it is even more emotionally laden; we even hear the claim (01:43), "at one point I even felt I was hard of hearing, that I was deaf." Bernstein didn't hear the second oboe and realized his error only when, as an afterthought, he looked at the orchestra and saw that the oboist was not playing (01:54). Throughout this recording Bernstein's sonorous voice gets even more under the listener's skin than in the film, probably because no images distract from its effect, and perhaps also because the film's German voiceover sounds more read than spoken and its mixture with Bernstein's original commentary somewhat ruins both. Its surprisingly personal, almost intimate character can be explained by the circumstances under which it was recorded.[25] Remarkably, both interviews dif-

---

23   The cast list: "Fidelio." https://de.wikipedia.org/wiki/Fidelio#cite_ref-7

24   "Katalog." http://catalog.phonogrammarchiv.at/sessions.php?id_sessions=5119&action =view&sortieren=signatur&vonBis=10-19. I thank Gerda Lechleitner, who is also the project leader for the Phonogrammarchive's cooperation with the *Telling Sounds* project, for giving me the opportunity to listen to this recording.

25   The following information about its production are taken from an interview with the Phongrammarchiv's former director, Dietrich Schüller, as well as from the recollections of Elisabeth Deutsch (born Pohl), who was the secretary of the Phonogrammarchiv at the time. My interview with Schüller (04.09.2019), stored in the Phonogrammarchiv (22:49–26:42), as well as an interview with Elisabeth Deutsch, recorded on 07.02.2020.

fer in some details regarding how the music recording in question had been arranged and where it took place. This is a good example of a characteristic that these kinds of sources have: views and attitudes, rather than mere documented facts, are provided. While Dietrich Schüller remembers the establishment where Elisabeth Deutsch had her second job at the time—the Loyalty Club[26]—as the location of her acquaintance with Bernstein, Deutsch herself confidently identifies her friend Sylvia (the secretary of the office of the Vienna Philharmonic at the time) as the one who had introduced her to Bernstein. Elisabeth eventually asked him to provide a recorded statement for the Phonogrammarchiv's unique collection of historical voice portraits. Bernstein agreed and the meeting was scheduled one morning at his lodgings at a downtown hotel,[27] where he was busily organizing his affairs. He seemed to have just wanted to get the task over with and gave a short, rather general statement. In retrospect it becomes obvious that Bernstein had already had to memorize his remarks for the documentary, which must have been filmed at the time of the staging's premiere in May. In fact, the Phonogrammarchiv recording tells the same story but in different words and in a different tone. The performative variation of the same narrative pattern, recorded more than a week after the documentary scene had been shot,[28] was obviously influenced by its very different circumstances of time and place. That said, the short voice portrait proves to be a telling example of the fundamental importance that performativity acquires in an audio(visual) recording. All its production and audio (as well as visual) details, such as tone of voice, articulation, and vocabulary, add meaning to the words which a written text doesn't possess. Bernstein's happy-go-lucky attitude gives his educational remarks a dimension that textbooks cannot achieve.[29] Another group of recordings, these on the topic of Bernstein's performance of the Piano Concerto No. 1 both as performer and conductor, helps support this argument. Its ramifications are additionally extended into the 21st century and broaden the scope of the

---

26 This club's name was, as Dietrich Schüller demonstrates (23:54), usually spoken with German rather than English pronunciation. It was allegedly founded by one Dr. Fellner.

27 Exactly which hotel this was is unclear; all parties involved identified different ones.

28 According to its identification code (19700601.M001) the recording date was June 1st 1970 at the latest.

29 Bernstein's Young People's Concerts (1958–72) where he maintains a conventionally 'serious' attitude. "Young People's Concerts." https://en.wikipedia.org/w/index.php?title=Young_People%27s_Concerts&oldid=938766812

sociocultural context of Bernstein's contribution to Beethoven's bicentenary celebration, reaching into Austria's political history.

Bernstein, Beethoven, and Bruno Kreisky

The performance of Beethoven's Piano Concerto No. 1 is also part of the above-mentioned documentary, both on screen and as part of the soundtrack to the brief sketch of Beethoven's life and fate. The documentary was additionally mentioned on TV several times in 1970, starting with a preannouncement of the performance at the Musikverein, broadcast in the cultural news program one day before the actual event (06.06.) with excerpts from a rehearsal; this was followed by a political news segment three days after the concert (10.06.) and later that year (03.10.), where it became the main subject of a special program (cf. table 2). The reason for its unexpected appearance in the ORF primetime news program[30] was another performance at the opening of the Social Democratic Party's annual convention, attended by 600 national and 70 international delegates. This was in many ways a special occasion, the first such meeting after the party had gained a relative majority in the national council elections in March, resulting in Bruno Kreisky's election to the office of federal chancellor in a minority government (established with the consent of the FPÖ, the national liberal party). To celebrate this achievement, the convention took place at the Wiener Konzerthaus, with Bernstein and the Vienna Philharmonic Orchestra performing.[31] In his opening speech during the first clip,[32] (02:15) Kreisky explains this by remarking not only on the *Vienna Festival* which had just taken place, but also on the "great tradition of the Social Democratic cultural movement," the *Arbeitersymphoniekonzerte*,[33] the last of which took place in that very same concert hall "on Saturday, February 10th 1934, two days before the dark night of dictatorship fell over Austria"

---

30   These two news excerpts from the ORF archive are marked as restricted and can therefore not be published but only viewed on-site.

31   The full program can be viewed in the Wiener Konzerthaus database. "Suche in der Archivdatenbank." https://www.konzerthaus.at/datenbanksuche

32   From its format I assume it was exactly what was shown in the news: it begins with a commentator's introduction of the event, then Kreisky begins his talk, followed by a recording of Bernstein's conducting the *Leonore Ouverture* No. 3.

33   Information about the *Arbeitersymphoniekonzerte*: "Arbeitermusik." https://www.geschichtewiki.wien.gv.at/Arbeitermusik

(00:46–01:15). A second clip from the same event (04:13) features another excerpt from Kreisky's speech, which begins with the statement, "Beethoven was an unbending and courageous confessor of freedom, not only in the musical sense as in his *Fidelio*"[34] (00:22–00:29). Kreisky reminds the viewers of the social conditions under absolutism and quotes Beethoven's self-confident statement to prince Lichnowsky: "Prince, what they are they owe to the circumstances of their birth, and what I am I owe to myself" (00:54).[35] Finally stating that he has answered the questions of "why this concert, why Beethoven, why the Philharmonic and Leonard Bernstein," he praises the latter, describing him as someone "who himself is also a deeply committed person in the truest sense of the word" (01:16).[36] Commitment to a similar cause might have also been the reason behind the alleged friendship between the two, a relationship that is said to have led to Bernstein's interference in political matters sixteen years later, an event which itself seems to have become a *lieu de mémoire* in the historiography of the Austrian Social Democrats.[37] Its background is the conflict that arose between Bruno Kreisky and Hannes Androsch, the minister of finance (1970–1981) as well as the vice chancellor (1976–1981). When a circle of friends wanted Androsch to succeed Kreisky as chancellor (who for his part would have become federal president, a representative rather than a powerful position), the latter searched for a reason to get his political rival out of the way.[38] A conflict of interests was claimed based on the fact that the minister of finance was also the owner or partner of a tax consultancy firm which, among other things, received orders from state-owned companies. In view of this discord, in 1986 Bernstein invited both men to his hotel room on the occasion of Yom Kippur, wishing to mediate between the two. In a 2010 interview, two decades after Bruno Kreisky's death,[39] Hannes Androsch claimed that Kreisky not only refused Bernstein's mediation but also stopped talking to the musician and composer from that point on. Androsch

---

34 "Beethoven war ein mutiger und unbeugsamer Bekenner der Freiheit, nicht nur im musikalischen Sinne wie etwa in seinem *Fidelio*."

35 "Fürst, was sie sind verdanken sie dem Zufall ihrer Geburt, was ich bin, verdanke ich mir selbst." This often-quoted letter was supposedly written in 1806 but may never have been sent to the prince. Lockwood, *Beethoven* 492.

36 "der selber auch ein im wahrsten Sinne des Wortes zutiefst Engagierter ist."

37 I thank *Telling Sounds* researcher Elias Berner for calling my attention to this.

38 "Die Welt bis gestern." https://www.diepresse.com/375875/die-welt-bis-gestern-androsch-mit-ihm-verlor-kreisky-sein-gluck

39 Rief, "Androsch: 'Es war nie eine Vater-Sohn-Beziehung.'" https://www.diepresse.com/543118/androsch-es-war-nie-eine-sohn-vater-beziehung

repeated the same story in an interview for another periodical the following year, the 100th anniversary of Kreisky's birth.[40] Later, in the second of a four-part TV documentary on Austria in the 1960s to the 1990s, *Es muss sich was ändern* (Something has to change), broadcast first in 2012 and then again in 2013, 2014/15, and in 2017/18, Androsch himself mentions this same event[41] (the clip is viewable on YouTube[42]). And in an interview given by Peter Pelinka for a tabloid in 2015, the meeting is again described, but in much more detail:

> "During one of his numerous visits to Vienna, the aghast Bernstein made an attempt at reconciliation: he persuaded the secretary general of the Konzerthaus, Peter Weiser (deceased in 2012), to invite Kreisky to the Hotel Bristol on 3 October 1986. He himself would 'bring in' Androsch and his former colleague Vranitzky (who had just moved from the Ministry of Finance to the Chancellery): 'I love them both and I want them to love each other again.' The evening went pleasantly enough at first: Bernstein had served up vanilla croissants, apple slices and honey, the guests discussed politics (a little), religion (more) and music (the most). As a farewell, Bernstein, deeply disappointed, took Weiser aside: Kreisky had told him never to invite him again along with these 'horrible guys.' Bernstein never saw Kreisky again. Four years later, 25 years ago, he died in New York on 14 October 1990—ten weeks after Kreisky."[43]

---

40   John, "100 Jahre Kreisky." https://www.derstandard.at/story/1293370216401/100-jahre-k reisky-androsch-kreisky-hat-die-rote-katze-ein-fuer-allemal-verbannt

41   *Wie wir wurden, was wir sind: Generation Österreich.* https://www.fernsehserien.de/wie-wir-wurden-was-wir-sind

42   "Österreich Geschichte 1976–2008." 56:05–56:44. https://youtu.be/rDGjWoTao8M

43   "Bei einem seiner zahlreichen Wien-Besuche unternahm der darüber entsetzte Bernstein einen Versöhnungsversuch: Er überredete den Generalsekretär des Konzerthauses, Peter Weiser (2012 verstorben), Kreisky am 3. Oktober 1986 ins Hotel Bristol einzuladen. Er selbst würde dort Androsch und dessen Exmitarbeiter Vranitzky (gerade vom Finanzministerium ins Kanzleramt gewechselt) 'einbringen:' 'I love them both and I want them to love each other again.' Der Abend verlief vorerst friedlich: Bernstein hatte Vanillekipferl, Apfelscheiben und Honig aufgetischt, man sprach über Politik (wenig), Religionen (mehr) und Musik (am meisten). Zum Abschied nahm Bernstein Weiser tief enttäuscht beiseite: Kreisky habe ihm gesagt, er solle ihn niemals wieder mit diesen 'horrible guys' einladen. Bernstein sah Kreisky nie wieder. Vier Jahre später, vor 25 Jahren, starb er am 14. Oktober 1990 in New York—zehn Wochen nach Kreisky." Pelinka, "Der Frust des Dirigenten." https://www.news.at/a/pelinka-leonard-bernstein-kreisky

Thus Kreisky's acquaintance with Bernstein, which is related to the latter's musical performance at the 1970 party convention, had not only resulted in a failed attempt at mediating a conflict, the consequences of which defined the Social Democratic Party's fate in Austria's subsequent political development, but also firmly positioned the two in an ongoing historical narrative, the narrative, as usual, taking on detail and structure in retrospect. The fact that related documentary video material is available online strengthens its presence as *lieu de mémoire* and makes it possible to recognize the further networks of sociocultural context to which it belongs or in the formation of which it participates.

One such network is centered around the work this chapter opened with, namely Bernstein's performance of the Piano Concerto No. 1 which was, as mentioned, performed a second time at the party convention. Its main performance was made the subject of a whole program, a sequel to the series *Die Wiener Philharmoniker in Probe und Konzert* (broadcast 03.10.), its significance emphasized by its being filmed in color. As the credits appear, Bernstein, sitting at the piano, conducts as the orchestra plays the stirring main theme of the concert's final *rondo* movement, then joins in as a soloist and plays with the orchestra until the movement's last sections, which end to enthusiastic applause (up to 01:48). Images of the performers bowing are accompanied by presenter Marcel Prawy's voice reminding viewers of the performance in June and its occasion, the Beethoven bicentenary. Corresponding to the composition's movements, the following documentary consists of three parts, separated by segments from Prawy's interview with Bernstein (at 02:48, 35:22, and 51:12), recorded on the occasion of the performance. Each part begins with Bernstein's rehearsal, followed by a cut to the performance itself, which is now and again further explained by inserts with Bernstein's comments on the composition, taken from the previously shown part of the interview. Thus the film's didactic task is achieved by the combination of Bernstein's performance (his facial expressions and gestures) as conductor and pianist, his spoken comments in the interview (often demonstrated with passages of music on the piano), several statements by presenter Marcel Prawy, and the repetition of Bernstein's main points inserted into the actual musical performance. It is remarkable that classical music education in such a tightly structured format was made with such care and broadcast at a popular time and day, on Saturday afternoon (03:10–04:00 pm). This seems to indicate that public broadcasting's fundamental task of education was in those times not regarded as unpopular but instead widely accepted.

In the abovementioned interview's last section (51:12–54:42), Prawy's introductory statements were dedicated, because of Bernstein's educational achievements, to "Beethoven today, tomorrow and in the future." This deserves closer examination because it is especially interesting both in terms of its explicit content and with regard to its performative subtext. As Prawy mentions, and as can also be deduced from Bernstein's attire, the interview was shot after the rehearsal. The musician, quite exhausted, lights a cigarette at the beginning of this section, and smoke drifts across the screen.[44] We see a considerable difference in the attitude and attire of Prawy and Bernstein; the former's hair is neatly styled, and he is wearing a dark grey suit with a white shirt and tie. He stands at the piano and looks down intently on Bernstein, who sits at the instrument in a checkered blazer and black turtleneck sweater, his hair rather disheveled, a cigarette in his hand. He answers Prawy's question about his view on Beethoven's contemporary importance with "[h]e's always the greatest—for everyone, for the youth too...there's a Beatles movie with Beethoven's Ninth"[45] (51:26) while slightly smiling, then turns his head to take a drag from the cigarette. When Prawy retorts with the question of whether he would judge this "a sacrilege," Bernstein replies in the negative, bowing his head and making a dismissive gesture, cigarette in hand, and emphasizes his subsequent words with his facial expressions (shot in close-up), gestures (just partly recognizable at the image's lower margin) and tone of voice: "No, it's common property, children, experts, connoisseur, amateur, dilettantes, doesn't matter—and he has something to say to everyone. The greatest connoisseur can always find something new in it, and amateurs, children can find something new in it"[46] (52:22). He also seems, at first, to not even understand Prawy's next question of whether today the composer still is ahead of mankind ("this I don't understand"[47]), and upon further

---

44   The interview was recorded on the stage of the Musikverein's Golden Hall, which is, in spite of its being empty, a striking if not shocking sight for (young) viewers of this interview today.

45   "Er ist immer der Größte,—für Alle, für die Jugend auch—es gibt einen Beatles-Film mit Beethovens Neunter." For a description of the respective scene in *Help* (Engl. 1965, dir.: Richard Lester). "Help! (film)." https://en.wikipedia.org/w/index.php?title=Help!_(film)&oldid=943912318

46   "Nein, es ist common property, Kinder, experts, connaisseur, Amateur, Dilettantes, macht nix—und er hat etwas allen zu sagen. Der größte connaisseur kann etwas immer Neues daran finden, und Amateurs, Kinder können etwas daran finden."

47   "Das versteh ich nicht."

insistence finally claims, starting in English (which might be taken as a sign of exhaustion) "It's not a question of ahead, it's timelessness, without period, it doesn't matter, it will always be something fresh, something new—it's like this—there is no composer—in the whole history—of music—like Beethoven [...]."[48] (52:43–53:07) During this part of the clip the close-up of Bernstein's face (repeatedly partially obscured by wisps of smoke), and as mentioned, his tone of voice, give his speech a certain intensity, his accented and sometimes 'broken' language adding to the effect.

One has to remind oneself that this interview was of course quite staged, the words prepared rather than spontaneous and the video material edited to fit the format. And one becomes even more impressed by how this constructed combination—Prawy's traditional 'old-world' personality and views[49] and Bernstein as a representative of the 'modern, new-world' way of teaching (reminiscent of what would later be labeled 'edutainment')—is made to fit its task. Written texts can never achieve such intensity as they lack the subtext of facial expressions and gestures. Neither can live presentations achieve the same effect because they cannot make use of camera angles (such as close-up shots), lighting, or careful editing. In addition to revealing the meanings created by their achronological, multilayered network, the closer, detailed analyses of the techniques and structure of video productions may reveal their particular significance.[50]

Bibliography (last accessed 16 April 2020)

Fritz, Walter. *Kino in Österreich 1945–1983: Film zwischen Kommerz und Avantgarde*. Wien: Österreichischer Bundesverlag, 1984.

---

48 "It's not a question of ahead, it's timelessness, zeitlos, ohne Periode, es macht nix, es wird immer etwas Frisches, Neues sein—es ist so—es gibt keinen Komponisten—in der ganzen Geschichte—der Musik—wie Beethoven [...]."

49 Beginning in 1962, he was popular for decades on Austrian TV as a presenter of classical music, especially opera (the series *Opernführer*, which began airing in 1965). "Marcel Prawy." https://de.wikipedia.org/w/index.php?title=Marcel_Prawy&oldid=19798989 9; "Marcel Prawy." https://www.geschichtewiki.wien.gv.at/Marcel_Prawy

50 Much in the manner of what Lawrence Kramer has called 'tropes' and defined as an approach to cultural-studies-informed analysis of music: "Under the hermeneutic attitude, there is and can be no fundamental difference between interpreting a written text and interpreting a work of music—or any other product or practice of culture." Kramer, "Tropes and Windows" 6.

John, Gerald. "100 Jahre Kreisky: Androsch: 'Kreisky hat die rote Katze ein für allemal verbannt.'" *Der Standard*, 07 January 2011. https://www.derstand ard.at/story/1293370216401/100-jahre-kreisky-androsch-kreisky-hat-die-rote-katze-ein-fuer-allemal-verbannt

Kramer, Lawrence. "Tropes and Windows: An Outline of Musical Hermeneutics." *Music as Cultural Practice 1800–1900*. Berkeley: Univ. of California Press, 1990. 1–20.

Landon, Howard C. Robbins. *Beethoven: sein Leben und seine Welt in zeitgenössischen Bildern und Texten*. Berlin: Dt. Buchgemeinschaft, 1976.

Lockwood, Lewis. *Beethoven: The Music and the Life*. New York: Norton, 2003.

Pelinka, Peter. "Der Frust des Dirigenten: Über den Versuch Leonard Bernsteins, Kreisky und Androsch zu versöhnen." *News*, 09 October 2015. http s://www.news.at/a/pelinka-leonard-bernstein-kreisky

Prawy, Marcel. *Die Wiener Oper*. Wien, München: Fritz Molden, 1969.

Racek, Fritz, ed. *Die Flamme lodert: Beethoven-Ausstellung der Stadt Wien: Rathaus, Volkshalle, 26. Mai Bis 30. August 1970*. Wien: Rosenbaum, 1970.

Racek, Fritz. "Zur Wiener Beethoven-Ausstellung." *Beethovenjubiläum – 100 Jahre Musikverein – Schauspielfestival*. Ed. Kurt Blaukopf. Wien et al.: Verlag für Jugend und Volk, 1970. 100–103.

Rief, Norbert. "Androsch: 'Es war nie eine Vater-Sohn-Beziehung.'" *Die Presse*, 28 February 2010. https://www.diepresse.com/543118/androsch-es-war-n ie-eine-sohn-vater-beziehung

Schmidt-Görg, Joseph, and Hans Schmidt, eds. *Ludwig van Beethoven*, London: Pall Mall, 1970.

Szabó-Knotik, Cornelia. "Zwischen Rückbesinnung und Aneignung: Bedeutungszuschreibungen von Aufführungen alter Musik in Wien zur Zeit der Ersten Republik." *Alte Musik in Österreich: Forschung und Praxis seit 1800*. Eds. Barbara Boisits and Ingeborg Harer. Wien: Mille Tre, 2009. 187–242. DOI: 10.2307/j.ctvdfomj3.11

"Die Welt bis gestern: Androsch: Mit ihm verlor Kreisky sein Glück." *Die Presse*, 11 April 2008. https://www.diepresse.com/375875/die-welt-bis-gestern-a ndrosch-mit-ihm-verlor-kreisky-sein-gluck

Wulff, Hans Jürgen. *Ludwig van Beethoven im Film: Mit Filmographie*. Westerkappeln: DerWulff.de 2018. DOI: 10.25969/mediarep/12813

Online Sources (last accessed 16 April 2020)

"Archive of Periodicals." *Documentary Archive Radio Communications*. http://ww
    w.dokufunk.org/upload/periodika_digitalisiert_20200117(1).pdf
Czeike, Felix. "Arbeitermusik." *Wien Geschichte Wiki*. https://www.geschichtew
    iki.wien.gv.at/Arbeitermusik
"Fidelio: List of Cast." *Wikipedia*. https://de.wikipedia.org/wiki/Fidelio#cite_
    ref-7
"Geschichte des Fernsehens in Österreich." *Wikipedia*. https://de.wikipedia.
    org/w/index.php?title=Geschichte_des_Fernsehens_in_%C3%96sterreich
    &oldid=194523170
"Help! (film)." *Wikipedia*. https://en.wikipedia.org/w/index.php?title=Help!_(
    film)&oldid=943912318
"Humphrey Burton." *Wikipedia*. https://en.wikipedia.org/w/index.php?title=
    Humphrey_Burton&oldid=946250094
"Ludwig van Beethoven, Beethoven's Opera Fidelio. German Text, with an
    English Translation [1805]." *Online Library of Liberty*. https://oll.libertyfun
    d.org/titles/beethoven-beethovens-opera-fidelio-german-text-with-an-
    english-translation
"Marcel Prawy." *Wien Geschichte Wiki*. https://www.geschichtewiki.wien.gv.at/
    Marcel_Prawy
"Marcel Prawy." *Wikipedia*. https://de.wikipedia.org/w/index.php?title=Marc
    el_Prawy&oldid=197989899
"Primetime Emmy Awards." *IMDb*. https://www.imdb.com/event/ev0000223/
    1972/1
"Suche in der Archivdatenbank." *Wiener Konzerthaus*. https://www.konzertha
    us.at/datenbanksuche
"Viennese Beethoven Events in 2020." *Vienna 2020*. https://musik2020.wien.
    info/en-us/beethoven-events-2020
Wie wir wurden, was wir sind: Generation Österreich, Part 2. TV ORF 3. Broad-
    casted December 29, 2013. https://www.fernsehserien.de/wie-wir-wurde
    n-was-wir-sind
"Young People's Concerts." *Wikipedia*. https://en.wikipedia.org/w/index.php?
    title=Young_People%27s_Concerts&oldid=938766812

Audiovisual Sources (last accessed 16 April 2020)

Perné, Walter. "Eine kleine Geschichte der Schallaufzeichnung." *Österreichische Mediathek*. https://www.mediathek.at/unterrichtsmaterialien/eine-kleine -geschichte-der-schallaufzeichnung/

"Voice Portrait Leonard Bernstein." *Österreichisches Phongrammarchiv*. http://catalog.phonogrammarchiv.at/sessions.php?id_sessions=5119&action= view&sortieren=signatur&vonBis=10-19

"Österreich Geschichte 1976–2008." *YouTube*. https://youtu.be/rDGjWoTaо8M

Appendix

Table 1: Beethoven Celebrations Vienna 1970; Dates – Events[51] – TV-Broadcasts

Sat 07.02.		Die große Glocke: Annual Preview
Sat 21.02		Tonopticum: 200 Years of Beethoven
Fri 27.02.		Famous Conductors: Karl Böhm and the Vienna Symphony. Rehearsals
Sun 22.03.	Recordings from the series of performances from 19.12.–21.12.1969	Die Wiener Philharmoniker in Probe und Konzert. Cond.: Eugene Ormandy; Presenter: Marcel Prawy. Beethoven, 'Egmont' Ouverture
Sat 04.04., Sun 05.04.	Konzerthaus. Vienna Phil.; Cond.: Leonard Bernstein. Beethoven, Symphony No. 9	
Sat 09.05.		Kultur aktuell: Beethoven, Incidental Music (= performance 30.05. Altes Rathaus)
Sun 10.05.		Die Wiener Philharmoniker in Probe und Konzert. Cond.: Eugene Ormandy; Sol.: Henryk Szeryng; Presenter: Marcel Prawy. Beethoven, Violin Concerto
Sat 23.05.	Opening of the Vienna Festival	Kultur aktuell
Sun 24.05.	Theater an der Wien. New Production: Beethoven, 'Fidelio' (repetitions. 27. u. 31. 05.)	

Sun 24.05.	Musikverein. Vienna Sym.; Cond.: David Oistrach; Sol.: Igor Oistrach. Beethoven, Violin Concerto; Prokofiev, Symphony No. 5	
Tue 26.05. to Sun 30.08.	The Vienna Beethoven Exhibition: 'Die Flamme lodert'	
Thu 28.05.	Künstlerhaus-Kino. Mauricio Kagel, Ludwig van	
Fri. 29.05.	Musikverein. Collegium musicum Pragense. i.a. Beethoven, Rondino	
Sat 30.05.		Kultur aktuell
Sat 30.05.	Musikverein. Jörg Demus. Beethoven, Piano Sonatas	
Mon 1.06.	Musikverein. Hermann Prey. Beethoven, Songs	
Mon 1.06.	Musikverein. Jörg Demus. Beethoven, Piano Sonatas	
Thu 4.06.	Musikverein. Jörg Demus. Beethoven, Piano Sonatas	

Fri 5.06 Sat 6.06. Sun 7.06.	Musikverein. Vienna Phil.; Cond. and Sol.: Leonard Bernstein. Beethoven, Piano Concerto No. 1; Bruckner, Symphony No. 9	Kultur aktuell
Sat 6.06.	Musikverein. Jörg Demus. Beethoven, Piano Sonatas	
Sun 7.06.	Musikverein. Vienna Phil.; Cond. and Sol.: Leonard Bernstein. Beethoven, String Quartet Op. 131 version for string orchestra; Piano Concerto No. 1	
Sun 7.06.	Musikverein. Octet of the Berliner Phil. Beethoven, Septet; Schubert Octet	
Tue 09.06. to Sun 14.06.	Musikverein. Berliner Phil.; Cond.: Herbert v. Karajan. Beethoven-Cycle	
Tue 9.06.	Staatsoper. Beethoven, 'Fidelio.' (Repetition of the New Production, cf. 24. 05.)	

Wed 10.06.	Konzerthaus. Convention of the SPÖ. Opening speech from the party chairman, Federal Chancellor Bruno Kreisky. Welcome addresses by the representatives of the Socialist International. Vienna Phil.; Cond.: Leonard Bernstein. Beethoven, Piano Concerto No. 1 and 3; 'Leonore' Ouverture; Josef Scheu: Lied der Arbeit; Austrian National Anthem	Zeit im Bild 1 (News Program): Convention of the SPÖ
Wed 10.06.	Theater an der Wien. Royal Ballet, London. Beethoven, 'Geschöpfe des Prometheus' (Chor.: Frederick Ashton); Repetition. 21.06.	
Wed 10.06.	Musikverein. Paul Badura-Skoda. Beethoven, Piano Sonatas	
Sat 13.06.	Musikverein. Paul Badura-Skoda. Beethoven, Piano Sonatas	
Tue 16.10.	Musikverein. Peter Schreier. Beethoven, Song Recital	

Thu 18.06.	Musikverein. Paul Badura-Skoda. Beethoven, Piano Sonatas	
Thu 18.06.	Musikverein. Vienna Sym.; Cond.: Eduard Serov; Cond.: Dmitrij Kitajenko (both had won the Herbert v. Karajan Conducting Competition). Beethoven, 'Egmont' Ouverture; Strawinsky, 'The Firebird;' Mozart, Symphony KV 550; Strauss, 'Don Juan'	
Sat 20.06.	Musikverein. Paul Badura-Skoda. Beethoven, Piano Sonatas	
Sat 20.06.		Kultur aktuell
Sun 21.06.	Musikverein. Vienna Phil.; Singverein; Cond.: Josef Krips; Sol.: Wilma Lipp, Anna Reynolds, Peter Schreier, Theo Adam. Beethoven, 'Missa Solemnis'	

Fri 26.06.	Musikverein. UN Gala Concert for the 25th Anniversary of the UN Charta (The net proceeds of the event benefited the United Nations disaster relief) ORF-Sym.; Cond.: Milan Horvat; Sol.: Alexander Jenner; Speaker: Fred Liewehr. Beethoven, Ouverture for the Ballet 'Die Geschöpfe des Prometheus.' The Preamble to the United Nations Charter. Beethoven, Piano Concerto No. 3; Ligeti, 'Apparitions' for Orchestra; Schubert, Symphony No. 6	UN Gala in Cooperation with the Austrian division of the UN – live broadcast
Sun 19.07.		The Creation of a Stage Design – 'Fidelio.' From Sketch to Premiere
Sat 01.08.		Kultur aktuell
Sun 23. 08.	Salzburg Cathedral. ORF-Sym.; ORF-Choir; Cond.: Gottfried Preinfalk; Sol.: Gerhard Zuckriegel, Rotraud Hausmann, Ingrid Mayr, Kurt Equiluz, Kurt Ruzizcka. Beethoven, Mass C major	Eurovision from the Salzburg Cathedral
Sun 27. 09.		Vienna – Home of Great Masters. In the footsteps of Ludwig van Beethoven

Sat 03.10.		Das ORF-Konzert. Die Wiener Philharmoniker in Probe und Konzert. Cond. and Sol.: Leonard Bernstein; Presenter: Marcel Prawy. Beethoven, Piano Concerto No. 1
Sun 11.10.		ORF-Sym.; Cond.: Milan Horvat. Beethoven, 'Geschöpfe des Prometheus'
Sat 17.10.		Das ORF-Konzert. Concertgebouw Orch.; Cond.: Rafael Kubelik. Beethoven, Symphony No. 2; 'Leonore' Ouverture No. 3 (no Viennese performance)
Sat 31.10.		Das ORF-Konzert. Vienna Phil.; Cond.: Claudio Abbado. Beethoven, Symphony No. 8 (recorded at the Musikverein 22. and 23.10.)
Sat 07.11.		Das ORF-Konzert. Berliner Phil.; Cond.: Herbert v. Karajan. Beethoven, Symphony No. 5 (recorded at the Musikverein 09.06.)
Sat 07.11.		Die Welt des Buches
Sat 14.11.		Das ORF-Konzert. Berliner Phil.; Cond.: Rafael Kubelik. Beethoven, Symphony No. 3
Sun 15.11.		Eurovision from Berlin. Gala-Abend der Schallplatte (Gala of Records)
Sat 21.11.		Das ORF-Konzert. Berliner Staatskapelle; Cond.: Kurt Masur. Beethoven, Symphony No. 1 and 4 (no Viennese performance)

Sun 22.11.		Opernführer. Marcel Prawy presents 'Fidelio' by Ludwig van Beethoven
Sun 22.11., 29.11., 06.12.,		Ludwig van Beethoven. Documentary for the Composer's 200th Anniversary (Dir. Barry Gavin)
Sun 13.12.		German Opera Berlin; Cond.: Karl Böhm; Sol.: Gwyneth Jones, James King, Gustav Neidlinger, Josef Greindl. Beethoven, 'Fidelio'
Tue 15.12.		Beethovens Geburtstag (Beethoven's Birthday). Wiener Musikfest with Leonard Bernstein. Co-production ORF, CBS, (dir.: Humphrey Burton)
Sat 19.12.		Das ORF-Konzert. Vienna Sym.; Cond.: Karl Böhm. Beethoven, Symphony No. 7 (no Viennese performance?)
Fri 25.12.		ORF-Konzert (in Farbe). Berliner Phil.; Choir of the German Opera Berlin; Cond.: Herbert v. Karajan; Sol.: Gundula Janowitz, Christa Ludwig, Jess Thomas, Walter Berry. Beethoven, Symphony No. 9 (the performance on 14.06. featured different soloists; therefore this is from another one, probably not from Vienna)

Table 2: Beethoven Vienna 1970 in TV: Leonard Bernstein's contributions
Dates – Broadcast formats – Contents

Sat 23.05.	Kultur aktuell	Opening of the Vienna Festival, scene excerpts from 'Fidelio'
Sat 6.06.	Kultur aktuell	Item 3 (10:15): Bernstein's rehearsal of Piano Concerto No. 1
Wen 10.06.	Zeit im Bild 1	Convention of the SPÖ speech Kreisky. Bernstein as Cond. and Sol. of Piano Concerto No. 1 (4:13); 'Leonore' Ouverture No. 3 (2:36)
Sun 19.07.	Ein Bühnenbild entsteht – 'Fidelio.' Von der Skizze zur Premiere.	Excerpts from the rehearsal and the performance, several interviews with people involved
Sat 03.10.	Das ORF-Konzert (in Farbe). Die Wiener Philharmoniker in Probe und Konzert	Excerpts from the rehearsal and the performance of Beethoven, Piano Concerto No. 1, Bernstein as Cond. and Sol., presenter Marcel Prawy (with interview)
Tue 15.12.	Beethovens Geburtstag (in Farbe). (Beethoven's Birthday). Ein Musikfest in Wien mit Leonard Bernstein	Bernstein's Viennese stay during the festival, excerpts from rehearsals; with his comments both diagetically and off-screen (in English) and with German voiceover

Women's Voices in Radio

Julia Jaklin (University of Music and Performing Arts Vienna)

Using audio(visual) sources to re-think (music) history raises a number of different questions. This article aims to discuss a case of biographical research and its relation to political, economic, and sociocultural matters, a case taken from the field of broadcasting, using audio sources and available metadata. The analysis of speech in these sources is an additional focus because it not only contains information about the content of the text that is spoken, but above all, information about the quality of the voice, e.g. its tone, articulation, pauses, and so on. There is a tension between *what* is said and *how* it is said, and the analysis of this tension is only made possible by the availability of the audio sources. In digital audio(visual) archives like the Österreichische Mediathek (Austrian archive for sound recordings and videos)[1] or the Phonogrammarchiv of the Austrian Academy of Sciences,[2] a wealth of different examples, especially of the spoken word, are available. Many of the sources in the Mediathek come from the Österreichischer Rundfunk (ORF, Austrian Broadcasting Corporation) and are recordings of news broadcasts or other radio shows as well as all manner of recordings on the topics of politics, literature, science, art, and everyday life.

To illustrate my arguments and at the same time reflect upon possible approaches to voice analysis, I will take a closer look at the ORF radio program *Von Tag zu Tag*, a live radio interview show, and one of its (more or less) regular presenters, Ilse Oberhofer. Oberhofer was among the first women to present news broadcasts on Austrian radio in the early 1970s.[3] Therefore, I also wish to understand how a woman's career and her activities in raising awareness of women's issues is presented via the medium in which both her professional development and its social effects are documented.

---

1   *Österreichische Mediathek.* https://www.mediathek.at/
2   "Phonogrammarchiv." https://www.oeaw.ac.at/phonogrammarchiv
3   "Ilse Oberhofer." https://oe1.orf.at/artikel/208892/Ilse-Oberhofer

The Radio Sound—Approaches to Analyzing the Voice in Radio

Radio is unmistakably recognizable as such because of its format, vocal delivery, and production techniques, which are all immediately and easily distinguishable from the auditory phenomena of everyday life as well as from other media—film, television, computer games, telephone advertisements, etc. Up until now, no systematic investigation has been made of the characteristics on which listeners base the identification of the 'radio sound,' how these characteristics are generated via editing and production, and how and to what extent the technology and environment of radio shapes their perception. In general, radio research is mostly regarded as a structural problem, and research is focused on the tension between listener ratings and the choice of topics and the journalistic presentation of the respective subjects.[4]

A very important factor in radio is the voice. It is a very personal and individual thing. We can easily distinguish people by their voices on the basis of pitch, timbre, volume, and other characteristic factors, such as dialectal coloring, speech defects, and age-related features.[5] For example, speaker recognition (and related fields like speaker diarisation[6] or speaker verification/recognition[7]) uses the acoustic features of a voice to automatically distinguish between different speakers in audio recordings.

When listening to the radio, especially news programs, there is, in Western culture, a strong preference for lower voices. They are seemingly perceived to be more 'objective,' 'calm,' and 'credible.' Higher voices, on the other hand, are regarded as 'exaggerated,' 'implausible,' and 'emotional.' This may be one reason why, up until the 1970s, women newscasters were rejected, mainly by men.[8] The show I want to analyze, however, is not a news program, but rather an informative interview program which, at times, deals with very personal topics. Nonetheless, the presenter needed to be perceived as being as neutral and credible as possible without appearing distanced and emotionless.

In his article *Radio als Sound*, Kiron Patka writes about the interaction of the room acoustics of the radio studio and the perception of the voice by radio listeners. Most studios have little to no reverberation, which contributes to

---

4   Föllmer, "Theoretisch-Methodische Annäherungen" 321, 325; Schröter, "Programmanalyse."
5   Meyer-Kalkus, *Stimme und Sprechkünste im 20. Jahrhundert* 1.
6   "Speaker diarisation," https://en.wikipedia.org/wiki/Speaker_diarisation
7   "Speaker recognition." https://en.wikipedia.org/wiki/Speaker_recognition
8   Sendlmeier, *Sprechwirkung* 15.

the radio voice's sounding as if it were spoken directly in the room where it is listened to, which is a typical aesthetic quality of radio that we so easily recognize.[9]

The use of the voice in a radio show generally depends on the type of show. In the more casual, informal interview setting, the voice sounds more 'natural' than in the more serious news broadcast setting. Depending on the target audience as well as factors such as the time of day—which contributes to the possible demographics of the listeners—or the type of radio station and its sound design, the voice of the speakers may vary. The 'sound design' of a radio station seems to be a very important factor, especially in determining and maintaining audiences.

There are several parameters that can be distinguished in voice analysis: pitch, dynamics, speed, pauses, volume/sound level, timbre, and word choice. The abovementioned parameters are interpreted differently with regard to women and men. Women's voices are typically higher than men's. Low voices are typically considered convincing, authoritative, competent, and dominant; high voices tend to be considered subordinate and less competent, even untrustworthy, and less capable.[10] This may also be a reason why women were denied positions as newscasters. In any case, it was not until the 1970s that women's voices were heard in the news.

Women at ORF

The position of women in radio is still underresearched, especially in the history of Austrian radio broadcasting.[11] To find out more about the beginnings of her career at the ORF, I interviewed Ilse Oberhofer in January 2020. She recalls her start at the ORF: In 1968 the ORF was looking for young journalists to fill positions in the newly founded news department 'Aktueller Dienst.' Oberhofer applied 'just for fun' and got a position as an aspiring journalist at Ö1 (the first ORF radio channel). During the oral examination she had to take as part of the application process, she remembers that there were about

9   Patka, "Radio als Sound."
10   Sendlmeier, *Sprechwirkung* 73.
11   Regarding the beginning of the radio in Austria as well as its postwar development: Pensold, *Zur Geschichte des Rundfunks in Österreich.*

15 to 20 applicants in total, two of them women. She also recalls that she was selected because of her unconventional ideas and her open mindset.

Most men on the editorial staff had a personal secretary— "of course they were all women, no man would do a job like that," says Oberhofer. She would soon find out that many of these women had a higher education and would have liked to do the job the men did. But there was almost no chance at all to 'escape' the secretary job and become an editor.

Oberhofer talks quite fondly about her start at the ORF, but there were also incidents where men behaved inappropriately.

Oberhofer started her career as a news editor, but she was, in the beginning, not allowed to read the news herself because Gerd Bacher,[12] the general director, did not allow women to do so. Roland Machatschke,[13] head of the news department, once let her take the microphone under the pretense that he had lost his voice; she convinced Bacher to let her host the news program. This development was founded on a broad women's rights movement which slowly seeped into the mainstream Austrian attitude.[14]

Von Tag zu Tag

The radio show *Von Tag zu Tag* ("from day to day") was an interview program which ran almost daily on Ö1, one of the three national radio channels operated by the ORF. The show was produced from June 1977 until 2017 under this name, but it still exists in a slightly modified form and with a new name: *Punkt eins*. The Österreichische Mediathek has made the *Von Tag zu Tag* shows from 1977 to 1989 available online.[15] The start of the series on October 3, 1977 was preceded by a two-week test run of the show during 'Schulfunk' (school radio) hours, from 9:05 to 9:30 in June 1977. From October on, the program was broadcast at 14:30.

The concept of the show is that a presenter has a half-hour live conversation with one or more (prominent) studio guests, including questions from the audience, who could phone in live, which was a new concept for Austrian

---

12   "Gerd Bacher." https://de.wikipedia.org/wiki/Gerd_Bacher
13   "Roland Machatschke." https://oe1.orf.at/artikel/208886/Roland-Machatschke
14   Mesner, "Zäsuren und Bögen."
15   "Sammlung Von Tag zu Tag." https://www.mediathek.at/oesterreich-am-wort/sammlu ngen/sammlung/col/11/cd/show/sc/Collection/gc/24/

radio.[16] Current topics are discussed, which means that there was usually a particular occasion for the program, e.g. an exhibition, a concert, a congress, or similar event. After the initial success of the program, non-profit organizations came on the show to talk about their work and introduce themselves to a wider audience. Ilse Oberhofer mentions in her interview that she tried to invite her guests on the news program as well, if possible, so that there would be a chance for a deeper discussion of some topics. Irmgard Czerny, the ORF staff member responsible for organizing the show, supported Oberhofer's efforts.

In the first 10 years of its existence, the program welcomed many famous actors, artists, as well as many Austrian ministers and high clergy. People working in the field of psychological counselling were especially popular guests and topics.[17]

The whole corpus of audio recordings of this program is, as mentioned, available online at the Austrian Mediathek. It comprises 2524 different shows from 1977 to 1989 together with the corresponding metadata. After downloading the metadata files in *.json format and preprocessing them, I ran several statistical analyses. For each show, the Mediathek provides the title, a subtitle ("Titelzusatz"), the length of the audio clip, the show's contributors/participants ("Mitwirkende"), categorized as interviewer/interviewee; the broadcast date; keywords as well as technical information regarding the type of recording (which, in this case, was always "audio"); the archive format (the format/medium in which it is stored in the archive); the shelf number ("Signatur"); and the current format ("Mp3-Audiodatei").

The metadata is not flawless, as is to be expected, but an especially problematic issue is that the airdates are not always correct; some are dated even before the conception of the show. I have (not yet) found a way to correct this, but there are most likely records of all shows in one of the available ORF archives; I have decided to focus on the available information for now. The data in the interviewer/interviewee category was also not always correct, but I was able to fix these classifications relatively easily (although I can't be completely certain that no mistakes remain).

The first set of information I was able to obtain from the available data is the amount of shows that each interviewer/presenter did. Volkmar

---

16   "Von Tag zu Tag: 10 Jahre 'Von Tag zu Tag:' 1. Teil." https://www.mediathek.at/atom/117
      42D66-153-00386-00000598-1173A532
17   Ibid.

Parschalk,[18] one of the founders of the show, hosted the most broadcasts by far, 360 shows in total. There are 185 different presenters listed in the metadata, some of whom only did 1 or 2 shows. The number of men is 153 and the number of women 32. Ilse Oberhofer hosted a total of 51 shows, about half of them on topics related to women.

Figure 1: Number of shows per person (more than 25 shows only).

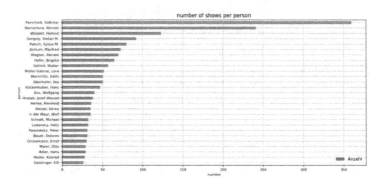

I also attempted to analyze the provided keywords in a graph analysis, but the results were not meaningful or significant in any way because the keywords the Mediathek uses are very generic and are often used to describe different topics. The resulting word cloud does show the more frequently occurring topics of the show more prominently, but correlations between shared keywords cannot be detected.

Every show starts with the theme song, a striking trumpet melody playing over the quickly repeating chords of a string section and a rising bass line. It is taken from a song on the soundtrack to the 1968 film *Barbarella*, overdubbed with the words "Von Tag zu Tag."

In order to demonstrate my findings and my analytical approach to the audio clips with an example, I would like to take a closer look at a show hosted by Ilse Oberhofer and broadcast on March 7th 1978 called *Von Tag zu Tag—Internationaler Frauentag* with the subtitle *Gespräch mit der Feministin Erica Fischer*, which translates to *The International Women's Day—An Interview with the Feminist*

---

18   "Volkmar Parschalk." https://de.wikipedia.org/wiki/Volkmar_Parschalk

Figure 2: Wordcloud with the visualization of the most commonly used keywords associated with the Von Tag zu Tag shows in the Mediathek.

Zivilgesellschaft   Kulturpolitik   Wirtschaftspolitik
Finanzpolitik   Porträt   Hilfe   Terror // SPÖ   Radio
römisch - katholische Kirche   Bildende Kunst
Drama   Ideen und Kulturen   Frauen
Arbeitsbedingungen   Gesundheitswesen und medizinische Versorgung
Natur   **Politik**
Politik Österreich   Medizin   Bauen
Kongress   **Wissenschaft und Forschung**
Wirtschaft
Bildung und Schulwesen   Religion
E-Musik   Theater   Medien und Kommunikation
Musik   Literatur   Soziales   Ökologie und Umweltschutz
Kultur   Politikwissenschaften
Kinder und Jugend   Technik
Bildung   Geschichtswissenschaft
Faschismus und Nationalsozialismus   Reise
Psychologie
Theologie und Religionswissenschaften

Erica Fischer. The metadata lists Erica Fischer as a guest and Ilse Oberhofer as the presenter.[19]

The structure of the show follows the usual *Von Tag zu Tag* format. After the theme song, Oberhofer opens with some welcoming remarks in her seemingly 'standard' radio voice, which is interspersed with deliberate pauses. Then there is a change in her voice and she begins to present the topic of the show: Erica Fischer is quickly introduced by Oberhofer and proceeds to speak about her organization, the AUF (Arbeitsgemeinschaft unabhängiger Frauen—The Association of Independent Women) which, among other things, provides support to women who are victims of domestic violence. During the show Oberhofer takes three calls from listeners.

---

19   "Von Tag zu Tag: Internationaler Frauentag." http://www.mediathek.at/atom/0BF6A33
      7-31B-000E6-00000D50-0BF5F1D5

Ilse Oberhofer presents the topic of the show as follows:

"Ich tu mir diesmal ein bissl schwer zu sagen, wen diese Sendung in erster Line angeht, wen sie vor allem betrifft, wer sich betroffen fühlen soll. Ganz sicher einmal die Frauen, aber vielleicht doch auch nicht ausschließlich nur die Frauen, vielleicht wär's auch gar nicht so schlecht, wenn sich auch die Männer angesprochen fühlten, als doch auch indirekt Mitbetroffene, als Mitschuldige, manchmal vielleicht sogar an dem, was wir heute da zur Sprache bringen wollen."[20]

Seemingly struggling for words, she explains that the following topic is not only addressed to women, but that even men should listen. Oberhofer does address the problem of a lack of male awareness of feminist issues in some of her other shows. In her search for the right phrase she uses three different wordings to describe 'whom this show should concern.'

Oberhofer uses a combination of pitch variation, deliberate pauses, and syllable stretches to emphasize important words. For example, in the phrase "ich tu mir diesmal ein bissl schwer" ("this time I find it a little difficult"), we hear a stretched "e" as well as a pitch variation in her pronunciation of "schwer." Comparing the opening remarks with the ones just mentioned, we find that the pitch of her voice changes slightly and she increases the amount of pitch modulation in her voice. Pitch variation as well as breaks and pauses can be analyzed using Praat, a piece of free software used for speech analysis in phonetics.[21]

She uses pauses before some words to emphasize them (e.g. before "Männer" and "indirekt"), perhaps with the intention of making (male) listeners more attentive.

The speed at which the words are spoken varies considerably. Some words or syllables are stretched out (e.g. in the word "schwer," the "e"), others delivered very quickly and connected to each other. In the first part, for example: "... Damen und Herren, ich freue mich ...", a phrase she presumably uses very

---

20   Ibid.: 00:26–00:56. "This time I find it a little difficult to say who this show primarily concerns, who it concerns above all, who should feel involved. Certainly, the women, but perhaps not only the women, perhaps it wouldn't be so bad if the men also felt addressed, as indirectly affected, as complicit, sometimes even in what we want to bring up today."

21   *Praat*. http://www.fon.hum.uva.nl/praat/

Figure 3: Screenshot of the Praat program. The pitch modulation in the word "schwer" is visualized as well as in the word "sagen."

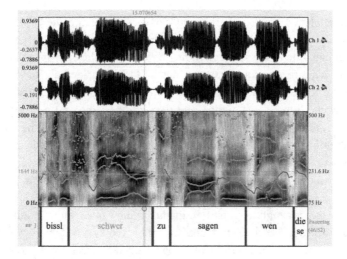

often in her shows, is spoken in a very condensed manner. However, Oberhofer uses pauses and breaks in most of her phrases to make the content of her speech clearly understood. A calm tone of voice is maintained during the interview with Erica Fischer, which contributes to the seriousness of the show's rather upsetting topic. The two women do not want to appear (too) emotional—a frequent accusation directed at women, as Oberhofer mentions in another episode of *Von Tag zu Tag*.[22]

Conclusion

Oberhofer consciously uses her voice to get attention: in the opening, mainly pauses and stretched-out syllables are used for this purpose. In radio, the voice is very powerful and emotions are indeed conveyed, but women are often labelled as too emotional; they have to remain very calm to be perceived as professional. Pitch is a concern as well. Women sometimes lower their voices

---

22   "Von Tag zu Tag: Alice Schwarzer über Feminismus." http://www.mediathek.at/atom/ 1084428D-186-0013E-00000F64-10836E0F

to be taken more seriously, or preference is given to women with naturally lower voices in the first place. I think it is important to listen to women and their speech and investigate if there are differences and specify what those are.

Oberhofer was criticized for her style of speaking on the radio.[23] She used to speak very freely, laughing often, seeming too emotional and personal. The combination of the women's rights movement in the early 1970s and Ilse Oberhofer's career as a newscaster is not, I think, coincidental. Having been put into a position where she could use her platform (e.g. *Von Tag zu Tag*) to talk about women's 'problems' and present them on the radio on a well-regarded show, she does get emotional, or rather uses the 'emotionality' of the topic to get attention—by using her voice. In the interview with her guest she remains more 'neutral' (or seems to be 'herself'). Both women do try to stay very calm, even when talking about abuse and sexual harassment; this is perhaps done on purpose to not seem 'hysterical' and hence be taken seriously.

The voice is a highly complex, individual thing whose timbre, volume, dialectal coloring, speech defects, etc. are influenced by a wide variety of factors which we unconsciously note in our everyday perception to recognize and classify people by their voice. This example analysis is intended to show that listening to audio clips, made possible by the (online) availability of AV sources, is an important part of historical research, and that it may be possible to gain further insights that can contribute to (music) historical research.

Bibliography

Föllmer, Golo. "Theoretisch-Methodische Annäherungen an die Ästhetik des Radios: Qualitative Merkmale von Wellenidentitäten." *Auditive Medienkulturen: Techniken des Hörens und Praktiken der Klanggestaltung*. Eds. Axel Volmar and Jens Schröter. Bielefeld: transcript, 2013. 321–38.

Mesner, Maria. "Zäsuren und Bögen, Grenzen und Brüche, Zeit- und Geschlechtergeschichte." *Bananen, Cola, Zeitgeschichte: Oliver Rathkolb und das lange 20. Jahrhundert*. Eds. Lucile Dreidemy, Richard Hufschmied, Agnes Meisinger et al. Köln, Wien: Böhlau, 2015. 1003–12.

---

23   "Ilse Oberhofer." https://oe1.orf.at/artikel/208892/Ilse-Oberhofer

Meyer-Kalkus, Reinhart. *Stimme und Sprechkünste im 20. Jahrhundert.* Berlin: Akad.-Verl., 2001.

Patka, Kiron. "Radio als Sound." *Von akustischen Medien zur auditiven Kultur 15,* 2 (2015): 113–25.

Pensold, Wolfgang. *Zur Geschichte des Rundfunks in Österreich.* Wiesbaden: Springer, 2018.

Schröter, Detlef. "Programmanalyse: Sehr gut, aber wie?" *Radiotrends: Formate, Konzepte, Analysen.* Eds. Hans-Jürgen Bucher, Walter Klingler and Christian Schröter. Baden-Baden: Nomos, 1995. 121–40.

Sendlmeier, Walter. *Sprechwirkung – Sprechstile in Funk und Fernsehen.* Berlin: Logos, 2005.

Online Sources (last accessed 16 April 2020)

"Gerd Bacher." *Wikipedia.* https://de.wikipedia.org/wiki/Gerd_Bacher

"Ilse Oberhofer." *ORF.* https://oe1.orf.at/artikel/208892/Ilse-Oberhofer

Praat: doing phonetics by computer. http://www.fon.hum.uva.nl/praat/

"Roland Machatschke." *ORF.* https://oe1.orf.at/artikel/208886/Roland-Machatschke

"Speaker diarisation." *Wikipedia.* https://en.wikipedia.org/wiki/Speaker_diarisation

"Speaker recognition." *Wikipedia.* https://en.wikipedia.org/wiki/Speaker_recognition

"Volkmar Parschalk." *Wikipedia.* https://de.wikipedia.org/wiki/Volkmar_Parschalk

Audiovisual Sources (last accessed 16 April 2020)

Österreichische Mediathek. https://www.mediathek.at/

"Phonogrammarchiv." *Österreichische Akademie der Wissenschaften.* https://www.oeaw.ac.at/phonogrammarchiv

"Sammlung Von Tag zu Tag." *Österreichische Mediathek.* https://www.mediathek.at/oesterreich-am-wort/sammlungen/sammlung/col/11/cd/show/sc/Collection/gc/24/

Vadim, Roger (Director). *Barbarella* (1968).

"Von Tag zu Tag: Internationaler Frauentag." *Österreichische Mediathek*. http://
www.mediathek.at/atom/0BF6A337-31B-000E6-00000D50-0BF5F1D5

"Von Tag zu Tag: Alice Schwarzer über Feminismus." *Österreichische Mediathek*. http://www.mediathek.at/atom/1084428D-186-0013E-00000F64-10836E0F

"Von Tag zu Tag: 10 Jahre 'Von Tag zu Tag.' 1. Teil." *Österreichische Mediathek*. https://www.mediathek.at/atom/11742D66-153-00386-00000598-1173A532

'Real Sound,' Readymade, Handmade: Musical Material and the Medium Between Mechanization, Automation, and Digitalization as an Impression and Expression of Reality
An Implicit Call for Real Interdisciplinarity

Hanns-Werner Heister

The point of departure and the central subject of the following considerations are 'real sounds.' These are the real noises and sounds *before and outside of music* in both inanimate and animate nature and society, from thunder to bird calls to machine and traffic noise. The way real sounds can be understood develops and shifts throughout the history of the music, technology, and media of the 20th century. Terms and concepts such as 'atmo'(sphere), even on the level of the industrial technical reproduction of the soundscape, lean toward the realm of noise, while 'original sound' in audiovisual montages primarily refers to the use of actually spoken words, but it can also mean all of the components of a film's soundtrack on-screen, i.e. within the depicted scene.[1]

In the following, I will attempt to shed more light on the category of 'real sound' or real tones and their artistic contexts between traditional, electroacoustic, and digitalized music with somewhat novel configurations and perspectives.

---

1   According to Szabó-Knotik within the framework of a meticulous analysis of the film *Amadeus*: The usual function of music as 'background' or else as an off-screen 'counterpoint' is infrequent. "All other music is directly provoked by Salieri's narration or by the plot of the film; even when the audience rather than the stage is on screen, the operatic music functions as *original sound* in the sense of 'belonging to the scene.' In extreme cases, even the relationship of image and music is reversed to such an extent that the mention of music requires images that serve only to illustrate it—one could also say to 'visualize' it." Szabó-Knotik, *Amadeus* 30f.

These real sounds are, 1.) first of all, simply real tones between sounds and noises in 'exterior' reality. They are a part of acoustic reality. They are used less often as an unconventionalized component of a musical work than 'realities,'[2] i.e. quotations from reality. Natural and societal sounds are normally assimilated into music and not adopted as a raw reality. Nevertheless, the incorporation of acoustic nature into musical culture does occur. A prime example from music is the scream, the uncadenced interjection in contrast to the cadenced interjection as an epitome of music according to Hegel's *Aesthetics*.[3]

Real sounds are 2.) subject matter to be processed that is external to music. Stylized by specific poiesis, they are conveyed in the musical mimesis. They have been a component of some music from its very beginning and remain so in many older and newer types of music, usually with a program-music dimension. This is the broad field of sound painting, or music as painting.

Film is thus blazing a trail for the change in that 3.) the entire soundscape that exists before and independently of art manifests as real sounds. This is because *music* existing *outside* of the film, which is prefabricated from the standpoint of the film, i.e. which is a readymade in the parlance of Duchamp's concept, becomes a component of its real sounds. The music heard at the recording locations as part of their acoustic local colour adds to it in the film; in other words, the on-screen music within scenes, and even the off-screen music, if it appears as a discovered, prefabricated musical object.

This is one of the bridges to the technically re/produced musical real sounds in discrete music, as is prototypical in 'musique concrète.' In this technical-medial determination, real sounds are 4.) readymades. They are preexistent and independent of their treatment in other subsequent works; in contrast to type 3, the real sound relates (only) to its integration into the new work or film. As such, it would become possible to convey them medially in film, radiophonic works, and later in television or video works as components of the soundtrack and to integrate them into independent

---

2   In a broad sense that, in contrast to the term used in translation studies, it is not culturally specific; 'realities' in this instance are material facts, i.e. sonically objectified, tangible, processual facts in reality, before and outside of art, including their medial embedding, transformation, resolution, in other words musical pieces as a whole or in parts, 'live' or fixed in technical reproduction by analogue or digital means, similar to the realities of 'reality studies' in the historical sciences; they could also be called real world objects.

3   See Hegel, *Ästhetik* Vol. II, part 3, chapter 2, 1.b.

music of the concert or musical theater type and into newer film and pop music.

A portion of medially conveyed nature is blended into music with real sounds. The readymade, the 'objet trouvé,' the found object, corresponds to them as a pictorial counterpart to the real sound in the visual arts. It is something similar but not identical, though, since the readymade is tangible, while music is essentially processual. Real sounds are not things, yet they can or could be presented and exhibited discretely by technical means. For this reason, an actual musical readymade exists only by means of the technical reproduction of sound, essentially since 1877 with Edison's phonograph, and on a mass scale with the advent of talking films using sound-on-film systems (Tri-Ergon process) and tape recording on the radio. The readymade is usually limited to objects from social reality, generally even only things industrially produced, from Duchamp's *Fountain* to Warhol's *Brillo*.

Duchamp places the urinal on a pedestal, thereby monumentalizing and museumizing it. He also tilts his *Fountain* by 90°. In so doing, he applies a kind of contrapuntal gimmick, which is then only made compositionally productive when serialized.[4] So he is doing nothing at all. The poiesis is not entirely eliminated, though. He does not leave the real thing as it was but rather firstly eliminates its utilitarian function; secondly, with his signature as "Mutt"[5] he transforms it into a work, albeit a simulated one, and thus defines art by virtue of his existence as an artist; and thirdly he transposes this work into the artistic context of an exhibit.[6] A minimum of poiesis is thus essential for

---

4   More on rotation and mirroring processes such as this in Springer, *Das verkehrte Bild*; for row rotation, see Eimert, *Grundlagen der musikalischen Reihentechnik*.

5   See Tomkins, *Marcel Duchamp*. The pseudonym is a type of portmanteau: Duchamp condenses company name 'J.L. *Mott* Iron,' where he purchased the urinal (214), and amalgamates it with the name from the comic strip *Mutt and Jeff*; the R. stood for Richard, which in French slang meant 'moneybags.' In the discussion at the time, the object was often referred to euphemistically-obfuscatingly as "bathroom accessory" (217) or even "drinking fountain" (219), possibly precisely because of the title "Fountain." What Tomkins characterized as "bigotry" was also still relevant later. "*Psycho* (1960) broke numerous taboos. Yet this is not directly about the depiction of violence [...]. *Psycho* (is) the first American film in which the flush of a toilet could be seen and heard—which at the time was enough to make censors blush." "7 Filme, die Tabus brachen." https://wieistderfilm.de/7-filme-die-tabus-brachen/

6   For more on the major controversies surrounding the exhibition in New York in 1917: Tomkins, *Marcel Duchamp* 212ff.

mimesis—even conceptual artists must at least write down the concepts that they do not execute.

The readymade is similar to the real sound in its origin and materiality. However, it differs fundamentally by virtue of its aesthetic functionality. For in the visual arts it is an isolated 'real thing as a work.' This is not the case in music, since the difference between useful object and art object does not exist—a piece of music could not be used as a urinal were one to reverse the independence of the work against its use.

The presentation of bird song as such, like the nightingale in Ottorino Respighi's *Pini di Roma*, can be imagined institutionally and aesthetically at best in exhibits or museums, but not on the concert stage. Furthermore, even in reality, animal noises like the nightingale song are not functional—for humans—like the urinal of *Fountain* is, and thus already analogous to art. In music, the readymade is an 'object in a work.'

Semiotically, real sounds are indexical signs that originate causally from that which is designated. This makes them especially significant for the question of the mimesis of reality.

From the outset, noise in particular is more unambiguously a part of reality than art-like sound *and* it demonstrates reality as an acoustic signal for something that exists and is acoustically perceptible. It occurs in this double function in music as well. It is indexical at its core, even if not exclusively. The origin of such art of a technical nature is hard to deny. Pierre Schaeffer attempted to do so with "'reduced listening'—the hearing of sound without reference to its source, cause, or meaning"—which George Antheil was already seeking in the 1920's as the ideal listening mode for his *Ballet Mécanique*.[7]

The complement and counterpart to the 'readymade' is the 'handmade.' I will permit myself to slightly re-accentuate and expand 'handmade' so as to be complementary to the established term 'readymade.' What is meant here is what is *created in art and as art*, specifically and in a manner intrinsic to art and music, and is not reproduced. In each case, it is newly *produced* and does not already exist before and outside of art. It is the realm of that which is classically called poiesis, 'making.' The traditional ways to convert real sounds into musical sounds are, as poiesis and mimesis at the same time, musical onomatopoeia and 'tone painting:' depiction and expression, but *not* 'impression.'

---

7   Epstein, *Sublime Noise* XIIf.

In view of the processes and methods of technical re/production, there are four technical principles or main forms, for each of which I have proposed figures from Greek mythology as a way to characterize them.[8] The decisive basic form of technical re/production is the 'true-to-life,' 'realistic' soundscape *re-production* of the 'phono-graphy' type: the *Echo principle*, named for that nymph who can only ever repeat what is said to her. Significantly earlier historically, at least since the time of Hellenistic antiquity, the *production* of sounds with instruments occurred in the form of automatophones or mechanical musical instruments, such as the musical clock or the barrel organ. The *Syrinx principle*, named for the nymph who was transformed into a reed, from which Pan makes a flute for himself and thereby calls to mind the vanished girl.[9] Finally, the fourth basic form is relevant for a perspective of 'digitalization;' it was already begun in the 'analogue,' in sampling, computers, etc., in the objectified, present- and future-determining integration of reproduction and production (thus the term re/production), of Echo and Syrinx—the *Daedalus principle*. It is named after Daedalus, the mythical inventor of the labyrinth for a monstrous combination of man and bull, the Minotaur; Daedalus was also the inventor of flight in order to escape from imprisonment, and as a sculptor and painter he created extremely lifelike works that appeared to be real and alive. The connection among the four basic forms should be considered even more systematically, particular in light of the new syntheses brought about by 'digitalization,' and it should be made productive for future research.

All of this—the modalities of production and reception as well as the historical development of the system—is ultimately also motivated and modelled by different and diverse social and individual needs, although they are not included here.

With the axis of production versus reproduction (handmade versus readymade, Syrinx versus Echo), a polarity comes into play that applies equally to mechanization, electrification, automation and digitalization. It is the same with the four-tiered configuration of mimesis and poiesis, supplemented by aisthesis and catharsis—which are not discussed here—i.e. representation,

---

8   More on conceptuality and object: Heister, "Mimetische Handlung und menschliche Natur."

9   Less important for our question is the third basic form, the entirely different principle of 'long-distance transmission,' such as telephone or radio: the Hermes principle, named for Hermes, messenger of the gods with winged shoes, and the guide of souls to the hereafter, as well as the god of knowledge, thieves, and merchants, including the 'banksters.'

production as well as perception and effect. The readymade is a real thing without poiesis and with minimal mimesis. Handmades, on the other hand, are intended to be poiesis without mimesis from the point of view of the denial of references of art to reality.

The closest thing to an identity of depiction and the depicted is the more or less 'automatic' impression[10] as a mechanical symmetrical reflection, be it a fossil in slate or a record album from the negative matrix. Nevertheless, there are differences here, too, as a result of material or technical blurring, as in the multi-stage 'printing' process of records, in casting and molding processes from hollow molds, etc. Yet in conscious, intentional reflection, there is a subjectively co-determined choice of criteria, which depends upon the motivation and the objective of the comparison—and which is not merely arbitrary, but also factually bound. Art is subject-mediated 'expression,' not the 'impression' of the real.

Often enough, however, expression and reality, art and life are identified with each other and thus confused for each other.

Structurally, it is always a matter—more specifically for art as mimesis—of confusing similarity for identity. In the face of such misleading identity, similarity forms a kind of compromise between identity and difference: The one Something is like and, at the same time, different from the other Something. This second Something is here primarily reality, in each case concretely in extracts.

Real sounds are such extracts. They represent reality as *pars pro toto*, but they *are* no longer reality as soon as they become art. Incidentally, the versatile futuristic painter Luigi Russolo was aware of this difference.

Real Sounds as the 'Object' of Musical Representation (Mimesis) and Production (Poiesis)

Before the age of mechanization and automation, real sounds were important in music not so much as a material component of music, but rather as its object, which was and is still appropriated sensually and ideologically by means of mimesis and poiesis. From the very beginning, in music as well as in spoken language, the process understood in a broad sense as sound painting has played a role for material and material development and for mimesis

---

10   Information and numerous aspects, Didi-Hubermann, *Ähnlichkeit und Berührung*.

through the filtering and abstraction process of taking real tones as *pars pro toto* for the thing or fact and transforming them into the respective musical material and idiom. Above all, it is determined in a way specific to the musical culture and epoch.

Musically, onomatopoeic stylization extends not beyond that in spoken language, but rather in a different direction: That which is noisy is translated into pitches; the natural sound as a whole is fitted into the respective idiom. In spoken language, onomatopoeic mimesis is generally limited by the principle of phonemes in general and by their respective individual linguistic characteristics in particular. Fuzziness in musical language is comparable. Sound painting likewise experiences a refraction and filtering, through styles, idioms, and the like, by the respective historical status of the material and its system, in particular pitch and rhythm systems.

In Rimsky-Korsakov's satirical fairy-tale opera based on Washington Irving's and Pushkin's *Le Coq d'or* (*The Golden Cockerel*, first performance: 1909), the title character appears in numerous forms. In keeping with his status, he is supposed to act as a warning watchman and spare the incompetent rulers further worry. His crowing has two variants. The first is the calming call.

Figure 1: Rimsky-Korsakov, Le Coq d'or.[11]

The three-tone core of the crowing is incorporated wordlessly into the orchestra as an echoed reply. The second variant is the warning call. It is similar, simply transposed, shifted to other pitches.

The mimesis of real sounds also includes the musically rather peripheral phenomenon that real *noises* are *imitated* as deceptively similarly as possible, not reproduced—a classic example is the wind machine in the theatre, which

11   Rimsky-Korsakow, *Le Coq d'or.* http://ks.imslp.net/files/imglnks/usimg/4/49/IMSLP5860
      95-PMLP45601-Coq_d_Or_Score.pdf
12   Ibid.

Figure 2: Rimsky-Korsakov, Le Coq d'or.[12]

has frequently been employed for 'sound painting' since Rameau, even in independent music, with that glissando, which then made a career in new music out of the system of discrete pitch orders for exterritorial continuous noise; for example in Strauss's *Eine Alpensinfonie* (*Alpine Symphony*).

Figure 3: Richard Strauss, Eine Alpensinfonie.[13]

Figure 4: *The thunder machine also comes in here.*

The wind machine was also used in film, albeit with a slightly shifted main function, namely not as an 'intonarumori,' i.e. a 'sound generator' in the sense of Italian Futurism, but to simulate air movement. The airplane propellers originally used for this purpose were certainly very loud and smelled quite bad. The former was welcome during its use in George Antheil's *Ballet Mécanique* (1924, with Ferdinand Léger and Dudley Murphy). The stench and noise were ameliorated by large fans—electrification replaced mechanization here

---

13   Strauss, *Eine Alpensinfonie*. http://ks.imslp.info/files/imglnks/usimg/6/6a/IMSLP51664-PMLP12189-StraussR-Op64.TimpPerc.pdf

as well; the "unavoidable wind noise is usually reduced by diverting the air-flow through sail canvasducts."[14] Only with the advent of sound film did the noise specifically also become a component of the soundtrack as wind, which was as elementary as the sounds of water (especially rain) or fire.[15]

Effects like this could also be produced with the Moog synthesizer from the 1960s onwards, although it was primarily designed for sounds. This electrification represents an early transition to the automation of sampling.

All of this is handmade—a traditional and still essential process of music as art, primarily instrumental, but also possible vocally with the traditional mimesis of real tones.

Nothing fundamental changes in futuristic noise music. Blinded by the loud racket of propaganda with the objectives of the New, the Futuristic was ignored, such as the fact that Luigi Russolo's 'intonarumori,' the 'noise makers,' were still producing instrumental sounds as musical material. From the point of view of poiesis they are traditional, only mechanical, neither electrified nor automated. 'Noise makers' are nothing but a particular form of musical instruments that, like body slaps, drums, sistrums, maracas, rattles etc., simply produce percussive sounds but not tones. A similar, converse argument applies to the numerous already electrified new musical instruments specialized for the production of *tones* since the end of the 19th century, such as the Theremin, ondes Martenot and Trautonium, but that also produce sounds. Be it noises, sound mixtures or tones—none of these instruments exceeds the bounds of musical instruments. Although they offer a much richer spectrum of sounds, tending almost to the orchestral, by combining several musical instruments, this also applies to the pre-electric mechanical musical instruments controlled by pin rollers, pin plates, perforated plates or perforated strips, such as the barrel organ, pianola, or all types of orchestrion, which usually contain their own instruments to produce sounds. A transitional form is the reproducing piano, the Welte-Mignon, first introduced in 1905, which was pneumatically controlled by punched tape, thereby permitting the recording, notating, and then playback of a particular interpretation, i.e. it corresponds to the Echo principle and already includes essential components of automated 'impression.' A digital potentiation was then represented by the Bösendorfer SE290 computer-controlled grand piano in 1986 and the Yamaha Disklavier

---

14   See "Windmaschine (Film)." https://de.wikipedia.org/wiki/Windmaschine_(Film); cf. Giesen, *Lexikon der Special Effects*.

15   E.g. Butzmann and Martin, *Filmgeräusch*.

in 1987. However, the sound 'impression' occurring here is not one of the universal soundscape, but only of the piano sound.

Attempts to incorporate other sensory areas such as smell into technical re/production, such as those following the model of Huysmans's smell organ in *À rebours*, go one step further. For example, Leon Thermen (1896-1993) in the Soviet Union of the 1920s strove to combine music with color, gesture, smell, and touch.[16] This is an extreme manifestation of the tendency of the avant-garde, which is almost always at least latent, to create a 'Gesamtkunstwerk.'[17] Initial attempts at an olfactory film or olfactory cinema have existed at least since the 1940s, but have always failed, probably ultimately because of the limits of both sensory physiology and anthropology as well as art ontology and thus practical limitations.

Based on his experience in a concert, including with Balilla Pratella's *Inno alla vita – sinfonia futurista*, Op. 30 in Milan in early 1913, Russolo wanted to extend the spectrum of sound production beyond the abilities of the orchestra. The parallels to the search for new sound generators are evident, especially in the field of microtonality, which was already expanding before the year 1900. Russolo first expressed his manifesto *L'arte dei rumori* in the form of a letter to Pratella in 1913 and published it in 1916, along with other texts, in a book with the same title.

The sound of the Futurists stands specifically for the 'modern, technical, industrial, urban world.'

It is remarkable, however, that Russolo, in his well-known classification of sounds into six types, prominently includes traditional types on the one hand, like the aforementioned wind in his "family of sounds" 2 as "whistling," "howling;"[18] on the other hand—and this is really innovative—he includes the instrumental production of specific vocal sounds as the sixth type: "Voices of animals and humans: calling, screaming, shouting, howling, laughing, wheezing, sobbing."[19]

Russolo's impressive description of—what at that time was—an urban soundscape contains an astonishing number of natural sounds:

---

16   Cf. Smirnov and Price, *Sound in Z* 46.
17   Cf. e.g. *Der Hang zum Gesamtkunstwerk*.
18   The well-known score by Russolo, *Il Risveglio della città* (1914), often includes glissandi. The oft-cited page of the score e.g. "Luigi Russolo: 'Intonarumori.'" http://www.medien kunstnetz.de/werke/intonarumori/bilder/2/
19   Russolo, *L'arte dei rumori*.

"To be convinced of the amazing variety of sounds, it is enough to think of the crash of thunder, the whistling of the wind, the rushing of a waterfall, the gurgling of a stream, the rustling of leaves, the trot of a horse as it moves away, to the wobbling of a cart on the pavement, and to the broad, solemn, and white breath of a city at night, to all the noises that wild animals and pets make and all those that the human mouth can produce without speaking or singing. Let us pass through a great modern capital city, the ears more attentive than the eyes, and we will find pleasure in distinguishing the swirls of water, air and gas in the metal pipes, the murmur of the engines, which undeniably snort and pulsate like animals, the knocking of the valves, the reciprocating of the pistons, the screeching of the mechanical saws, the bumping of the trams along their rails, the crackling of the whips, the crackling of the curtains and flags. We will discuss orchestrating the din of the merchants' shutters in our concept, the doors slamming open and closed, the babble of voices and the shuffling of the crowds, the various noises of the railway stations, the ironworks, the weaving mills, the printing works, the electrical centers, and the underground railways."[20]

What is new about Futurism in relation to music is not the use of sounds as such—that is ancient—but its revaluation (and overvaluation in relation to the sounds) on the one hand and its semantic accentuation as an expression of the industrial world on the other hand, with a specific accent on aggressive to military sounds between racecar and mitrailleuse. These, too, are not unfamiliar in music to this day, but they have not played such a prominent role—similarly, onomatopoeia prefers the sounds of guns, rifles, military orders as exemplified in Marinetti's poem glorifying war, *Il Bombardamento di Adrianopoli* (1912). Following the sentence: "Nor must we forget the completely new sounds of modern war,"[21] Russolo's list of the components of urban sounds leads into an enthusiastic essay on this poem, which depicts "in wonderful *parole in libertà*[22] the orchestra of a great battle."[23] These are fine examples of that barbaric aestheticism which already had a glorious history at that time and to which an even greater future opened up in the 20th century,

---

20   Ibid. The passage is shorted in Asholt and Fähnders, *Manifeste und Proklamationen der europäischen Avantgarde.*

21   Ibid.

22   These *parole in libertà*, words in freedom, are preferably free of syntax and human sense.

23   Ibid.

continuing into the 21st. Russolo, with music as his sound weapon, thus also wants to "generously share tonal slaps in the face."[24]

This revaluation, without the intensification of Italian Futurism, sparked a trend in music beginning in the 1920s. The new, positive evaluation of real sounds is shown, for example, in Honegger's *Pacific* 231 (1923) for an orchestra with traditional instrumentation. Although he was an ardent fan of locomotives (as was Dvořák, incidentally), Honegger found the objectives embarrassing; he insisted that his *Mouvement Symphonique* No. 1 was a study of tempo acceleration and deceleration merely by the diminution or augmentation of note values without tempo changes while also being a chorale variation. The railway, as handled in Honegger's traditional mimesis, is not one of the truly new real tones.

Compositionally, the noises come to themselves as independent material, so to speak, and thus become futuristic composition only with Edgard Varèse's *Ionisation* (1931), probably the first work for percussion orchestra alone. Here, too, the composer attaches importance to the fact that this is not mimesis. The technical innovation of electroacoustic music after 1945 does not change this aesthetic position. However, the range of the spectrum of the sounds produced in this way does change. As one of its pioneers, Varèse used the term "organized sound" "for what he predicted as the future of music, when electronic instruments would be liberated from the dictates of conventional music to produce any type of sound."[25]

One consequence of this is then a compositionally available continuum between noise and sound, sinusoidal tone and white noise.

Thus the *acoustic* reality content potentially increased, but not the *aesthetic-artistic* content; the opposite occurs, in fact. "Before the advent of electronic music, musical imitations were necessarily constrained by the limitations of musical instruments, whose timbres did not necessarily approximate nonmusical sounds with any precision. Thanks to sampling and synthesis, however, electronic music can produce mimetic representations that are virtually indistinguishable from their real-world counterparts."[26]

This was largely not realized, though. To the extent that music becomes painting at all in this context, then it is mainly as abstract, non-objective,

---

24   Ibid.
25   Demers, *Listening Through the Noise* e.g. 174.
26   Ibid. 172.

non-figurative painting—once again as the aforementioned distinction from the technical reproduction of real sounds.[27]

Arseny Avraamov's *Symphony of Sirens*, 1922 and 1923. Real Noises and Sounds in a New Type of Open-Air Music

Arseny Avraamov's work *Simfoniya Gudkov* (*Symphony of Sirens*), which premiered in Baku on November 7, 1922, the 5th anniversary of the October Revolution, then in Moscow in 1923, takes a completely different approach to the use and design of real sounds with a remarkable interweaving of new and old.

The foghorns of the entire Caspian fleet took part, all the factory sirens, two batteries of artillery, several infantry regiments, a machine gun unit, numerous hydroplanes, and finally choirs, to which all of the spectators contributed. The celebration is said to have been very impressive; it is not surprising that this 'music' could be heard far beyond the city walls of Baku.[28]

Avraamov had arranged the open-air symphony, which was divided into movements or 'acts,' even including an intermission, to be site-specific, carefully programed in space and time and with choreographed movements of the masses. "Human crowds sang workers' and revolutionary anthems in chorus as they moved to and from key nodes of entry and ceremony in the city: from the shipping docks to the ferry docks, from the ceremonial square to the Transcaucasus Railroad terminus, and from the military academy, factories, and music conservatory."[29]

As with the coupling of music and image in film, considerable synchronization problems obviously occurred in augmented form due to the pre-electric, pre-digital mechanical control system.[30] Fülöp-Müller calls the work a

---

27   Demers criticizes the identity illusion associated with this: "Although any act of recording necessarily involves some editorial decisions on the part of the recordist, many field recordings also aspire toward an unmediated representation of reality." Ibid. 170. And apodictically Sterne: "Recordings do not reproduce sound, they represent sound." Sterne, *The Sound Studies Reader* 218.

28   Fülöp-Müller, *Geist und Gesicht des Bolschewismus* 163. Further material on this subject can be found *inter alia* in Smirnov and Sterneck.

29   Wendel, "The 1922 'Symphony of Sirens' in Baku" 549. The traditional location is thus included.

30   Ibid. 553.

"factory whistle symphony." The performance in Moscow also reportedly did not produce "especially pleasing results:"

> "On the one hand, the modulation capability of the 'instruments' that were used was not exactly great, on the other hand [sic] the 'compositions' performed were much too complicated. Although the 'conductors,'[31] positioned on high command towers, regulated the use of the various sirens and steam pipes, which were located very far apart, by waving flags, it was not possible to achieve a uniform acoustic impression; the distortions were such that the audience was not even able to recognize the 'Internationale' that was so well-known and familiar to them."[32]

Efforts to "improve the modulation capability and tonal purity of the 'monumental instruments,' as well as the accuracy of joint conducting" continued during the formative phase of the 1920s. Fülöp-Müller previously reported on "noise orchestras" with "engines, turbines, sirens, horns, and similar noise instruments," with which "noise orgies" were held in the Moscow Trade Union Palace, for instance, i.e. not as open-air music, followed by "noise symphonies, noise operas, and noise festivals."[33] He attributed these tendencies to the "period of economic war communism," while the events in Baku and Moscow were in line with the reconstruction, including "electrification,"[34] which according to Lenin's formula, when added to "Soviet power," was supposed to result in "communism," progress through the unity of economic and political development.[35] Both types form a notable combination of avant-garde and otherwise rather anti-avant-garde 'proletkult.'

In her fairly comprehensive account, Wendel deems the event "Soviet internationalism"—hence the city on the periphery, the industrialization of the country, the Russian-Soviet and other avant-gardes, and the 'Gesamtkunstwerk' tendencies. The *Siren Symphony* was "one of the first realizations of a

---

31 A picture appears on page 160 of the conductor directing with signal flags, which appears frequently in literature; this is Avraamov. Fülöp-Müller, *Geist und Gesicht des Bolschewismus* 160.

32 Ibid. 163.

33 Ibid. 162.

34 Ibid.

35 "Communism – that is Soviet power plus the electrification of the whole country" (as stated at the 8th All-Russian Soviet Congress on 22 December 1920). Wallis, "Elektrifizierung." http://www.inkrit.de/e_inkritpedia/e_maincode/doku.php?id=e:elektrifizierung

socialist Gesamtkunstwerk, defined otherwise as a radical unity of the arts, technology, urban space and human labor. [Avraamov's Symphony of Sirens] belongs to a genre of avant-garde practices that synthesized disparate artistic modalities and modern technologies in the form of mass spectacles, theatrical performances, and music and filmic compositions."[36]

In the context of the festive occasion, everyday sounds are part of reality, yet at the same time they are symbolic references to it through the particular context. Because of the open-air character, everything that makes noise tends to be used for acoustic reasons alone. Industrialization as a catch-up development was as vital for the early Soviet Union as it remains today for the so-called 'developing' countries. Since people are a decisive productive force in this context, Avraamov also used sounds and words beyond noises. The fact that military sounds, speaking of 'Soviet power,' also belong to this is regrettable but understandable, since the phase of civil war and foreign intervention had only just ended.

The open-air concert as a festive event thus does not simply repeat the sounds of the urban landscape but condenses them, selects and accentuates socially relevant components that were important for proto-socialist industrialization as forward-looking landmarks, complemented by politically progressive music, thus actively changing and concentrating the sound of a new, proto-socialist city. Everything was handmade, and in particular in the pre-electrical stage of mechanization.

Respighi's Nightingale in *I pini del Gianicolo*, 1924. Technically Reproduced Sounds and Noises *in* Music

'Real sounds' bring the world of things most immediately into the music, but still convey it through the material and methods of music. The innumerable birds that 'sing' in music, presumably in all eras and regions, are not songbirds but artificial and artistic imitations of this special form of animal communication with its mating, advertising and warning calls.

1.) One exception as a readymade is Ottorino Respighi's programmatic musical work *Pini di Roma* (1924): There, in the third movement, *I pini del Gianicolo*, a 'real' nightingale appears on the concert stage, albeit not in the flesh

---

36   Wendel, "The 1922 'Symphony of Sirens' in Baku" 565.

but in a technically reproduced form: Its singing is played on a record in the concert hall.

Figure 5: Ottorino Respighi: Third movement, I pini del Gianicolo, the nightingale song from record is overlaid, from 13ᵗʰ bar before the end of the movement.

★ Nᵒ *R. 6105* del "Concert Record Gramophone: Il canto dell'usignolo.

Respighi wanted to present these real sounds as 'real' as possible. The 'authenticity' is underlined by the probable 'authentic' recording location, which is identical to the area described in the sentence: "The nightingale was recorded in the yard of the McKim Building of the American Academy in Rome situated on Janiculum Hill."[37]

Respighi's pioneering act of technically reproducing animal sounds as 'real sounds' and incorporating them into musical works has found many imitators in an expanded form, especially since the lasting structural crisis from 1971 onwards and growing environmental awareness.[38] One work that became especially popular was the musically traditional and simply arranged *Missa Gaia/Earth Mass* from 1982 by soprano saxophonist Paul Winter with PaulHall ey, JimScott, OscarCastro-Neves, and KimOler.[39] Original sounds that can be heard include "the voices of wolf, whale, eagle, harp seal, Amazonian musical wren, Russian loon."[40] In addition, however, the composers transform the animal sounds into musical material and incorporate them into it: "In *Sanctus*,

---

37   "Pines of Rome." https://en.wikipedia.org/wiki/Pines_of_Rome

38   Several examples in "Biomusic." https://en.wikipedia.org/wiki/Biomusic

39   "Missa Gaia/Earth Mass." https://en.wikipedia.org/wiki/Missa_Gaia/Earth_Mass

40   "Missa Gaia – Earth Mass." http://www.paulwinter.com/projects/missa-gaia-earth-mas s/

the whale songs describe the vastness of heaven and earth [...]. The howling of the wolf becomes a *Kyrie* melody."[41]

2.) Another type of musical use of animal-biological real sounds are "sounds made by humans in a directly biological way [...] created by the brain waves of the composer [...] by neurofeedback [...]. An Electroencephalophone [...] was first designed by Erkki Kurenniemi in the 1960s. David Rosenboom, the Brazilian composer Eduardo Reck Miranda or Alvin Lucier followed. With the help of modern digital technology, it is even possible to elicit music from a plant, a bonsai tree, as a musical instrument, thus—almost—directly transforming nature into art: "To determine the key I used the lowest note I could play and recorded the rest around it. Besides playing the leaves, I used bows of different sizes, a piano hammer and a paint brush. As far as microphones I used my Røde NT6, a customized stethoscope and tiny MEAS piezo transducers. I played all the sounds and rhythms only with the bonsai, I didn't use any synthesizer or samplers to create or modify the sounds."[42]

Diego Stocco intervenes in the process in which nature is supposed to be and creates art in such a way that he incorporates arbitrary components into the indexical and iconic relationship between plants and music. He *produces* sounds, so it is the Syrinx principle, not the Echo principle. The plant serves as a musical instrument; its sound is not re-produced.

Kurt Weill's *Tango Angèle*, 1927. Technically Reproduced *Musical* Pieces as Musical-Dramatic Material

A further stage of the described relationship is to make technically reproduced music into a component of music and musical theatre instead of the ready-made natural sounds of inanimate nature or animals. Kurt Weill achieves this with a record played within the scene. He was not the first to do so, however.

A counterpart to Respighi's nightingale reproduced on record is the prospective hit song *Tango Angèle* in Kurt Weill's one-act opera buffa (1928, libretto: Georg Kaiser) *Der Zar lässt sich photographieren (The Czar Has His Pho-*

---

41   "Missa Gaia – Weltmusik zur Weltklimakonferenz." https://www.evangelisch-beuel.de/wordpress/?p=1130

42   Self-commentary by Diego Stocco, "Diego Stocco – Music from a Bonsai." https://youtu.be/qvyHHX6hNkY

tograph Taken). This tango is also a real sound in the form of the readymade, in the theatre on stage, analogous to film.

Figure 6: Kurt Weill, *Tango Angèle*.

The situation seems simpler than it is: A piece of music from a record is played on stage.[43] This is incorporated into a complex game of illusions, however.

A group of conspirators lures the tsar into the renowned Angèle photo studio. The camera is rigged up in such a way that, instead of taking a picture of the person to be portrayed, it triggers a pistol that shoots him dead. All conspirators are 'excellent copies' of the studio staff.[44] When the conspiracy is uncovered and the police arrive, the false Angèle puts on the record—supposedly to 'undress' out of sight, but in reality to remove her disguise and escape. The aesthetic bridging of the preparation for the act of love masks the sounds of escape.

The music thus acts as the classical 'retarding moment' for the drama, which in turn justifies its long duration, in this case, the side of a shellac record. The piece within the piece is musically not very distinctive, since Weill also uses elements of the Foxtrot and other fashionable dances. However, he

---

43   This can also be considered intermediality. Cf. *inter alia* Mücke, *Musikalischer Film – Musikalisches Theater*.

44   Weill, *Der Zar lässt sich photographieren* 10. Since the subject here is not to improve the technique of assassination attempts, it should only be noted that Kaiser's protagonists proceed rather awkwardly and amateurishly according to the motto "Why make it simple if it can be complicated?"

saves "saxophone and jazz sound"[45] for the tango and, moreover, the gramophone sound itself provides a distinctive tone quality.[46]

It is dramaturgically motivated incidental music, theatrically functional, not a component of mimesis, as in the case of Respighi. The tango is not a foreign work, though, but a piece of music by Weill. Thus it is a fictitious, ostensible readymade, while in fact it is a handmade, art within art rather than reality in art or, outside of the theatrical context, not a quotation but a pseudo-quotation. With this ambiguity, he inserts himself into the play with identities by 'switching persons'[47]—which implies differences. Many in the play are not who they seem: The second, "false Adele" is not a photographer, but, like her two assistant characters "the false assistant" and "the false boy," she is part of the group of conspirators, a pseudo-ancient "male choir in the orchestra,"[48] so to speak, who rarely comments on what is to be seen and heard anyway, but doubles it. Ultimately, the tsar is not really a tsar either, and is discreetly referred to in the list of persons as "Tsar of *."[49] An actual joke results from the fact that this tango, recorded in early 1928 for UA, was Weill's first record release and became a hit, so reality is catching up and realizing that which art fiction had only insinuated.

---

45 Weill, n.d., cited by Kogelheide, *Jenseits einer Reihe 'tönender Punkte'* 128.

46 Ibid. 129; music sample 128.

47 Weill, *Der Zar lässt sich photographieren* 14. Like the preceding one-act *The Protagonist*, the *Czar* deals with "tensions between the false and the true, between deception and honesty, pretense and reality. The ultimate artistry for the protagonist is to lose himself in the role he plays; the Czar's great desire is to escape his role of functionary." Eaton, "Director's Notes for a Kurt Weill Double Bill" 10f., cited by Geulen, *Von der Zeitoper zur Broadway Opera* 167.

48 Cook, "'Der Zar lässt sich photographieren:'" 91ff. refers to parallels in neoclassical operas by Wellesz, Milhaud, Prokofiev, and Stravinsky's *Oedipus* (1927).

49 The doubling of Angèle into the proper and 'the false Angèle' anticipates the divisive doubling of the main character of *The Seven Deadly Sins of the Bourgeoisie* (April/May 1933) into Anna I and Anna II. Bertolt Brecht takes the comedy motif very seriously, of course. The division of the person expresses the reversal that human virtues have become 'market economy' sins.

Walter Ruttmann's *Weekend*, 1930. The Totality of the Soundscape as a Soundtrack Without a Film

Ruttmann's *Weekend* is an eleven-minute radio play in the spirit of 'New Objectivity.' Ruttmann, originally a painter, then a filmmaker, used the sound-on-film method here. The radiophonic work, an invisible sound film, consists of mounted sound film recordings using the Tri-Ergon process, which was the only way to cut image or sound tracks with precision before tape was available. It is a purely acoustic counterpart to Ruttmann's purely acoustic silent film *Berlin: Symphony of a Metropolis* from 1926.

The starting point there are individual film sequences, which, as in the advanced handling of real sounds, become a whole through montage. For example, in a self-commentary from 1927: "Every day the shots were developed, and very, very slowly, visible only to me, the first act began to take shape."[50] This means: "The post-production is claimed to be the actual and creative process of film."[51] Contrary to the actual facts, Ruttmann staged himself as the sole 'auteur.' As the title suggests, music, particularly as rhythm, is the common denominator, integrator and model:

> "He makes the category of the symphonic his own without further ado, all his central formal terms are equally musical terms, and he prefers to describe his montage technique with musical metaphors. Cinematic practice and technical action are presented as being permeated by music; even thinking about film is deeply immersed in music. All of this is essentially part of the romantic, music-focused artistic phase that is typical of Ruttmann. As a consequence, Edmund Meisel's accompanying music is then merely the expression, rendering audible what is already at the core of the images and the sequences of images as sound and rhythm."[52]

The advance notice of the radio play *Weekend* in early 1930 describes very precisely the components and progression of the scenes. The work-free weekend, for example, is set against the working week in a semi-documentary form:

> "Ruttmann's photographic radio play
> In the following we present the progression of the radio play outlined by

---

50   Cited by Prümm, "Die Montage als alles durchdringendes Prinzip der Stadtsinfonie" 62.

51   Ibid.

52   Ibid. 64.

Ruttmann, which acoustically reproduces the events of the weekend from the end of work on Saturday to the resumption of work on Monday.

WEEKEND

1) Jazz of work
Material:
Typewriters Telephone bell Cash register
Various machines Hammering Saws
Files Forging Dictating Commands

Progression:
a) Cheerful, almost entirely musical jazz of working sounds; rhythmically heavily arranged counterpoint
b) Simpler counterpoint: the individual sounds are more distinctly characterized in their materiality.
c) The groaning machinery of work: weariness, agony of work, exhaustion. Machine *ritardando*.

2) Closing time
Clock strikes. Other clocks strike like canons, factory sirens: far – near – near.

Liberated final cadence of the typewriter. Desks are closed. Drawers, roller shutters, scissor grids closed, bunch of keys clanging, doors slamming into the lock, keys creakingly rotated.

In between human voices: giggling girls, laughing men, shouts: 'Goodbye!' etc., echoing: hurried steps in the staircase. [...]"[53]

Frisius, in his very detailed analysis extending to the level of sonograms, emphasizes the technical advancement *and* the unusual realism of the work:

"*Weekend* is the first radically experimental composition of montaged sounds. This production anticipated tendencies that would only be taken up again decades later in French 'musique concrète' and in the West German 'New Radio Play'—for example, by Pierre Schaeffer and Ferdinand Kriwet. In Ruttmann's audio film, Schaeffer's early 'musique concrète' and Kriwet's audio texts, approaches to the content-related selection, combination and

---

53   *Film-Kurier*, Berlin (No. 41), 15 February 1930. Cited by: "Walter Ruttmann, 'Weekend.'" http://www.medienkunstnetz.de/quellentext/96/

processing of sounds are evident, as they remained largely singular until the end of the 20th century."[54]

The real sounds of the urban, industrial soundscape appear completely and acoustically vivid in an imageless soundtrack. The artfully assembled, quasi-documentary radio play without a plot is an audio image. It is a glimpse of the later independence of independent musical works in 'musique concrète.'

Historically, the soundtrack of the film even includes the imitation/*creation*, also called Foley after the name of a pioneer of 'sound-making,' *before* the mechanical-automatic real sound recording, which only became conveniently possible with the electric microphone starting in 1924.[55] Aesthetically and artistically as well, the Syrinx principle of imitation/*creation* has priority over the Echo principle of 'lifelike' reproduction.

Due to recording problems, even in the age of electrification, artificially produced sounds are used for film noises in addition to or instead of the real or 'original' sounds. These artificial real sounds often seem more real than the real sounds. Similarity by similarity, such as the imitation of the clattering of horse hooves by rattling coconut shells, for example, merges[56] into similarity by otherness, even dissimilarity. Gunfire can be represented by beans crackling against the lid in a cooking pot, for instance. So there is an analogy in the sense of biology. And what was indexical becomes iconic in this way.

---

54   See "4. Analyse erfahrungsorientierter Musik," in: Frisius, *Forum Analyse*. http://www.fri sius.de/rudolf/texte/txhorend.htm. A broad embedding of the work into various artistic and ideological currents is undertaken by Hagen, *Walter Ruttmanns Großstadt-Weekend*. http://www.whagen.de/PDFS/11010_HagenWalterRuttmannsGro_2005.pdf

55   See inter alia Stinson, "Real-time Sound Effects: The Foley Way." https://www.videomak er.com/article/7220-real-time-sound-effects-the-foley-way; Prendergast, "The Aesthetics of Film Music." http://web.archive.org/web/19970516041845/http://citd.scar.utoronto .ca/VPAB93/course/readings/prenderg.html; "Game Sound Design." http://www.filmsou nd.org/game-audio/. A practically endless list of links at "Theoretical Film Sound Texts." http://www.filmsound.org/theory/. A long alphabetic list with tips on sound production: David Filskov, "The Guide To Sounds Effects." https://www.epicsound.com/sfx/. For example, for horse hooves, in addition to the obligatory coconut halves, "by beating two potatoes in a 3-beat rhythm in a pan filled with sand, rice, and crushed crackers. Pitch adjusted to suit" or more simply "cup your hands and clap them against your thighs to the running horse rhythm." Product placement is a free extra: "Works best when you're wearing denim pants."

56   Cf. parody by *Monty Python and the Holy Grail* (1975).

Pierre Schaeffer's *Étude aux chemins de fer*, 1948. Technically Reproduced, Compositionally Reprocessed Sounds as Music

Real tones as readymades are the unstylized, preexisting material of the 'musique concrète' produced by Schaeffer and others since about 1945.[57] However, they become stylized and assembled into the raw material of the composition. In contrast, they are not used in 'electronic' or 'electro-acoustic' music by Herbert Eimert, Henri Pousseur, Karlheinz Stockhausen, and so on. However, both originally antagonistic currents soon converged. Stockhausen's *Gesang der Jünglinge (Song of the Youths)* from 1955/1956 represents the synthesis. In Pierre Henry and Pierre Schaeffer, as well, the instrumental is then supplemented by the human voice, first in the jointly produced *Symphonie pour un homme seul (Symphony for One Man Alone*, 1950).

Schaeffer preferred real sounds from the realm of transportation that are more traditional than the racing cars and airplanes or the military means of destruction in Futurism. *Chemin de fer* then appears in several of his titles. He mainly uses industrial real sounds taken from reality—'found audio footage.' These sounds are not 'exhibited' or performed in isolation, but are processed as musical material, assembled to form larger contexts and composed as a work. But the ideal was not similarity. Schaeffer's earliest concrete works used recognizable sounds, although Schaeffer advocated 'reduced listening' as a way of bypassing external associations to focus on a sound's inherent qualities. A point of contention in post-Schaefferian electroacoustic music is whether materials can be mimetic or should adhere to the modernist ideal of abstraction.

His decision was against mimesis, and his successors liked to imitate him in it. He wanted real sounds, but not mimetic relations to reality. It was important to him to remove sigmatics and semantics as far as possible: "the sound object (*objet sonore*) is sound isolated from its means of production or notation as well as the state of mind of the listener. Schaeffer's conception of the sound object is a reduction, a bracketing out of external information in order to arrive at a pure phenomenological experience. The concept of the sound object has held wide sway among post-Schaefferian electroacoustic musicians."[58]

---

57   See *inter alia* Schaeffer, *Musique concrète*.
58   Demers, *Listening Through the Noise* e.g. 174.

The sources of the sounds should also be deliberately faded out in the reception, contrary to the spontaneous listening experience, in a form of listening that is correctly called 'reduced listening:' "Schaeffer's term for listening
that ignores the source and origins of sound. Schaeffer advocated reduced
listening for his 'musique concrète,' a genre that often relied on recognizable
footage of everyday sounds such as trains. Several composers, including many
of Schaeffer's own students, have criticized or rejected reduced listening for
placing unrealistic expectations on listeners."[59]

The Winstons' *Amen, Brother*, 1969. Sampling–Technically Reproduced Pieces of Music as Musical Material

'Sampling' in this context represents a collective term, perhaps even as a basic
term for a wealth of procedures that are applied by the collage and montage
processes that has been heretofore outlined, but which first became predominant with the synthesizer and then again with a qualitative leap in many
segments of newer pop music. To name but a few between quotation and
plagiarism: Pre- and transitional forms such as covers or mashups—basically
each time a new interpretation or/and the traditional parody process in digital
form—recycling, remix, copy and paste, looping, 'plunderphonics,' 'appropriation literature,' etc. We could call all of this music 'second-handmade.'

Probably one of the most used samples is an excerpt from *Amen, Brother*
by the American soul band The Winstons, released in 1969 as the B-side of a
single and a modest commercial success. Only with its re-release in 1986 did
the piece came into the focus of the pop musicians of the time. "The four bars
of 'Amen, Brother' quickly became known as the 'Amen Break.' The producers
extracted the drum solo, slowed down its tempo, played the file endlessly over
and over again and let rappers loose on it [...]. As a result, complete micro-
genres were based on the four bars by the drummer Coleman. According to
the statistics from the website Whosampled.com, the mini drum solo appears
in more than 2,400 songs to date."[60]

---

59   Ibid.
60   Sievers, Florian. "Die hohe Kunst des Copy and Paste." https://www.fluter.de/geschicht
      e-des-samplings

The technical prerequisite for rampant sampling was the availability of inexpensive digital samplers from 1987 onwards.[61] In this way, preexisting music and not just real-world noises function as readymade and real sounds. On the one hand, Duchamp's concept of art was setting a precedent, while on the other hand, and probably more importantly, it was the development of the soundtrack in film—and in reality. The proliferation of the readymade received another huge boost in neo-liberal postmodernism since the late 1970s. Sampling,[62] Appropriation Art[63] and similar currents and genres use as material something that is already art and no longer extra-artistic reality.[64] In this respect, real sound and Readymade are an analogy above all else. For it is something that has already been artistically formed, which is now being transported into the new context as material and language.

In 'Plunderphonics,' which is more of a trademark of composer John Oswald than a term, sampling obtains a challenging element of cultural criticism, seemingly progressive in the name of freedom and democracy, but rather backward-looking because it is ultimately a violation of copyright law to be able to plunder rights-free authors without questioning the 'market economy.'

From a digital standpoint, 'analogue' then retrospectively seems 'vintage' and like the nostalgic 'retro.' Thus, the use of quotation-like methods in more recent electroacoustic music sometimes takes a peculiar turn: "Electronica often propagates metaphors linking different types of sounds with larger concepts. For instance, the sounds of synthesizers, especially vintage instruments of the 1960s and 1970s, frequently evoke science fiction and futurism."[65]

In another variant, sounds of past media, in this case the record, serve as a kind of ennobling of music by historical dignity. Yet the old is then usually similar at best, reproduction is a construction, and identity is an illusion: "Phonographic noise such as the pops and scratches of a record player's needle

---

61   Ibid.
62   Ratcliffe, "A Proposed Typology of Sampled Material within Electronic Dance Music" attempts an enlightening typology. It could be differentiated and expanded. For sampling in hip-hop, see Kautny, "Talkin all that Jazz."
63   In general, but especially in relation to currents in the 1980s in the USA, see "Appropriation." https://www.tate.org.uk/art/art-terms/a/appropriation
64   Cf. Döhl and Wöhrer, Zitieren, appropriieren, sampeln.
65   Demers, Listening Through the Noise e.g. 171.

can serve as a metaphor for the age of the underlying music, even if those noises were artificially constructed rather than innate to the material."[66]

The handmade of instrumental playing itself supports or else substitutes for and simulates digitized pedals for electric guitars in real instrumental playing: "The amps have the 'sought-after old sound' with an extremely high dynamic range. The only concession to modernity is a 'post phase-splitter master control,' which allows for a great *vintage distorted sound* even at moderate levels. The circuit reacts extremely *honestly* to everything you input and responds exceedingly well to all kinds of effect devices."[67]

It is a winding, spiral path from mechanization to electrification to digitalization, zigzagging between the mechanical, almost automatic impression of the real on the one hand and the technical re/production of the real on the other, i.e. in the interplay between the Echo and Syrinx principles, of readymade and handmade. The kicker is that, even before digitalization, the readymade principle had been generalized through sampling and collage in such a way that the difference between genuine, documentary real sounds, processed real sounds, and preexisting handmade sounds had been blurred.

Composing Goes Beyond Collaging

Real sounds, as actual noises, are not entirely aesthetically and artistically equivalent to art noises, art sounds and artificial tones, nor are preexisting readymades, which are transformed as readymade quotations that are already within the art. The handmade, the composition, regardless of whether by hand and head or with a computer, whether 'analogue' or 'digital,' is ultimately what is essential in terms of art ontology and aesthetics.

Relatively novel would be to not only declare *interdisciplinarity*, but to practice it and to understand the references of music to reality, inter alia in social, cultural, literary, theatrical, art, cinematic, image, neuro- and technical sciences, biological, anthropological, psychological, psychoanalytical, economic, sociological, media, semiotic, linguistic, epistemological, and generally aesthetic methods, to incorporate findings and develop them independently in a way that is specific to music.

---

66   Ibid.
67   Advertisement: *Kammler.* http://www.kammler-cabinets.de/

Bibliography (last accessed 16 April 2020)

Asholt, Wolfgang, and Walter Fähnders, eds. *Manifeste und Proklamationen der europäischen Avantgarde: 1909–1938*. Stuttgart, Weimar: J.B. Metzler, 1995.

Belli, Gabriella. *Sprachen des Futurismus: Literatur, Malerei, Skulptur, Musik, Theater, Fotografie*. Berlin: Jovis, 2009.

Boone, Christine E. *Mashups: History, Legality, and Aesthetics*. Doctoral dissertation. Austin: Univ. of Texas, 2011.

Butzmann, Frieder, and Jean Martin. *Filmgeräusch: Wahrnehmungsfelder eines Mediums*. Hofheim: Wolke, 2012.

Cook, Susan C. "'Der Zar lässt sich photographieren.' Weill and Comic Opera." *A New Orpheus: Essays on Kurt Weill*. Ed. Kim H. Kowalke. New Haven, London: Yale Univ. Press, 1990. 83–102.

Der Hang Zum Gesamtkunstwerk: Europäische Utopien seit 1800. Aarau: Verlag Sauerländer, 1983.

Demers, Joanna. *Listening Through the Noise: The Aesthetics of Experimental Electronic Music*. New York, Oxford: Oxford Univ. Press, 2010.

Didi-Huberman, Georges. *Ähnlichkeit und Berührung: Archäologie, Anachronismus und Modernität des Abdrucks*. Köln: Dumont, 1999 (1997).

Döhl, Frédéric, and Renate Wöhrer. *Zitieren, appropriieren, sampeln: Referenzielle Verfahren in den Gegenwartskünsten*. Bielefeld: transcript, 2014.

Eaton, John. "Director's Notes for a Kurt Weill Double Bill." *Kurt Weill Newsletter* 11, 1 (1993).

Eimert, Herbert. *Grundlagen der musikalischen Reihentechnik*. Wien: Universal, 1964.

Epstein, Josh. *Sublime Noise: Musical Culture and the Modernist Writer*. Baltimore: Johns Hopkins Univ. Press, 2014.

Frisius, Rudolf. "Musique concrète." *Die Musik in Geschichte und Gegenwart*, Vol. 6. Ed. Ludwig Finscher. Kassel: Bärenreiter, 1997. 1834–1844.

Fülöp-Müller, René. *Geist und Gesicht des Bolschewismus: Darstellung und Kritik des kulturellen Lebens in Sowjetrussland*. Reprinted as: *Fantasien und Alltag in Sowjet-Rußland: Ein Augezeugebericht von Rene Fülöp-Miller*. Ed. Eckhard Siepmann. Berlin, Hamburg: Elefantenpresse, 1978.

Geulen, Heinz. *Von der Zeitoper zur Broadway Opera: Kurt Weill und die Idee des musikalischen Theaters*. Schlingen: Argus, 1997.

Giesen, Rolf. *Lexikon der Special Effects: Von der ersten Filmtricks bis zu den Computeranimationen der Gegenwart*. Berlin: Schwarzkopf and Schwarzkopf, 2001.

Gredig, Mathias. *Tiermusik: Zur Geschichte der skeptischen Zoomusikologie*. Würzburg: Königshausen and Neumann, 2018.

Großmann, Rolf. "Xtended Sampling." *Sampling: Arbeitsberichte der Lehrkanzlei für Kommunikationstheorie* 4 (1995): 38–43.

Harenberg, Michael: *Neue Musik durch neue Technik? Musikcomputer als qualitative Herausforderung für ein neues Denken in der Musik*. Kassel: Bärenreiter, 1989.

Hegel, Georg Wilhelm Friedrich. *Ästhetik*. 2 vols. Berlin, Weimar: Aufbauverlag, 1965 (1842).

Heister, Hanns-Werner. "Musik/Geräusch: Soundtrack im Sprechtheater und anderswo." *Zwischen Aufklärung [und] Kulturindustrie: Festschrift für Georg Knepler zum 85. Geburtstag*. Vol. 2. Eds. Hanns-Werner Heister et al. Hamburg: Bockel 1993. 271–286.

Heister, Hanns-Werner. "Systematische Rückgriffe aufs Elementare (Entgrenzungen und Verselbständigungen I: Das Optische als Ausgangspunkt /Entgrenzungen und Verselbständigungen II: Das Akustische als Ausgangspunkt.)" *Geschichte der Musik im 20. Jahrhundert: 1945–1975* (Handbuch der Musik im 20. Jahrhundert Band 3). Eds. Hanns-Werner Heister et al. Laaber: Laaber, 2005. 199–212.

Heister, Hanns-Werner. *Hintergrund Klangkunst. Ein Beitrag zur akustischen Ökologie*. Mainz: Schott, 2010.

Heister, Hanns-Werner. "Mimetische Handlung und menschliche Natur: Überlegungen zur historisch-logisch ersten Ausprägung von Sprache." *'Der Mensch, das ist die Welt des Menschen…' – Eine Diskussion über menschliche Natur*. Eds. Hanns-Werner Heister and Lars Lambrecht. Berlin: Frank and Timme, 2013. 9–28.

Heister, Hanns-Werner. "Hände und Stimme: Zum Verhältnis von instrumentaler und vokaler Musik." *International Review of the Aesthetics and Sociology of Music* 50, 1–2 (2019): 87–104.

Kautny, Oliver. "Talkin all that Jazz: Ein Plädoyer für die Analyse des HipHop-Sampling." *Sampling in Hip-Hop, Samples* 9 (2010).

Kogelheide, Ralph. *Jenseits einer Reihe 'tönender Punkte:' Kompositorische Auseinandersetzung mit Schallaufzeichnung, 1900–1930*. Doctoral dissertation. Hamburg: Univ. of Hamburg, 2017.

Kutschke, Beate. "Geräuschkonzepte: Das Bedeutungsfeld des Geräuschs im Vorfeld des italienischen Futurismus." *Archiv für Musikwissenschaft* 63, 3 (2006): 241–255.

Loers, Veit, et al., eds. *Okkultismus und Avantgarde: Von Munch bis Mondrian: 1900–1915*. Frankfurt: Tertium, 1995.

Maur, Karin, et al., eds. *Vom Klang der Bilder: Die Musik in der Kunst des 20. Jahrhunderts*. München: Prestel, 1985.

Mücke, Panja. *Musikalischer Film – Musikalisches Theater: Medienwechsel und szenische Collage bei Kurt Weill*. Münster: Waxmann, 2011.

Prümm, Karl. "Die Montage als alles durchdringendes Prinzip der Stadtsinfonie: Anmerkungen zu Walter Ruttmanns Berlin: Die Sinfonie der Grossstadt und die Folgen." montage AV: Zeitschrift für Theorie und Geschichte audiovisueller Kommunikation 20, 1 (2011): 61–71. DOI: 10.25969/mediare p/366

Ratcliffe, Robert. "A Proposed Typology of Sampled Material within Electronic Dance Music." Dancecult: Journal of Electronic Dance Music Culture 6, 1 (2014): 97–122.

Rietveld, Hillegonda. "Im Strom des Techno: 'Slow-Mix.' GDJ-Stile in der Dance Music der 90er-Jahre." *Rock- und Popmusik* (Handbuch der Musik im 20. Jahrhundert, Vol. 8). Eds. Peter Wicke et al. Laaber: Laaber, 2001. 267–300.

Rimsky-Korsakow, Nikolai. *Le Coq d'or*. Moscow, Leipzig: P. Jurgenson, 1907. http://ks.imslp.net/files/imglnks/usimg/4/49/IMSLP586095-PMLP4 5601-Coq_d_Or_Score.pdf

Russolo, Luigi. *L' arte dei rumori*. Milan: Edizioni Futuriste di Poesia, 1916.

Saxer, Marion, ed. *Spiel (mit) der Maschine: Musikalische Medienpraxis in der Frühzeit von Phonographie, Selbstspielklavier, Film und Radio*. Bielefeld: transcript, 2016.

Schaeffer, Pierre, Michel Chion and Josef Häusler. *Musique concrète: Von den Pariser Anfängen um 1948 bis zur elektroakustischen Musik heute*. Stuttgart: Ernst Klett, 1974 (1967).

Smirnov, Andrey, and Matt Price. *Sound in Z: Experiments in Sound and Electronic Music in Early 20th Century Russia*. London: Koenig, 2013.

Springer, Peter. *Das verkehrte Bild: Inversion als bildnerische Strategie*. Delmenhorst: Aschenbeck and Holstein, 2004.

Stern, Dietrich. *Musik und Film: Aneignung der Wirklichkeit: Filmkomposition zu Beginn der Tonfilmzeit*. Doctoral dissertation. Berlin: Technical Univ. Berlin, 1981.

Sterne, Jonathan, ed. *The Sound Studies Reader*. Abington, New York: Routledge, 2012.

Sterneck, Wolfgang. *Der Kampf um die Träume: Musik und Gesellschaft*. Hanau: Komista, 1998.

Strauss, Richard. *Alpine Symphony.* http://ks.imslp.info/files/imglnks/usimg/6/6a/IMSLP51664-PMLP12189-StraussR-Op64.TimpPerc.pdf

Supper, Martin. *Elektroakustische Musik und Computermusik: Geschichte – Ästhetik – Methoden – Systeme.* Hofheim: Wolke, 1997.

Szabó-Knotik, Cornelia. *Amadeus: Milos Formans Film als musikhistorisches Phänomen.* Graz: Akademische Druck- u. Verlagsanstalt, 1999.

Tomkins, Calvin. *Marcel Duchamp: Eine Biographie.* München, Wien: Hanser, 1999 (1996).

Toop, David. *Ocean of Sound: Klang, Geräusch, Stille.* St. Andrä-Wördern: Hannibal, 1997.

Ungeheuer, Elena, Martha Brech and Herbert Brün, eds. *Elektroakustische Musik* (Handbuch der Musik im 20. Jahrhundert, Vol. 5). Laaber: Laaber, 2002.

Ungeheuer, Elena, and Martin Supper. "Elektroakustische Musik." *Die Musik in Geschichte und Gegenwart*, Vol. 2. Ed. Ludwig Finscher. Kassel: Bärenreiter, 1995. 1717-1765.

Wagner, Manfred, Hans Heinz Fabris and Ingo Moerth. *über alle? gegen alle? für alle? Kultur: Animation am Beispiel der Ars Electronica des Linzer Brucknerfestes.* Linz: Trauner, 1982.

Weill, Kurt. *Der Zar lässt sich photographieren: Opera buffa in einem Akt von Georg Kaiser.* Wien: Universal, 1927.

Wendel, Delia Duong Ba. "The 1922 'Symphony of Sirens' in Baku, Azerbaijan." *Journal of Urban Design* 17, 4 (2012): 549–572. DOI: 10.1080/13574809.2012.706366

Wescher, Hertha. *Die Geschichte der Collage: Vom Kubismus bis zur Gegenwart.* Köln: DuMont, 1987 (1968).

Online Sources (last accessed 16 April 2020)

"Appropriation." *Tate.* https://www.tate.org.uk/art/art-terms/a/appropriation

"Biomusic." *Wikipedia.* https://en.wikipedia.org/wiki/Biomusic

"Diego Stocco – Music from a Bonsai." *YouTube.* https://youtu.be/qvyHHX6h NkY

Filskov, David. "The Guide To Sounds Effects." *epicsound.* https://www.epicsound.com/sfx/

Frisius, Rudolf. *Forum Analyse: Medienspezifische Analyse – Analyse medienspezifischer Musik*. http://www.frisius.de/rudolf/texte/txhorend.htm

"Game Sound Design." *FilmSound.org*. http://www.filmsound.org/game-audi o/

Hagen, Wolfgang: "Walter Ruttmanns Großstadt-Weekend: Zur Herkunft der Hörcollage aus der ungegenständlichen Malerei." *Hörstürze. Akustik und Gewalt im 20. Jahrhundert*. Conference of the Graduate College, Codierung von Gewalt im medialen Wandel [Codification of Violence in Medial Transformation] at Humboldt University Berlin. 1 November 2005. http:// www.whagen.de/PDFS/11010_HagenWalterRuttmannsGro_2005.pdf

Kammler. https://www.kammler-cabinets.de/

Lexikon der Filmbegriffe. Universität Kiel. http://filmlexikon.uni-kiel.de/

"Luigi Russolo: 'Intonarumori.'" *Medien Kunst Netz – Media Art Net*. http://www. medienkunstnetz.de/werke/intonarumori/bilder/2/

"Missa Gaia/Earth Mass." *Wikipedia*. https://en.wikipedia.org/wiki/Missa_Ga ia/Earth_Mass

"Missa Gaia – Earth Mass." *Paul Winter. Celebrating the Cultures & Creatures of the Whole Earth*. http://www.paulwinter.com/

"Missa Gaia – Weltmusik zur Weltklimakonferenz." *Evangelische Kirchengemeinde Beuel*. https://www.evangelisch-beuel.de/wordpress/?p=1130

Oswald, John. "Plunderphonics, or Audio Piracy as a Compositional Prerogative." *plunderphonics.com*. http://www.plunderphonics.com/xhtml/xplund er.html

"Pines of Rome." *Wikipedia*. https://en.wikipedia.org/wiki/Pines_of_Rome

Prendergast, Roy A. "The Aesthetics of Film Music." *archive.org*. https://web. archive.org/web/19970516041845/http://citd.scar.utoronto.ca/VPAB93/ course/readings/prenderg.html

"7 Filme, die Tabus brachen." *wieistderfilm?de*. https://wieistderfilm.de/7-film e-die-tabus-brachen/

Sievers, Florian. "Die hohe Kunst des Copy and Paste: Dr. Dre macht's, Kanye West macht's und Jay Z widmet ihm ein ganzes Album: Sampling. Eine kurze Geschichte des musikalischen Recyclings." *fluter*. https://www.flute r.de/geschichte-des-samplings

Sterneck, Wolfgang. "Der Rhythmus der Maschinen: die Musik des Futurismus." *Sterneck.net*. http://www.sterneck.net/stern/futurismus/

Stinson, Jim. "Real-time Sound Effects: The Foley Way." *Videomaker*. https:// www.videomaker.com/article/7220-real-time-sound-effects-the-foleyway

"Theoretical Film Sound Texts." *FilmSound.org*. http://www.filmsound.org/theory/

Wallis, Victor. "Elektrifizierung." *Berliner Institut für kritische Theorie: InkriTpedia*. http://www.inkrit.de/e_inkritpedia/e_maincode/doku.php?id=e:elektrifizierung

"Walter Ruttmann, 'Weekend.'" *Medien Kunst Netz – Media Art Net*. http://www.medienkunstnetz.de/quellentext/96/

"Windmaschine (Film)." *Wikipedia*. https://de.wikipedia.org/wiki/Windmaschine_(Film)

Sonic Icons in *A Song Is Born* (1948): A Model for an Audio History of Film

Winfried Pauleit (University of Bremen)

The production of film sound forms part of the aesthetics of film. Voice, music, and sound in film production are subject to historical modes and conventions that are in turn in constant interaction with history. These processes do not only produce sound with differing acoustic qualities, but are also marked by periods of large-scale upheaval, such as the introduction of synchronized sound, stereo sound, and sound design. Since the introduction of sync sound, the recording of voice, music, and sound via microphone established a number of procedures for intentionally shaping the sound of film—procedures which continue to be used in today's digital sound design. Historical markers and sound events also found their way into these recordings, including, for example, the voices of actors or known historical personalities, pieces of music, as well as the inevitable artifacts of the recording process itself, which one might refer to as 'the noise of the real;' sounds such as hiss or feedback, i.e., the aspects of the sound production process that emerge at random or unintentionally as a result of the technology used during the recording.[1] At the same time, these noises enable inferences to be made about the time and circumstances of a given film's production as well as about the history of technology, which is both a part of the production history of the film in question as well as a part of history itself. In modern film productions, both of these areas fall under the category of sound design. The reciprocal relationship between media history and history can be observed and investigated by examining the treatment of film sound.

Soundtracks for film are produced by means of the abovementioned procedures along with subsequent processing. The fact that one talks of sound-*tracks* here likely has to do with the original placement of sound on the ana-

---

1   Kittler, *Gramophone, Film, Typewriter* 14.

logue film strip used for sound film. In order to ensure that the sound was played in sync, an additional track was set up next to the image track which, as well as creating a fixed connection between sound and image on the film strip, also set up a unified gauge—akin to the use of standardized gauges in train tracks—i.e., a fixed distance between the sound and image tracks. Yet the addition of a soundtrack to the film strip during the birth of sound film also changed the temporality of the entire production practice for sound. Until the end of the 1920s, film sound was created by live performances put on during the film screening itself, which made use of a film narrator, sound effects, and musical accompaniment. With the introduction of synchronized sound, this sort of performative sound production became separated from the actual film screening. Since then, the sound for a film (much like the images) is produced in advance at a different location and then scanned from the film strip during screening or, as is the case today, read from digital data packets as the trace of a track left behind by a production process inscribed onto it in the past. The concept of the soundtrack thus expresses this aspect of the temporality of sound (i.e., inscription and scanning).

When microphones, loudspeakers, and sound recording equipment appear in films, their appearance creates a self-reflexive potential which links the reception of the film back to the cultural actions carried out during its production process. This serves to characterize film sound as the product of sounds from the real world, which are recorded and subsequently processed. These forms of self-reflexivity bear historical witness to and provide historical models for the setups and techniques used in film sound production and enable them to be experienced via the film itself. They also verify these cultural actions, that is, the history of the performative process of working with the techniques and various apparatuses used for creating sound. This sort of cinematic self-reflexivity represents the starting point for the following investigation. These analyses are concerned with, on the one hand, the idea that listening is an integral component of film perception. On the other, they emphasize that what is heard can be decoded and reflected upon in view of its historical production, that is, this investigation examines film sound both in terms of the complex aesthetic of film as well as in terms of how it taps into history. This dual perspective on film sound enables an audio history of film to become conceivable. It places a focus on the relationship between aesthetics and history, and while the examples from film and the discourses surrounding them may not allow it to be 'heard' directly, it can certainly be studied, tapped into, and described. In this way, the approach presented here is fundamentally different from the sort of proposals that assume history exists directly and can be accessed just as directly in sound recordings, such as, for example, the approach taken by Gerhard Paul and Ralph Schock in their book *Sound des Jahrhunderts*.[2]

Rick Altman explicitly points out that film sound cannot simply be reduced to sound events from the outside world.[3] Over the course of that discussion, he mounts a fundamental critique of the idea of the indexical film sound. According to Altman, this debate has been marked by the idea that the conception of indexicality employed in photography can be transposed onto the procedures used in film sound without the need for any further reflection. The basic assumption here—which is itself hardly uncontroversial—is that photography is generally accepted as the historical trace of past occurrences and has already become a part of the study of history in the form of visual history.[4] In photography discourse, the idea of the historical trace of an event has been expressed most pointedly by Roland Barthes's dictum "this has been."[5] Without wishing to discuss the validity of such postulations here, it should be noted that the presence of microphones, sound recording equipment, etc. represents an obvious analogy to the presence of photographic equipment in film—both shaping an experience of cinematic self-reflexivity. Microphones in particular demonstrate, for example, that a similar quality of inscription or indexicality is attached to sound recording as to the capture of photographic images—if nothing else due to the fact that film sound is produced in advance (and at a different location).

In his critique *Four and a Half Film Fallacies*, Altman emphasizes the broad reach of the conclusions based on this analogy in the section entitled *Half a Fallacy*.[6] Altman's fundamental criticism here is aimed at the sort of conceptions of indexicality that are based on a naïve representational realism, conceptions which are then subsequently transposed onto sound. He also brings the theme of digitization into play, which makes actual image and sound recordings increasingly unnecessary, which for him means that the era of indexical inscription via the use of cameras or microphones increasingly belongs to history and thus loses its validity. Yet Altman's criticism is still only presented as

2   Paul and Schock, *Sound des Jahrhunderts*.
3   Altman, "Four and a Half Film Fallacies" 35–45.
4   Paul, "Von der Historischen Bildkunde" 7–36.
5   Barthes, *Camera Lucida* 96.
6   Altman, "Four and a Half Film Fallacies" 42–45.

a 'half fallacy' because it doesn't apply to more complex conceptions of index-icality, which assume that historical events don't simply remain accessible in image and sound recordings like events of the present but can only actually be tapped into in the sense of a difference—as past events that are not directly accessible. Roland Barthes speaks of a 'madness' here in relation to photography in the sense of a dual temporal codification.[7] When this idea is applied to sound, the resulting implication is that film sound can indeed reveal historical traces under certain circumstances. At such moments, what is heard during film perception is encoded in a dual fashion and thus at once apprehended as a sound in the present and as an (inaccessible) trace. Altman's hypothesis that the use of cameras and microphones loses its relevance in the process of digitization thus also remains a half fallacy; to this day digital sound design hasn't yet bid a full farewell to working with sound recordings. In order to create specific sound effects, sound recordings of the physical world (voices, screams, animal cries, or other sounds) are still made and/or processed further.[8]

Film sound is not regarded in isolation here but rather as one element of the texture of a film, which is what produces the actual experience of viewing. To use a term from the work of Michel Chion, this can be referred to as 'audio-logo-visual.'[9] Chion's term describes "all the cases that include written and/or spoken language." Chion then goes on to describe the five relations between the said and the shown.[10] In this process, Chion's considerations emphasize the simultaneously unified and hybrid nature of film perception and thus pave the way for the concept of 'sonic icons.'

Brian Currid introduces this concept to describe characteristic sound phenomena that function as acoustic markers for political history or serve to represent it.[11] Currid's term essentially adapts an art history approach that draws on political iconography for subsequent use in musicology and cultural history. My focus in the following is to apply the concept of 'sonic icons' to film and film studies. The emphasis here is less on the iconic film quotes that have been taken out of the context of their respective films via repetition and thus left their mark in collective memory as independent aesthetic sound figures,

7   Barthes, *Camera Lucida* 113–16.
8   Flückiger, "Sound Effects" 228–36.
9   Chion, *Film, A Sound Art* 468.
10   Ibid. 473, 489.
11   Currid, *A National Acoustics* 102.

but rather on self-reflexive moments in specific films where the sound comes to the fore and reveals specific historical references.

This perspective also expands on Chion's theoretical concept of film, moving beyond his classifications in order to refer to specific and unique moments in films. Sonic icons can thus be described as unique aesthetic moments. They are aesthetic figures in films and cannot as such be reduced to their sound alone, functioning instead as a hybrid category full of tension, as part of a 'soundimagetext.'[12] They reveal their relationship to history by conjuring up the past or by allowing the recollection of something, becoming themselves a site for the potential transformation of history in the process.[13] The term refers neither to the restaging of historical sounds nor to the assertion that authentic historical sounds can be made accessible or carried into the present. The defining quality of a sonic icon lies instead in the reference to something from the past, in a trace that enables something absent to be identified.

The investigation of sonic icons is also linked to a particular understanding of modern film, for here too it is possible to identify the autonomy of sound, image, and text as unfolding within a form of tense aesthetic play where sound may be heard out of sync with or independently of the image.[14] The way that modern film makes this aesthetic play visible and audible or even treats it discursively (in certain cases) emphasizes the importance of sound as a part of film aesthetics. The study of sonic icons is thus heavily indebted to an aesthetics of modern film. Sonic icons are therefore grasped as aesthetic figurations first and foremost, albeit ones which are marked or pervaded by historical inscriptions. The investigation of sonic icons thus aims to develop this connection between aesthetic production and historical inscription in order

---

12   Mitchell grasps the 'imagetext' less as a concept for classifying hybrid aesthetic forms and more as a theoretical figure (analogous to Derrida's 'différance'), as a place of dialectic tension and transformation which connects aesthetics with history. For Mitchell's concept of 'imagetext,' see Mitchell, *Picture Theory* 83–107, for a discussion of this concept and how it can be extended to the idea of 'soundimagetext,' see Nessel and Pauleit, "Constructions of the Digital Film" 219–34.

13   In her book about Alain Resnais's *Nuit et Brouillard*, Sylvie Lindeperg refers to Alain Fleischer in describing a similar aesthetic procedure, calling it as an "art of deposition" and explaining it as follows: "because film is a place of absence, of fissure, of distance, it doesn't appear in place of the event, it receives it." Lindeperg, *Nacht und Nebel* 10. (Translation by W.P.)

14   This reference to modern film can, for example, be found in different manifestations in the following: Deleuze, *Cinema 2*; Gregor and Patalas, *Geschichte des modernen Films*; Metz, *Language and Cinema*.

to lay the foundations for an audio history of film—an approach that differs from merely registering and describing iconic film sounds.

From Nightclub to Research Library: A Utopian Encounter with Louis Armstrong

Howard Hawks' *A Song Is Born* (1948) depicts the production of a phonographic music encyclopedia. The film is about an academic project with the goal of creating a music encyclopedia, which has been worked on over a period of nine years by seven professors. The undertaking is being funded by a foundation—it is what would be referred to today as an 'external project'—and headed by Professor Hobart Frisbee (Danny Kaye). What is special about the project is that a considerable part of the encyclopedia is being compiled in the form of phonographic recordings, which the academics—who are also musicians—record themselves. The musical comedy begins—similar to *Bringing Up Baby* (1938)—when the real world intrudes on the isolated academic world in the form of nightclub singer Honey Swanson (Virginia Mayo).

The comedy doesn't just give an account of an attempt to create a revised version of music history that incorporates the popular musical styles of the time—in particular Afro-American gospel, blues, and jazz—but also depicts the innovative practice of creating an encyclopedia by means of the phonograph and music recordings. At times, Hawks' comedy appears like a making-of for this phonographic undertaking. It presents sonic icons in the making, as it were, and not only because Hawks places musical legends such as Louis Armstrong, Benny Goodman, Lionel Hampton, and many others in front of the microphone and the camera, but rather because it serves as an example of how a phonography of music history (and thus ultimately an audio history of film) can take concrete form.

The musical can be seen as the preferred subject for studies on early sound film, as it is one of the most significant film genres to become established with the introduction of sound. Unlike the western but like the comedy, it is not necessarily regarded as a genre which seeks to grapple with history and is frequently instead relegated to the realm of light entertainment, with a tendency to suppress any references to reality as such. In the following, my initial focus is on investigating several aspects of the historicization of the musical's production contexts in order to then discuss it as more of a media-aesthetic hybrid formation generated by media industries than as a film genre. Film exhibits very clear references to modern aesthetics in the sense of cinematic self-reflexivity while also revealing connections to history. The specific focus here is on the appearance of Louis Armstrong's singing voice, which features prominently in one of the musical numbers, as well as on the depiction of scat singing that follows it—which basically functions as a tribute to Armstrong. Both of these events receive additional emphasis because they are depicted as specific sound recordings created via phonograph within the film itself.

The film studios' investment in new sound technologies and their attempts to appropriate the record industry (and the licensing rights linked to it) played a significant role in the ascendancy of the musical in Hollywood. David Bordwell and Kristin Thompson sketch out the different production strategies of the various studios in this context.[15] While the prestigious MGM studio continued to throw its weight behind stars and production design, Warner Bros. invested in the development of the Vitaphone sound system at an early stage and established itself as one of the big Hollywood players with the success of *The Jazz Singer*. In this case, the initial production idea was to bring vaudeville plays and song numbers to the big screen as revue films, with the studio becoming specialized in the production of gangster films and musicals as a result. By contrast, the RKO studio developed the musical into more of a narrative genre over the course of the 1930s after having bought up the declining vaudeville theatres and converted them into cinemas. In his study *The Sound of Commerce: Marketing Popular Film Music* Jeff Smith shows how Hollywood was concerned with building up its own business models, independent of the music industry, at a very early stage. Motivated by the legal situation governing the use of music in film, Warner began buying up record companies in the 1930s to be able to record the music for their films themselves and market it as the rights holder. MGM followed this trend from the mid-1940s onwards.[16]

Thomas Elsaesser and Malte Hagener emphasize both the popularity of the musical with audiences as well as the interest it generated among the theorists of the time. They also point out that the genre already exhibited numerous examples of self-reflexivity at the beginning of the 1930s which reflect the interplay of image and sound.[17] This shows that this genre already contains the qualities of aesthetic play normally attributed to modern cinema.

---

15   Bordwell and Thompson, *Film Art* 472.
16   Smith, *The Sound of Commerce* 28.
17   Elsaesser and Hagener, *Film Theory* 129–48.

Kay Kirchmann also highlights this quality in his investigation of Hawks's comedies by emphasizing the autonomy of the speech acts in this genre (in reference to Gilles Deleuze) as a form of autonomous, aesthetic play on the auditory level.[18] The sort of modern and self-reflexive moments that appear in this genre were, however, also produced as part of an interaction with other media. The rapid pace of the speech acts in the screwball comedy and the design of the song numbers in the musical were also designed to compete with radio, a circumstance to which the numerous references to contemporary radio shows in these films allude.[19]

Rick Altman goes one step further and fundamentally questions the entire historical identity of film and cinema during the silent film era against the backdrop of the intertwining of the media industries. With regard to sound, he already confirms the multiple identities of silent-era cinema, which he describes as a series of historically alternating forms: "Cinema as Photography [...] Cinema as Illustrated Music [...] Cinema as Vaudeville [...] Cinema as Opera [...] Cinema as Radio [...] Cinema as Phonography [...] Cinema as Telephony."[20] I regard this repeated focus on the qualities and contexts of the film musical of the time as evidence for the idea that these film productions should not be understood first and foremost as a nascent film genre, but rather as media aesthetic hybrid formations against the backdrop of their complex production, economic, and legal history, formations that are as indebted to stage, radio, records, and other entertainment industries as they are to cinema.

In the following, I take a closer look at Howard Hawks's *A Song Is Born* as an example of such a media aesthetic hybrid formation. The film's composite form is particularly evident in how it makes use of its stars. The film's main draw, actor and singer Danny Kaye, doesn't actually sing in this musical—apart from the exaggerated caricature of a non-Western love song at the beginning of the film.[21] By contrast, large portions of the film are dedicated to musicians like Benny Goodman, Lionel Hampton, and Louis Armstrong, with singing ultimately left to the latter as well. The film's stridently composite nature, which borders on inner turmoil, might be the reason why it has only received cursory attention from film critics and historians, particularly in comparison to other films by the same director, and is usually discredited

---

18   Kirchmann, "Der Körper" 255–84.
19   Hagen, *Das Radio*.
20   Altman, "Four and a Half Film Fallacies" 114–21.
21   Exactly which countries are being referenced here remains unclear, Polynesia, Samoa and the West Indies are all mentioned.

as an artistic work. It is referred to, for example, by Peter John Dyer, as super-
ficial, inflated, uninventive, and not made with enough care; by Robin Wood
as an obviously weaker remake of Hawks's previous *Ball of Fire* (1941).[22] Gerald
Mast is one of the few to defend the film's qualities albeit with a few caveats:

> "Despite the rancid Mayo (and Kaye) of *A Song Is Born*, the film contains sev-
> eral spectacular musical sequences (a familiar Hawks strength) with Benny
> Goodman, Lionel Hampton, Louis Armstrong, Tommy Dorsey, Charlie Bar-
> net, Mel Powell, and the Golden Gate Quartet. Hawks delights in document-
> ing the way that musicians make music—in the same way he documents
> the ways that people fly planes, catch tuna, drive cattle, chase game. No film
> with all those musicians can be all bad."[23]

Mast attempts to explore the specific qualities of the film here, which are
linked to the musical sequences staged by Hawks and the specific performances of the musicians—albeit without grasping the stand-out moments
as sonic icons. Mast's biography of Hawks also emphasizes the unusual position that the director was in; he tried to secure the greatest degree of independence possible from producers and usually produced his films himself as
well. For this reason, *A Song Is Born's* composite nature may well have stemmed
from the conflict of interest between Hawks the director and Sam Goldwyn
the producer, a conflict that was publicized in interviews with Hawks, which
in turn only increased the film's stigmatization as a failed project.[24] In his
biography of Hawks, Todd MacCarthy also gives an account of the various
conflicts during the shooting of the film and emphasizes that Hawks was primarily interested in the musicians and not in the two actual stars Danny Kaye
and Virginia Mayo, who had been allocated to him by Goldwyn. At the same
time, it is also worth mentioning that the film was regarded as a success with
audiences and a box office hit when it was released in theaters, topping the
list of most-seen films for a whole week and staying within the top twelve for
over two months.[25]

Yet *A Song Is Born* occupies a different position from the perspective of jazz
music and its respective discourses. Krin Gabbard sketches out how the view
of jazz music changed radically in the specialist press from the middle of the

---

22   Dyer, "Sling the Lamps Low" 78–93, 90; Wood, *Howard Hawks* 105.
23   Mast, *Howard Hawks* 353.
24   Blumenberg, *Die Kamera in Augenhöhe* 42.
25   MacCarthy, *Howard Hawks* 433–44.

1940s onwards;[26] jazz came to be considered an art form. For a short period in the late 1940s, Hollywood reacted to this trend by accepting the legitimacy of this musical style and ascribing to it a specific aesthetic and history in two films in particular: *New Orleans* (1947) and *A Song Is Born* (1948). As Gabbard however emphasizes, the music historiography in question is a revisionist one in which the history of the slave trade and racial segregation doesn't appear, and jazz greats such as Louis Armstrong are actually being exploited by the film industry as a means of authenticating a sanitized version of history, and the origins of the blues are at most reduced to a sigh.[27]

A Song Is Born can almost be seen as providing a blueprint for how an audio history of film can be created—not least due to its composite nature and work with sonic icons and in spite of its story, which is not entirely satisfactorily narrated. This leads to at least one chapter in the history of music being revised via the incorporation of contemporary popular music styles such as jazz, bebop, and boogie-woogie. In this part of the film's plot, the two stars then play more of a subordinate role among the 'genuine' musicians invited to the research facility.[28]

The film also finds ways of depicting this innovative practice of composing an encyclopedia by way of audio recordings. This begins with the mise-en-scène. The research project library (just like the neighboring seminar room) is the central plot location and is equipped with a state-of-the-art phonograph, which stands in clear contrast to the room's otherwise venerable, bibliophilic décor. As a technical device (and central figure), the phonograph stands in the middle of the room and also forms the focal point of numerous visual compositions. The color scheme (in Technicolor) also serves to accentuate the black, metallic tones of the phonograph and marks it as an element of media self-reflexivity. The phonograph also vies for attention in the frame with the leading actress (Mayo), who wears a red coat when she appears in the library for the first time. This configuration already reveals an initial difference to Hawks' previous *Ball of Fire*, which tells the story of a similar encyclopedia project (in black and white). There too, the world of academia is contrasted with the

26   Gabbard, *Jammin' at the Margins* 222.
27   Ibid. 117–20.
28   Most of the jazz musicians appear as themselves under their own names. It is only Benny Goodman who plays the role of Professor Magenbruch, an expert in classical clarinet, who has allegedly never heard of jazz musician Goodman, but quickly develops a passion for jazz when playing with the jazz greats.

language of contemporary slang and similarly shaken up the unexpected appearance of a nightclub singer (Barbara Stanwyck) in the academic setting. In *A Song Is Born*, the figure of the phonograph appears as an additional foreign body alongside the female star, which binds together the desires of the (white) male academics. It shifts and directs their interest onto the ecstasy of jazz music and, by extension, Afro-American music, which with the help of the phonograph can be captured differently than by means of traditional notation—which the professors still repeatedly attempt to use in a futile attempt to capture the melodies and chords.

The presentation and use of the phonograph as a recording device receives explicit emphasis in two scenes. In the first of these (in the seminar room), a history of popular music is delineated on the blackboard with the help of numerous guests and star musicians. Afterwards, the findings are expressed in both words and music and recorded with the phonograph. The recording for the encyclopedia begins like a documentary radio feature on music history headed by Prof. Frisbee—who is also operating the phonograph—and compiled using various illustrative musical examples. The undertaking then quickly becomes an audio essay structured by music, with the nightclub singer taking over from the professor and continuing the historical account as a song. It's at this point that the performance finally becomes a musical number. Yet the lead is passed on one last time, to the jazz musicians themselves. Now the leading voice is that of Louis Armstrong, augmented by his physical performance and his trumpet playing—both of which stand out not just from the film's point of view, but also from musical conventions. In my view, what is relevant here is less that Louis Armstrong is narrating a specific history of jazz, accompanied by his colleagues, and more that the vocal number is revealed to be a model for another historical connection, which is incorporated into the academic, phonographic undertaking that makes up the film's plot. Armstrong's vocal performance is central here, creating a prominent moment hard to put one's finger on and which is seemingly pervaded by Hollywood's ambivalence towards the history of jazz. The scene presents a sonic icon in the making, as it were, as it is also encoded as a specific sound recording on the phonograph. The sonic icon created at this moment is thus particularly complex; having already been accentuated as the material for a phonograph recording and a musical number within a musical, it finally comes to the fore as a sonic icon once again as a specific sound event generated by Armstrong's voice.

It is thus only at a surface level that this scene is about the specific narration of a history of music led by an African-American musical icon, which—as Gabbard rightly comments—is 'revisionist' and thus appeared sanitized.[29] At the same time, Gabbard comments that Armstrong was portrayed as a serious jazz musician in *A Song Is Born* in a manner previously unseen, a fact that can't simply be attributed to the film's documentary qualities, which are emphasized by Gerald Mast. Here too the sonic icon emerges from the interplay of differences between sound, image, and text. As such, Benny Goodman appears with a book by music critic Winthrop Sargeant entitled *Jazz: Hot and Hybrid* before the scene described above, which he—in the role of Professor Magenbruch, who knows nothing about jazz—read in order to learn about the musical genre.

What is so special about this scene, however, is that this prominent moment with all its accompanying ambivalence is phonographically recorded for inclusion in a music encyclopedia within the fiction of the film—and has indeed been captured in sound and image for this film and thus preserved in film history. The aesthetic production of this song number is tied to history in the process. As one element of a media aesthetic hybrid, the titular song *A Song Is Born* refers to how the film and recording industries are interconnected and displays this, in model fashion, as the context for a version of history that incorporates the Afro-American experience, regardless of how distorted. The academic seminar and the music recording studio become superimposed on one another in the film as two locations of historical production.

In the second scene with the phonograph (in the library), the other group of professors—all specialists in classical music—conduct a second recording a short time later. It is led by the nightclub singer, with support from vaudeville duo Buck and Bubbles. The duo appears here under their own name, although their unlikely appearance is explained by their being window cleaners who just so happen to be excellent musicians and jazz connoisseurs. They are introduced by the professors as good friends who had already conveyed the different styles of jazz to them. The goal of the exercise is to capture a jam session as it's being performed. Unlike the first recording session, which takes the form of an audio essay whose ultimate aim is to create a well-ordered (revisionist) historical narrative according to a sanitized 'it starts here and ends there'

---

29   Gabbard, *Jammin' at the Margins* 117–22. Gabbard also claims that Louis Armstrong's presence seems to have been bought by the film industry as a commodity in order to pass on the necessary authentication to a new generation of white swing musicians.

trajectory, the second recording frustrates this setup via the introduction of narrative nonsense. This is initiated in particular by the fact that the song lyrics are being read from random newspaper snippets. This improvisational procedure, which is known as scat singing, deconstructs the meaning of language and transforms the words and syllables being sung into autonomous, poetic sounds. This performance once again pays tribute to Louis Armstrong as one of the early representatives of this art form (even if he himself is not actually present in this scene). It also depicts the jam session as playing with aesthetic difference, as a utopian space of encounter where racial, class, and gender boundaries can be transcended—and which is transported here from the nightclub (where such borders can traditionally be crossed) to a research library.

This second phonography scene contains another unique feature: although it is branded as excessive and "a prairie fire of orgiastic events" (by housekeeper Miss Bragg) before being immediately reprimanded and ended by Prof. Frisbee (as a responsible historian), it had already been inscribed as a utopian trace in the phonograph recording, and no less one with an excessive physical lust for aesthetic play. Within this context, the phonograph is thus not just a recording device that preserves the traces of this excess and allows it to be accessed later on[30] but also changes what happens from the very beginning by virtue of recording it. This is because historiography is now confronted with the non-narrative, tonal elements of language and thus also the body's entire auditory sensuality and desire within the phonographic recording of the jam session and scat singing. And with the help of the microphone, phonography is able to capture these utterances in a particularly clear fashion. This is where the challenge to classical historiography represented by the media of film and phonography comes into view, which Hollywood imagines in model, utopian fashion.

It took 25 years for a similar fantasy to actually make its way into academic libraries: with the final sentence in Roland Barthes' *The Pleasure of the Text*. Barthes bases his "aesthetic of textual pleasure" on precisely the same tonal elements of language, such as the "grain of the voice," the "patina of consonants," and the "voluptuousness of the vowels." Surprisingly, he derives his model from sound film: "it suffices that the cinema capture the sound of speech close up [...] and make us hear in their materiality, their sensuality,

---

30   It is only the recording of the reprimanded jam session that is actually played again from the record player as a gag.

the breath, the gutturals, the fleshiness of the lips, a whole presence of the human muzzle [...], to succeed in shifting the signified a great distance and in throwing, so to speak, the anonymous body of the actor into my ear: it granulates, it crackles, it caresses, it grates, it cuts, it comes: that is bliss."[31]

A Song Is Born's unique nature now emerges when the two phonograph scenes in the two opposite rooms are placed in a configuration and related to one another like the two sides of record. While the jam session in the seminar room is tied to a didactic narration, the library scene makes the film's narrative context splinter into the different song numbers (familiar from vaudeville) or into fragmented sonic images. By setting off what happens in one room from what happens in the other, the film flaunts its own complex hybridity and reflects upon its own nature as part of an entertainment industry that produces stories and history based on two opposing techniques: as the sort of easily narratable, linear, and sanitized version of history that is subject to the specific interests of the industry and its consumers on the one hand, and as a performative expression of aesthetic play of a certain physicality that is interspersed with moments of ecstatic distraction on the other.[32]

The phonograph scenes ultimately also juxtapose two different configurations of knowledge. The recording scene in the seminar room represents the production of a narrative work with a beginning and an end, previously symbolized in the film as a tree diagram on the blackboard. By creating an audio essay, the recording session essentially implements this diagram, working in the same classically narrative mode as a history book. The nonsense arrangement that makes up the recording scene in the library is structured in opposing fashion, functioning either as an individual number that others may follow, or as a soundtrack, which, together with others, produces an ensemble, a music album. The jam session, scat singing, and the splitting off of particular quotes in the library scene makes reference to an ordering principle referred to by Roland Barthes as the 'album' in *The Preparation of the Novel*, which involves quotes or fragments being collected in such a way that Barthes

---

31 Barthes, *The Pleasure of the Text* 66–67.
32 The linking of the two rooms is flaunted as a hybrid formation once again and inverted when the gangster plot overlaps with the musical. A shotgun wedding ceremony is conducted in the seminar room, whose speech acts are transformed into a series of slapstick moments and sonic images thanks to the hearing aid worn by the master of ceremonies, while in the library, the professors and musicians of all colors start jamming together, which is successfully able to ward off the threat of violence from the gangsters.

sees as being distinct from a book, which he sees as constituting a work. He does, however, refer to the relationship of mutuality between the work and the album whereby the work tends towards the album and vice versa.[33] Hawks creates a similar connection between the two phonograph scenes by presenting them as artwork and album respectively and displaying them as two interrelated orders of knowledge. These two orders of knowledge employed by Hawks and Barthes can now be drawn on for use in what we have called an "Audio History of Film."[34] On the one hand, the audio history of film takes its orientation from the main historical development of film and its treatment of sound. On the other, it is revealed to be a technique akin to archival work, proceeding from the various singular moments—sonic icons—which emerge from the 'soundimagetext' (in this case, the voice of Louis Armstrong and the tribute to him in the scat singing scene).

Bibliography

Altman, Rick. "Four and a Half Film Fallacies." *Sound Theory, Sound Practice*. Ed. Rick Altman. New York: Routledge, 1992.

Barthes, Roland. *The Pleasure of the Text*. New York: Farrar, Straus and Giroux, 1975 (1973).

Barthes, Roland. *Camera Lucida: Reflections on Photography*. New York: Farrar, Straus and Giroux, 1989 (1980).

Barthes, Roland. *The Preparation of the Novel*. New York: Columbia Univ. Press, 2011.

Blumenberg, Hans C. *Die Kamera in Augenhöhe: Begegnungen mit Howard Hawks*. Köln: DuMont, 1979.

Bordwell, David, and Kristin Thompson. *Film Art: An Introduction*. New York: Univ. of Wisconsin, 1993.

Chion, Michel. *Film, A Sound Art*. New York: Colombia Univ. Press, 2009.

Currid, Brian. *A National Acoustics: Music and Mass Publicity in Weimar and Nazi Germany*. Minneapolis: Univ. of Minnesota Press, 2006.

Deleuze, Gilles. *Cinema 2: The Time Image*. London: Continuum, 1989.

---

33   Barthes, *The Preparation of the Novel* 182–99.
34   Pauleit, Greiner and Frey, "Audio History of Film." https://film-history.org/approaches/audio-history-film

Dyer, Peter John. "Sling the Lamps Low." *Focus on Howard Hawks*. Ed. Joseph McBride. Englewood Cliffs, NJ: Prentice-Hall, 1972.

Elsaesser, Thomas, and Malte Hagener. *Film Theory: An Introduction Through the Senses*. New York: Routledge, 2010.

Flückiger, Barbara. "Sound Effects: On the Theory and Practice of Film Sound Design." *Sound Art: Between Avant-Garde and Pop Culture*. Eds. Anne Thurmann-Jajes, Sabine Breitsameter and Winfried Pauleit. Bremen, Köln: Salon, 2006.

Gabbard, Krin. *Jammin' at the Margins: Jazz and the American Cinema*. Chicago: Univ. of Chicago Press, 1996.

Gregor, Ulrich, and Enno Patalas. *Geschichte des modernen Films*. Gütersloh: Mohn, 1965.

Hagen, Wolfgang. *Das Radio*. München: Wilhelm Fink, 2005.

Kirchmann, Kay. "Der Körper des Gelehrten: Leiblichkeit und Sprache in Howard Hawks' screwball comedies." *Uni literarisch: Lebenswelt Universität in literarischer Repräsentation*. Ed. Reingard M. Nischik. Konstanz: UVK, 2000. 255–284.

Kittler, Friedrich. *Gramophone, Film, Typewriter*. Stanford: Stanford Univ. Press, 1999.

Lindeperg, Sylvie. *Nacht und Nebel: Ein Film in der Geschichte*. Berlin: Vorwerk 8, 2010.

MacCarthy, Todd. *Howard Hawks: The Grey Fox of Hollywood*. New York: Groove, 1997.

Mast, Gerald. *Howard Hawks, Storyteller*. New York, Oxford: Oxford Univ. Press, 1982.

Metz, Christian. *Language and Cinema*. Berlin: De Gruyter, 1974.

Mitchell, William J. Thomas. *Picture Theory: Essays on Verbal and Visual Representation*. Chicago: Univ. of Chicago Press, 1994.

Nessel, Sabine, and Winfried Pauleit. "Constructions of the Digital Film: Aesthetics, Narrative, Discourse." *Expanded Narration*. Eds. Bernd Kracke and Marc Ries. Bielefeld: transcript, 2013.

Paul, Gerhard, and Ralph Schock, eds. *Sound des Jahrhunderts: Geräusche, Töne, Stimmen 1889 bis heute*. Bonn: BpB, 2013.

Paul, Gerhard. "Von der Historischen Bildkunde zur Visual History: Eine Einführung." *Visual History: Ein Studienbuch*. Ed. Gerhard Paul. Göttingen: Vandenhoeck and Ruprecht, 2006.

Smith, Jeff. *The Sound of Commerce: Marketing Popular Film Music*. New York: Columbia Univ. Press, 1998.

Wood, Robin. *Howard Hawks*. London: Secker and Warburg, 1968.

Online Source (last accessed 16 April 2020)

Pauleit, Winfried, Rasmus Greiner and Mattias Frey. "Audio History of Film."
    Research in Film and History (2018). https://film-history.org/approaches/au
    dio-history-film

Audiovisual Sources

Crosland, Alan (Director). *The Jazz Singer* (1927).
Hawks, Howard (Director). *A Song Is Born* (1948).
Hawks, Howard (Director). *Ball of Fire* (1941).
Hawks, Howard (Director). *Bringing Up Baby* (1938).
Lubin, Arthur (Director). *New Orleans* (1947).

The Production, Reception and Cultural Transfer of Operetta on Early Sound Film

Derek B. Scott (University of Leeds)

In this essay, I investigate the way early sound films of operettas were received in domestic and international markets. I explore the changes that occurred when operettas from the German stage were adapted for British and American films. The meanings that audiences drew from them, and their impact on social and cultural history have been matters of debate. In order to reflect on interpretations that relate only to musical films of the period and not to general questions of adaptation, I am going to begin with a brief look at an example of a German screen operetta; in other words, an operetta composed directly for the screen and not a filmed version of a stage work. I am choosing *Die Drei von der Tankstelle*, which was directed by Wilhelm Thiele and released by Ufa (Universum-Film Aktiengesellschaft) in 1930. My reason for selecting this is because it proved to be Ufa's most popular film of the 1930s. It tells of three bankrupt friends who buy a filling station but, subsequently, fall in love with the same woman motorist. In the end they manage to resolve their differences and remain good friends (one of the film's hit songs was "Ein guter Freund").

Films such as this have given rise to contradictory interpretations. For Siegfried Kracauer operetta films were simply an escapist genre, and one that benefited enormously from the advent of sound. While noting the novelty of its contemporary setting, he calls *Die Drei von der Tankstelle* "a playful day-dream" with a "half-rational" plot.[1] I maintain, however, that many films of this kind did not disguise their character as a form of entertainment, and, on occasion, made their artificiality explicit. The end of the film makes an audience very aware that what they are watching is screen entertainment. When an actor refers to the watching audience, as happens here, it alerts that

---

1   Kracauer, *From Caligari to Hitler* 207.

audience to the fact that the audience cannot in reality be seen by that actor. What is more, the two leading actors, Lilian Harvey and Willy Fritsch, express their surprise at seeing that the audience has not gone home, in spite of the fact that the film has ended. Then, they begin to realize that a crucial audience expectation has been denied. The absence of a 'proper operetta finale' has supposedly created confusion, and so an extravagant and overblown conclusion follows that the audience would recognize as a parody of an operetta finale.

Lilian Harvey was English-born but became a great star in Germany for Ufa. It was odd that, despite her acting and dancing skills, she failed to succeed in Hollywood, and was perhaps constrained by constant Ufa promotion as "the sweetest girl in the world."[2] Willy Fritsch first appeared with Harvey in a silent film of Jean Gilbert's *Die keusche Susanne* in 1926, and there were to become a 'dream couple,' as operetta singers Jeanette MacDonald and Nelson Eddy did later in Hollywood. Both couples were admired for their positive on-screen energy and resilience as social and financial problems grew increasingly bleak in the off-screen world.

Most operetta films rejected the present day in favor of what Kracauer described as "lucrative speculation in romantic nostalgia," pointing to Erik Charrell's *Der Kongreß tanzt* of 1931 as a prime example.[3] He sensed in them a deluding fantasy that made the Weimar Republic vulnerable to the rise of Nazism. Richard Dyer countered this view by arguing that they responded to social needs in a time of depression by offering utopian visions.[4] It is an idea picked up more recently by Rainer Rother, who has also emphasized that irony is employed in order to stimulate laughter.[5]

Occasionally, a screen operetta might be the subject of a stage adaptation, the earliest example being the first German screen operetta, Robert Stolz's *Zwei Herzen im Dreiviertel-Takt*, which premiered at the large Ufa-Palast cinema in Berlin on 13 March 1930.[6] This film enjoyed international success. Indeed, Ufa presented the only serious European challenge to Hollywood, and it built its international success by producing operettas and comedies, shooting versions in several languages (German, English, French, and sometimes Italian) to facilitate international distribution. Kracauer, however, condemns *Zwei Herzen im Dreiviertel-Takt* for selling the public "standardized dreams of an

2   Pehla, "Harvey, Lilian" 131; Bock, *The Concise Cinegraph* 186.
3   Kracauer, *From Caligari to Hitler* 208.
4   Dyer, "Entertainment and Utopia."
5   Rother, "Genreblüte ohnegleichen."
6   Holm, *Im 3/4 Takt durch die Welt* 283.

idyllic Vienna."[7] This became the first example of a screen operetta transferring successfully to the stage when it was performed in Zurich as *Der verlorene Walzer* in 1933. Transfers were, and continued to be, almost always the other way round. The move from film to stage can have uncertain results. Two later examples are the 1958 film musical *Gigi* (Lerner and Loewe), which had little success on stage in 1973, and, in contrast, the stage adaptation of the 1933 film musical *42nd Street* (Dubin and Warren), which triumphed as a musical on Broadway in 1980.

In Hollywood, English-language versions were made of operettas from the German stage, and these films often prove illuminating regarding the changes that were found necessary to ensure a similar emotional response from audiences raised in differing cultural contexts. There are also lessons to be learned about the ways in which performers needed to respond to the differing demands of film compared to theatre. *The Smiling Lieutenant*, a Hollywood film directed by Ernst Lubitsch and released in 1931, became the first sound-film adaptation of a stage operetta to enjoy international success. It starred Maurice Chevalier as Lieutenant Niki, Claudette Colbert as Franzi, and Miriam Hopkins as Princess Anna. It was based on *Ein Walzertraum* (Vienna, 1907), which had music by Oscar Straus, and a libretto by Leopold Jacobson and Felix Dörmann. Joseph W. Herbert had written the book and lyrics for the Broadway production of 1908, but the film had a screenplay by Ernest Vajda and Samson Raphaelson, and new song lyrics by Clifford Grey. Additional musical arrangements were made to Straus's music by Johnny Green and Conrad Salinger (uncredited), and the uncredited musical director was Adolph Deutsch.

It was normal practice for arrangers to update and re-orchestrate the music and for the libretto to be revised to suit the medium of film. The changes that were made in such adaptations provide insight into the workings of cultural transfer. The Hollywood operetta films helped to shape understandings of European operetta in the USA, and, in order to do so, they found ways to relate the time of their original stage productions to the cultural context of the period in which they were now being released as films.

The plot of *The Smiling Lieutenant* revolves around an incident in which Lieutenant Niki, on street duty in Vienna during the arrival procession of King Adolf XV of Flausenthurm and his daughter, smiles and winks at his sweetheart Franzi. Unfortunately, Princess Anna thinks it was meant for her.

---

7   Kracauer, *From Caligari to Hitler* 207–08.

He finds himself having to marry the Princess and move with her to Flausen-thurm. He remains fond of Franzi, but, in the end, Franzi teaches Anna how to win Niki over to herself.

Early in the film there is an illustration of how continental European operetta was transcreated for the American market; in the stage operetta Lieutenant Niki romances Franzi with a song in waltz rhythm "O du Lieber," but in the Hollywood film he sings, instead, a new song in fox-trot rhythm: "Breakfast Time—It Must Be Love!" The following scene begins with a steam train emerging from a tunnel. This is the director Ernst Lubtisch's cheeky suggestiveness, but, interestingly, it is also an effect that is possible only on film and not on the theatre stage. A little later, there is another interpolated song, "Toujours l'Amour in the Army," which had been specially tailored for Maurice Chevalier, the actor playing Niki. A little French vocabulary is included because, of course, the audience knows Chevalier is French—even if he is cast in the role of an Austrian lieutenant (and, besides, he is never able to disguise his French accent).

Later in the film, there is another example of a change that was made to respond to a new cultural context. In the stage operetta, Franzi had to teach the princess about the lively temperament that makes Viennese women so attractive, and encourages her, also, to cater for his love of Viennese food. In Ludwig Berger's 1925 silent film of the operetta, Franzi goes further, and teaches the princess to play a Viennese waltz on the piano. In Lubitsch's film, Franzi has rather different advice: she plays ragtime piano and sings "Jazz up Your Lingerie." Clearly, the vivacious, emancipated American woman is an equivalent of the Viennese woman and her fiery temperament. Yet, while Niki is discovering his wife's change of behavior, the film's underscore is of the trio "Temp'rament" from Act 2 of the Viennese version. So, two qualities, one urban American, the other Viennese, are equated, which tells us that women of differing cultures are able to attract and domesticize men, but not necessarily by using the same means.

The historical period of the film's production is evident in Chevalier's occasional gaze to camera. This is a mode of address linked to what Tom Gunning has termed the "cinema of attractions" in reference to the emphasis on showing and exhibiting in early cinema. It is a feature of early European film that was rejected in classical Hollywood practice because it ran counter to the creation of realistic illusion.[8] At the very end of *The Smiling Lieutenant*, Chevalier

8   Gunning, "The Cinema of Attraction" 64.

sings blatantly to the camera, emphasizing the performance act and, therefore, breaking with the naturalistic illusion that was soon to be the hallmark of Hollywood practice.

Lubitsch went on to direct *The Merry Widow* with Chevalier and MacDonald in 1934. It was MGM's second film of the operetta, the first being Erich von Stroheim's *Die lustige Witwe* (1925), starring John Gilbert as Danilo and Mae Murray as the widow, which departed considerably from the operetta. This silent film contains what would now be called a 'backstory' of the widow as an ex-vaudeville American girl who arrives in the small kingdom of Monteblanco and later goes to Paris. Lehár's music was re-arranged by William Axt and David Mendoza for a silent cinema orchestra. Lubitsch's film starred Chevalier as Danilo and Jeanette MacDonald as the widow, the screenplay was by Ernest Vajda and Samson Raphaelson, and new lyrics were provided by Lorenz Hart (with some additional lyrics by Gus Kahn). The musical arrangement was by Herbert Stothart, with help from orchestrators Paul Marquardt, Charles Maxwell, and Leonid Raab. Herbert Stothart, who had enjoyed plenty of Broadway experience, was a composer, arranger, and musical director for MGM in the 1930s. Discovering that her forthcoming marriage to Danilo had been a plot to obtain her wealth, the widow calls it off, and Danilo returns to Marshova, where he is imprisoned for failing in his task. She goes there too, to vouch for his innocence, and they are finally reconciled in his prison cell.

There are several differences between the stage operetta and the film version: in the former, it is money that creates distrust for a couple in love; in the film, seduction scenes are important. Lubitsch has a characteristic fascination about seduction and power relations, the latter being different during the seduction process when sexual desire is the focus.[9] Maurice Chevalier is the same charming seducer he was in *The Smiling Lieutenant*. Surprisingly, *The Merry Widow* was not a box office success and that prompted MGM to find a new partner for MacDonald in the shape of Nelson Eddy.[10]

The British film *Blossom Time* of 1934 was a screen operetta based on Schubert melodies arranged by G.H. Clutsam and differed from his earlier West End success *Lilac Time*, which had been a reworking of Heinrich Berté's *Das Dreimäderlhaus*. The director Paul Stein was Viennese but had worked for five years in Hollywood.[11] The cast included Richard Tauber, one of the first op-

9   Vincent, "'Lippen schweigen, 's flüstern Geigen'" 272–74.
10   Henderson, *Red, Hot & Blue* 124.
11   Ames, *A Critical History of the British Cinema* 85.

eretta singers to become a sound-film star. An examination of the scene in which Tauber accompanies himself on piano singing "Once There Lived a Lady Fair"—the music of which is by Clutsam rather than Schubert—reveals that his mimetic and gestural signs are in accord with operatic performance practice (as is his wide dynamic range) and contrast with the naturalistic code adopted by the members of the drawing-room audience in the film: his gestures are theatrical, whereas theirs are restrained.[12] The success of *Blossom Time* persuaded Alfred Hitchcock to try his hand later that year with the operetta *Waltzes from Vienna*, which Oswald Stoll had presented at his Alhambra Theatre in 1931–32.

The next year a British film titled *I Give My Heart* (1935) gave viewers an opportunity to see and hear the Hungarian coloratura soprano Gitta Alpár, who had been the star of the related stage version, *Die Dubarry*, four years earlier in Berlin. Operetta films like to feature a hit song during the opening credits, and this film not only begins with a hit song from *Die Dubarry* but also takes its title from that song. The film is an English version of Theo Mackeben's musical reworking of Millöcker's *Gräfin Dubarry* of 1879, which had been provided with a new libretto by Paul Knepler, Ignaz Michael Welleminsky, and E. M. Cremer.[13] The film version was created by Frank Launder, Roger Burford, Paul Perez, and Kurt Siodmak, but the lyrics by Desmond Carter and Rowland Leigh for the English stage production of 1932 were retained. The arrangement of the music for the film was by Theo Mackeben. No doubt because of its French theme, British International Pictures (BIP) engaged a French director, Marcel Varnel. However, Gitta Alpár, in the role of French milliner Jeanne, speaks her English lines with a Hungarian rather than French accent. Alpár had left Germany with her daughter for England before she made this film. Her husband, the film star Gustav Fröhlich, divorced her because she was Jewish and he wanted to remain in favor with the Nazi Party. Disappointingly, *I Give My Heart* made little money at the box office and Alpár's film career was short-lived. She became a singing teacher and died in Los Angeles in 1991.

The momentum for operetta films in the UK continued. In 1937, courtesy of British Unity Pictures, came *The Girl in the Taxi* (1937), directed by André Berthomieu. It was based on the 1912 English stage version by Frederick Fenn and Arthur Wimperis of the 1910 operetta *Die keusche Susanne* (music by Jean Gilbert and a libretto by Georg Okonowski). For the film, a screenplay was

---

12   Scott, "Song Performance in the Early Sound Shorts" 190–94.
13   Its earlier libretto was by F. Zell [Camillo Walzel] and Richard Genée.

devised by Austin Melford, after a screen story by Fritz Gottfurcht, and Frank Eyton wrote some additional lyrics. The British film industry now had the confidence to look beyond the German stage for its lead singer and chose Frances Day. She was actually American but had made her home as a cabaret artist in England in the 1920s and, by the time of this film, had become a popular West End star. British Unity Pictures, having taken care to hire a French director, also made a simultaneous French version of *The Girl in the Taxi* as *La Chaste Susanne*, the title by which the operetta was known in France. The only member of the cast to play in both versions was Henry Garat (as René), a Paris-born actor who had earlier taken the role of Tsar Alexander I in the English and French versions of Erik Charell's *Der Kongress tanzt* (1931).

The American version of *Walzer aus Wien* was staged on Broadway in 1934 and renamed *The Great Waltz*. It had a revised book by Moss Hart but retained many of the lyrics Desmond Carter had written for the West End production. In 1938, it became an MGM movie, directed by Julien Duvivier. It starred Louise Rainer, Fernand Gravet (as Johann Strauss Jr), and coloratura soprano Miliza Korjus. Moss Hart's book was replaced with a screenplay by Samuel Hoffenstein and Walter Reisch (with uncredited help from Joseph L. Mankiewicz and Vicki Baum). Lyrics by Oscar Hammerstein II replaced those of Desmond Carter. The musical arranger and composer of additional music was Dimitri Tiomkin, who later became celebrated for his scores to Hollywood Westerns, especially *High Noon* (1952).

The film begins with on-screen announcement:

"In Vienna in 1844 'nice people' neither danced the waltz ... nor kissed their wives in public ... nor listened to new ideas ...
In 1845 came Johann Strauss II and his immortal melodies ..."

It is unhistorical nonsense, of course, but an excuse follows: "We have dramatized the spirit rather than the facts of his life, because it is his spirit that has lived—in his music." There follows a scene of Strauss's first performance with his orchestra at Dommayer's Casino. It is poorly attended and going badly. An aristocrat enters with a 'famous opera singer' Carla Donner in his party, and she is immediately attracted to young Strauss. Around twenty minutes into the film, there is a dramatic cut from the sensual abandon of the waltz to a decorous minuet in an aristocratic hall. Carla has invited Strauss, who has brought a new song. Carla sings it, tactfully avoiding announcing that it is a waltz. The polite audience looks a little shocked as the waltz rhythm kicks in, but—predictably—they are soon won over. Evidently, none of these people had ever listened to the music of Strauss's father or that of Joseph Lanner during the past ten years, even though the latter had been music director for court balls at the Hofburg Imperial Palace until his death in 1843.

During a scene in the Wienerwald, sounds of the environment (such as birdsong) give Strauss the inspiration for his waltz "Tales from Vienna Woods." He even benefits from Carla's assistance. The mixing of music and sounds of the environment is hard to realize on stage, but it can be achieved easily and effectively in the medium of sound film. In particular, film allows a familiar melody to emerge from the diegetic sounds of the scene, as happens here. Hitchcock had used the same kind of sonic technique when he included a scene in which a dough-making machine inspires the "Blue Danube" waltz in *Waltzes from Vienna*. Strauss and Carla's carriage ride is indebted to Erik Charell's pioneering example in *Der Kongress tanzt*, when Lilian Harvey as Christel travels to see Tsar Alexander I (Willy Fritsch). In that film, unlike *The Great Waltz*, it is not a stationary carriage with a background film that creates the illusion of motion. The camera shows an onlooker touching the moving carriage, as well as Lilian Harvey reaching up to touch one of a bunch of balloons held by a bystander, and women at the flower shop throwing flowers into the carriage.

Tracking shots produce a sense of space and motion that is difficult to recreate on stage, unless some sort of screen projection onto the backcloth is employed as an alternative. However, a tracking shot, which requires a camera dolly on rails, is costly for filmmakers. Therefore, a decision may be taken on economic grounds to film a couple sitting in a carriage against a screen showing scenery that has been filmed previously by a camera operator riding on the back of a vehicle of similar size to that in which the couple sit. That will give the impression of the vehicle's being in motion (induced movement), but it allows no interaction with the surroundings since those are merely screen images. Use of tracking shots, or simulated tracking shots is common when a stage scene involving a mode of transport is transferred to the screen. A later example occurs in the 1955 film version of Rodgers and Hammerstein's 1943 Broadway musical *Oklahoma!* during the song "The Surrey with the Fringe on Top." In the song the ride in the Surrey—a four-wheeled carriage—is seen in a cutaway scene as the characters imagine their ride.

Later in *The Great Waltz*, there is a domestic scene with Strauss playing the tune of the bullfinch duet from *Der Zigeunerbaron* on the piano and becoming irritated with his wife Poldi for disrupting his work. They decide to leave Vienna, and they inform a gathering of their friends. Strauss then sings "One Day When We Were Young" to the bullfinch tune. This furnishes an example of how music could be updated to the meet the musical expectations of the 1930s in contrast to those of the 1880s. The original was constructed in verse and refrain form, the typical popular song structure of the later nineteenth century, but the later version was converted into the typical Tin Pan Alley 32-bar song structure AABA. To achieve that, the verse music is scrapped, and the 16-bar refrain becomes the basis of the entire song. It is stated and repeated, then a new melodic passage is added for the B section before section A is repeated again.

Carla happens to look in on the farewell gathering, and her look indicates that she knows she is the inspiration for Strauss's new song. She has come with an operatic commission, and Poldi persuades Strauss that he must stay in order to compose for the Imperial Theatre. Not only did a performance of a Strauss operetta in the Imperial Theatre never take place, but the piece he writes now is *Die Fledermaus*, which was actually composed many years before *Der Zigeunerbaron*. Poldi goes to the performance and tells Carla in emotional tones that she is not standing in her way, because she loves Strauss deeply and recognizes his manly needs as an artistic genius. Strauss leaves in a carriage with Carla, but she is suddenly struck with the realization that Poldi will always be between them. She tells him so and catches the Danube boat to Budapest alone. In the film's closing scene, it is forty-three years later, and Strauss, accompanied by Poldi, has an audience with the Emperor, who escorts him to his balcony to show him a cheering crowd of grateful, cheering Viennese citizens who adore his music.

When a stage operetta became a film, the change from the stage play to screenplay was affected by the scenario, shooting script, and use of montage, and that led to blurred distinctions about authorship between the screen writer and the film director from the 1920s on. The operetta film containing the most far-reaching changes is MGM's *The Chocolate Soldier* (1941), directed by Roy Del Ruth and starring Nelson Eddy and Risë Stevens. When Rudolf Bernauer and Leopold Jacobson adapted Bernard Shaw's play *Arms and the Man* (1894) as a German libretto in 1908, he had given consent. A year later, he had grudgingly permitted performances of the stage operetta on Broadway, then London, in an English version by Stanislaus Stange, provided the program announced that it was an unauthorized use of his play. However, he was no longer willing to allow his play to be used for a new film version in English and demanded a hefty fee from MGM.

MGM was not prepared to pay any royalties to Shaw, and so Leonard Lee and Keith Winter were commissioned to devise a screenplay based on *The Guardsman* (*A testőr*, 1910), a play by Ferenc Molnár that had already been made into a film by MGM in 1931. Naturally, MGM retained the score by Oscar Straus, which went through some modification in the hands of the musical directors and arrangers Herbert Stothart and Bronislau Kaper, and the orchestrator Murray Cutter (uncredited).

In addition to a changed plot in which a jealous husband flirts with his wife while disguised as a Russian guardsman, there are two interpolated operatic numbers: Camille Saint-Säens's "Mon Coeur s'ouvre á ta voix" from *Samson et Dalila* (1877) and "O du mein holder Abendstern" from Richard Wagner's *Tannhäuser* (1845). Another interpolated number was Mussorgsky's "Song of the Flea," and there was also some additional music by Bronislau Kaper with lyrics by Gus Kahn. The number of reprises of the song "My Hero" in the film make up for Straus's failure to provide a single one in the stage operetta—he had not expected it to be the huge hit it became.

Concluding Remarks

Austrian film director Arthur Maria Rabenalt commented on the various advantages screen adaptations possessed over the stage originals: the libretto became the basis of a scenario with montage, complicated intrigues could be edited in a way that made them more credible, awkward scene changes could be effected quickly, and characters could be made more convincing by rendering certain dramatic situations more visible.[14] Another means of removing stage rigidity in screen adaptations was to reduce the quantity of music and be flexible about the sequence of an operetta's musical numbers. Musical numbers can often seem static and undramatic on film, so the tendency was to increase the amount of dialogue. However, short instrumental reprises could be used for scene transitions, and new numbers could be specially composed for the film version.

Rabenalt insists that operetta scenes filmed outside of the studio provided the viewer with more than a travel brochure and the beauty of landscape. Its naturalistic effect was really decisive for the success of the new genre both at

---

14   Rabenalt, *Der Operetten-Bildband* 33.

home and abroad. The stage operetta, he maintains, was always pseudorealistic in its apparent naturalism and rather artistic in its decorative offer of illusion by means of stylistic stage extensions.[15]

In many cases, screen adaptations of operettas were far from being filmed versions of the stage production: the music would be reworked, updated and re-arranged, and new music, or the music of other operettas, might be included. In addition to all this, it was necessary to facilitate the border crossing of operettas by including features which an audience in another country could recognize and empathize with, and to ensure that any unfamiliar historical context was explained. As such, they offer examples of the way cultural meanings adapt to different media contexts at different times.

Bibliography

Ames, Roy. *A Critical History of the British Cinema*. London: Secker and Warburg, 1978.

Bock, Hans-Michael, and Tim Bergfelder, eds. *The Concise Cinegraph: Encyclopedia of German Cinema*. New York: Berghahn, 2009.

Brown, Julie, and Annette Davison, eds. *The Sounds of the Silents in Britain: Voice, Music and Sound in Early Cinema Exhibition*. New York, Oxford: Oxford Univ. Press, 2013.

Dyer, Richard. "Entertainment and Utopia." *Movie* 24 (Spring 1977): 2–13.

Gunning, Tom. "The Cinema of Attraction: Early Film, Its Spectator and the Avant-Garde." *Wide Angle* 8, 3–4 (1986): 63–70.

Henderson, Amy, and Dwight Blocker Bowers. *Red, Hot & Blue: A Smithsonian Salute to the American Musical*. Washington D.C.: Smithsonian Institute Press, 1996.

Holm, Gustav. *Im 3/4 Takt durch die Welt: Ein Lebensbild des Komponisten Robert Stolz*. Linz, Pittsburgh, Wien: Ibis, 1948.

Kracauer, Siegfried. *From Caligari to Hitler: A Psychological History of the German Film*. Princeton: Princeton Univ. Press, 1947.

Pehla, Karen. "Harvey, Lilian." *The BFI Companion to German Cinema*. Eds. Thomas Elsaesser and Michael Wedel. London: BFI, 1999. 131.

Rabenalt, Arthur Maria. *Der Operetten-Bildband: Bühne, Film, Fernsehen*. Hildesheim: Olms, 1980.

---

15   Ibid. 39.

Rother, Rainer. "Genreblüte ohnegleichen: Die deutsche Tonfilmoperette." *Kunst der Oberfläche: Operette zwischen Bravour und Banalität*. Eds. Bettina Brandl-Risi, Clemens Risi and Rainer Simon. Leipzig: Henschel, 2015. 177–83.

Sala, Massimiliano, ed. *From Stage to Screen: Musical Films in Europe and United States (1927–1961)*. Turnhout: Brepols, 2012.

Scott, Derek B. "Song Performance in the Early Sound Shorts of British Pathé." *The Sounds of the Silents in Britain*. Eds. Julie Brown and Annette Davison. New York, Oxford: Oxford Univ. Press, 2013. 183–99.

Vincent, Delphine. "'Lippen schweigen, 's flüstern Geigen: Hab mich lieb!' Seduction, Power Relations and Lubitsch's Touch in *The Merry Widow*." *From Stage to Screen: Musical Films in Europe and United States (1927–1961)*. Ed. Massimiliano Sala. Turnhout: Brepols, 2012. 271–87.

Audiovisual Sources

Berthomieu, André (Director). *The Girl in the Taxi* (1937), after the operetta *Die keusche Susanne* (1910) by Jean Gilbert.

Charell, Erik (Director). *Der Kongress tanzt* (1931).

Del Ruth, Roy (Director). *The Chocolate Soldier* (1941), after *A testőr* (*The Guardsman*, 1910) by Ference Molnár and after the operetta *Der tapfere Soldat* (1908) by Oscar Straus.

Duvivier, Julien (Director). *The Great Waltz* (1938).

Hitchcock, Alfred (Director). *Waltzes from Vienna* (1934), after the operetta *Walzer aus Wien* (1930) by Heinz Reichtert, A.M. Willner and Ernst Marischka, with music of Strauss Sr. and Strauss Jr. arranged by Erich Korngold and Julius Bittner.

Liebman, Max (Director). *The Chocolate Soldier* (1955), after the operetta *Der tapfere Soldat* (1908) by Oscar Straus.

Lubitsch, Ernst (Director). *The Smiling Lieutenant* (1931), after the operetta *Ein Walzertraum* (1907) by Oscar Straus.

Lubitsch, Ernst, and Otto Preminger (Directors). *That Lady in Ermine* (1948), after the operetta *Die Frau im Hermelin* (1919) by Jean Gilbert.

Stein, Paul L. (Director). *Blossom Time* (1934).

Thiele, Wilhelm (Director). *Die Drei von der Tankstelle* (1930).

Varnel, Marcel (Director). *I Give My Heart* (1935), after the operetta *Die Dubarry* (1931) by Carl Millöcker and Theo Mackeben.

von Bolváry, Géza (Director). *Zwei Herzen im Dreiviertel-Takt* (1930).

The Address of the Ear: Music and History in *Waltz with Bashir*

Rasmus Greiner (University of Bremen)

The exploration of film sound as a part of films which make the past experienceable continues to be a new field of research. Gerhard Paul, who had already proclaimed a paradigm shift from the dominance of writing to the dominance of images with the term 'visual history,' dared to make a first attempt on the part of historians. In his rich and comprehensive collection *Sound des Jahrhunderts* (Sound of the Century), together with Ralph Schock, he compiles articles on the cultural history of sound, the historical relevance of the auditive in the 20th century, and the sound of political history.[1] As with visual history, however, the specifics of film are largely excluded here as well. On the other hand, in film studies, interest in the auditive has intensified since the 1980s, generating an added value as a particular level of meaning.[2] Further studies focused on sound design as well as the aesthetics and meaning of film sounds.[3] The article *Audio History of Film* is a first attempt to combine these studies in the intersection of film and history. It opens up a field of research that acts as a missing link between the approaches of film studies, sound studies, and historical science.[4] It aims to "investigate how film sound can generate and shape audiences' experience of history."[5] Here, both the aesthetic dimension and its potential for the production of history, as well as the material, technical, and cultural dimensions of film sound are examined with regard to historical modeling and figuration. Research on film music has, admittedly, taken some tentative steps in this direction: for example, Annette

---

1   Paul and Schock, *Der Sound des Jahrhunderts*.
2   Chion, *La voix*; —, *Le son*; —, *Audio-Vision*; Altman, *Sound Theory*; Kamensky, *Ton*.
3   Flückiger, *Sound Design*; Butzmann, *Filmgeräusch*.
4   Pauleit, Greiner and Frey, "Audio History of Film." https://film-history.org/approaches/1418
5   Ibid.

Kreuziger-Herr and Rüdiger Jantzen's consideration of Miklós Rózsa's music (and its desire for authenticity) in historical films such as *Quo Vadis* (1951), or Stephen C. Meyer's book *Epic Sound: Music in Postwar Hollywood Biblical Films*.[6] The impact of film music on the production of experiences of the past requires, however, further far-reaching research.

In this article, I will explore how film music enables historical experience by means of film experience. Scholars like Vivian Sobchack understand the experience of film as an embodied process. Adapting her theory, I will show how historical films make palpable the experience of history not simply by means of intensely affective images but also by synaesthetically combining the visual and auditory levels. Though the soundtrack is crucial for establishing the mood of film sequences, it elicits emotional reactions to historical processes, events, and situations. It structures the cinematic narration of history by creating continuities and breaks, connections, conjunctions, and oppositions. Film music, I claim, plays a special role in this process. According to Birger Langkjær, "the music does not refer to an already given meaning but contributes to its creation."[7] This impact can be explained by the special mode of perception to which film music is subject. As the music is inseparably merged with the film images, we both hear and feel it. Cognitive and embodied perception are closely interrelated and lend themselves especially well to reflection in the phenomenology of film.

In order to further develop these claims, I will discuss selected sequences from the animated documentary drama film *Waltz with Bashir* (2008). The film's plot draws on director Ari Folman's war memories. Just like Folman himself, the protagonist, an Israeli soldier, witnessed the Sabra and Shatila massacre, in which members of the Lebanese Phalange militia tortured and killed large numbers of civilians in the Lebanon War of 1982. However, he has lost his memories of the massacre, and the film tells the story of his quest to recover them. Using interviews, flashbacks, and imaginary visions, it shows "narrative microactivities that the protagonist (and hence the film itself) connects to a macronarrative of the Lebanon War."[8] The soundtrack is dominated by electronic music. The composer, Max Richter, is a late descendant of the renewal movements in both film and music that mainly took place at the beginning of the 1970s. In those years, a revolution began in American film production that

---

6   Kreuziger-Herr, "Mittelalter in Hollywoods Filmmusik;" Meyer, *Epic Sound*.
7   Langkjær, "Der hörende Zuschauer" 110.
8   Hasebrink, "Das gezeichnete Gedächtnis" 20.

film historians later termed 'New Hollywood.' Inspired by European avant-garde movements such as the French New Wave, a new generation of film-makers (including George Lucas, Francis Ford Coppola, Steven Spielberg, and Martin Scorsese) elevated the status of sound design. They shared an enthusiasm for the contemporary music industry's "electronically modified sounds that blurred the boundary between noise and music"[9] and attempted to "develop a similar vocabulary for film soundtracks."[10] The profession of sound designer was born. Sound design was pivotal in turning film sound into an autonomous dimension of expression with a status equal to images by organizing the production of auditory signs and increasing their scope for expression and complexity. Today, film music and sound design merge and one can become part of the other. In the following exploration of the address of the ear, I will therefore include considerations not only regarding film music and the phenomenology of film but also the interaction between the different components of a soundtrack in terms of mood, memory, self-referential structures, and reflection.

The Phenomenology of Film

The image still dominates most of the discourses in film studies. Parts of musicology, in turn, consider film music detached from the other audiovisual elements and structures of the medium. Both approaches are not suitable for a theory of film music as a medium of historical experience. Instead of thinking in hierarchies, the visual and auditory dimensions should be examined in their interaction, which produces specific cinematic experiences. Consequently, in the following reflections, I do not treat the auditory level in isolation, but consider how it interacts with moving images, montage, aesthetics, and narration. In terms of film theory, Vivian Sobchack's *The Address of the Eye. A Phenomenology of Film Experience* is crucial.[11] Sobchack understands the experience of film as an embodied process that addresses the synaesthetic structure of our perceptual apparatus. The existential phenomenology of Maurice Merleau-Ponty and its projection onto film by Vivian Sobchack provide an explanatory model based on the interrelation between the living body and the

---

9   Flückiger, *Sound Design* 17.
10   Ibid.
11   Sobchack, *The Address of the Eye*.

lived world.[12] This phenomenological framework makes the cinematic figuration of a historical world appear in a new light. In her reflections, Sobchack proceeds from two levels of film perception: as a systematic communicative competence, the primary structures of film are based on conscious experience, while the secondary notion of distortion can be identified as ideology, rhetoric, and poetics.[13] Her approach complements, and contrasts with, popular film analysis techniques. Instead of abstracting the 'wild meaning' of the film into individual codes, it argues for the thesis that the film creates meaning by virtue of its own being as an embodied experience.[14] The film's sensual and meaningful expression of experience becomes an experience for the viewer himself. "A film," Sobchack argues, "is an act of seeing that makes itself seen, an act of hearing that makes itself heard, an act of physical and reflective movement that makes itself reflexively felt and understood."[15] Against this background, the processes of film analysis with their small-scale approaches not only lead to a shortening but also to a misunderstanding: they analyze the film based on its production and design; they make it theoretically writable. Phenomenology, on the other hand, aims at a holistic perception that creates a pre-reflexive, comprehensive impression. Here, the relationship between image and sound comes into play. In film, the visible and the audible can create different meanings, but both senses influence each other in our perception. Hence the title of Michel Chion's book *Audio-Vision*; we do not see and hear a film, we hear/see it.[16] Film music in particular bonds together the soundtrack and the moving images as the latter are very differently perceived if we hear a melody while watching them.

Since Sobchack stresses that seeing "is an act performed by both the film (which sees a world as visible images) and the viewer (who sees the film's visible images both as a world and the seeing of a world),"[17] we may add the word 'hearing' in every place where the word 'seeing' is used: "Seeing/*hearing* is an act performed by both the film (which sees/*hears* a world as visible images *and audible sounds*) and the viewer (who sees/*hears* the film's visible images *and audible sounds* both as a world and the seeing/*hearing* of a world)." Hence, this approach could serve as the basis for a new understanding of the relationship

12   Ibid. 38.
13   Ibid. 8.
14   Ibid. 12.
15   Ibid. 3–4.
16   Chion, *Audio-Vision*.
17   Sobchack, *The Address of the Eye* 56.

between film sound and history. Assuming that historical films build a space-time structure that models a historical world and opens it up to embodied experience, I would like to suggest the term 'histosphere' for this purpose.[18] In a histosphere, the spectator's perceptions oscillate between a supposedly objective external view *of* a historical world and the subjective experience *of* the film and its characters *in* this world. Film sound plays a special role in this process. It structures the cinematic narration of history by creating continuities and breaks, connections, conjunctions, and oppositions. The auditory level is also crucial in determining the mood of film sequences, and elicits emotional reactions to historical processes, events, and situations.[19] In order to emphasize the importance of sound in this context, I introduced the notion of a 'sonic histosphere'.[20] Within this framework, film music can be considered a key factor in the intersection of the audience's perception, emotional response, and experience.

The crucial importance of the soundtrack as part of a synaesthetic experience of history can also be derived from the analogies between the embodied film experience and historical experience. The historian Frank R. Ankersmit emphasizes that the moment of historical experience creates the illusion of being able to physically touch the past.[21] Based on Aristotle's epistemology and Maurice Merleau-Ponty's phenomenological concept of 'tentative seeing,' he assigns the historical experience to the sensory channel of the tactile.[22] Thus, he refers not only to the haptic perception of the physical world, but also to a simultaneous form of self-experience.[23] The 'tentative seeing' makes tangible not only the past in historical experience but also our own embodied existence.[24] Ankersmit therefore describes the characteristics of the sense of touch as immediacy, experience through self-experience, and contiguity

---

18   Greiner, *Histospheres.*
19   Michel Chion understands film sound as a subtle means of emotional and semantic manipulation that directly influences the spectator's physiology and perceptions. Chion, *Audio-Vision* XXVI.
20   Greiner, "Sonic Histospheres." https://film-history.org/approaches/sonic-histospheres
21   Ankersmit refers to Jo Tollebeek and Tom Verschaffel, who state that historical experience makes the past "palpable and visible," as well as Johan Huizinga, who describes historical experience as "the contact with the essence of things." Ankersmit, *Die Historische Erfahrung* 71; Tollebeek, *De vreugden* 18; Huizinga, *Verzamelde werken* 56.
22   Ankersmit, *Die Historische Erfahrung* 63–68.
23   Ibid.
24   Ibid. 68.

of object and subject.[25] He then assigns individual human senses to the different approaches to history: historical experience is like "being touched by the past," while the historical text is more about dominating and structuring the past.[26] Written historiography—as Ankersmit puts it—is therefore allocated the metaphor of seeing.[27] Historical debate in turn testifies to the relativity of all historical insight and is therefore linked to the metaphor of hearing.[28] These allocations make clear that Ankersmit does not want to play the historical text and the historical debate against historical experience.[29] The metaphorical division into different sensory channels points to mutual exchange and to a synaesthetically generated insight in the mode of self-experience.[30] This sheds light on the special connectivity of history to film. In historical films the particular sensory channels of seeing and hearing not only generate meaning, as written historiography does, but also tangible historical worlds. Film music, as I will show below, acts like a catalyst that drives the fusion of these dimensions. In turn, investigating the causes of this phenomenon may be very helpful for our understanding of how film experience creates historical experience.

Mood and Memory

Right from the start, the soundtrack to *Waltz with Bashir* operates on its own level of meaning. The repetitive structures and the sustained, haunting sounds of the score begin creating a trance-like mood even before the opening credits, displayed against a black background, are over. The bass-heavy beat that begins as the picture fades in acts as an auditory paraphrase for the sequence that then ensues, in which an animated pack of dogs rampages through the streets with teeth bared. Hyperrealistic breathing, growling, and panting sounds contribute to creating a sense of danger. A wild race through the city begins until the furiously barking dogs gather below a window. After a hard cut we see Ari's friend Boaz, who recounts this dream in a bar. But then the music resumes, indicating that the dream sequence is not

---

25   Ibid. 98.
26   Ibid. 74.
27   Ibid.
28   Ibid.
29   Ibid.
30   Ibid.

over. When the film cuts back to the dream, the switch from the on-screen conversation to Boaz's voiceover commentary is not marked by a change in the sound. On the contrary, sounds hinting at his spatial surroundings can still be heard in the voiceover: for example, a faint reverberation and ambient noise. Sound maintains a link to the filmic present even during the dream and memory sequences presented as such by the score. Thus, the filmic present, memory, and imagination are depicted as fundamentally equal elements of historicization that are in a state of constant interchange.

Moreover, the haunting music creates a certain atmosphere of unrest which covers the filmic present with a dark shadow from the past. In order to better understand this function, we should take a closer look at the theoretical background of cinematic atmospheres which surround all forms and structures of the histosphere like a "misty primal substance" or an "exhalation."[31] According to Béla Balázs's concept of an "anthropomorphic world," "every figure [...] has an emotional effect (mostly unconscious to us), a pleasant, unpleasant, calming or threatening one—because, however distant, it reminds us of human or animal physiognomy."[32] Baláz's considerations make it clear that cinematic atmospheres can cause emotional reactions in the viewer based on the recognition of human traits. In the spirit of Paul Ricoeur, the atmosphere must therefore be understood as part of the 'configuration' of the cinematic world while a mood is only generated in a specific interaction with the viewer which Ricoeur calls 'refiguration.'[33] Furthermore, as holistic experiences, moods cannot be reduced to their individual parts.[34] The aesthetic figuration of the film, in particular the music in relation to the moving images, forms a constellation which, in the case of historical film, is expanded by imaginary historical references. This also applies to ambient sounds. Composed of different tones and aural elements, these sounds enliven the cinematic image and refer to a continuous historical world that extends far beyond the boundaries of the image. Embedded in an associative network of "memories, thoughts, tendencies to act, physiological reactions, and vocalizations,"[35] ambient sounds in *Waltz with Bashir* evoke emotions and moods that are in a complex interrelation.[36] For example, after

---

31   Balázs, *Der Geist des Films* 30.
32   Balázs, *Der Film* 89.
33   Ricoeur, *Zeit und Erzählung* 103–14.
34   Balázs, *Der Geist des Films* 33–34.
35   Kappelhoff, "Das Zuschauergefühl" 83.
36   Ibid.

the conversation in the bar, Ari watches Boaz staring at the turbulent sea. The ocean, the drumming of the rain, and the roar of the waves symbolize the release of disordered flows of memory mixed with imaginary visions. The aural dimension of the atmosphere not only reflects the inner mood of the characters in the film, but also creates an emotional reaction in the viewer. In particular the music, composed of elongated melancholic soundscapes, makes this resonance physically perceptible. It partly takes on the role of ambient sounds so that, in the sense of the auditory revolution of New Hollywood, no exact boundary can be drawn between the music and the other elements of the soundtrack. The protagonist's personal, subjective mood is mixed with the film's claim to model an experienceable historical world. Thus, by involving the viewer in reenacted historical events and making them physically experienceable, the film can potentially activate embodied memories and project them onto the historical content, as I will show in the next paragraph.

Reminiscence Triggers

The conversation between Ari and Boaz at the beginning of *Waltz with Bashir* opens up a complex interaction with film-inherent memories, historical knowledge, and the embodied memory of the viewer. When Ari drives away in his car afterwards, this release gives way to a process of reflection. The regular sound of the windscreen wipers functions like a metronome, giving structure to the haunting soundscapes of the score, which now grows in intensity. On the one hand, linking sounds that are audible in the cinematic world to the musical score metaphorically reflects Sobchack's theory of a double experience: I see and hear the pictures and sounds of the movie as both, *as* a world and the seeing and hearing *of* a world.[37] On the other hand, sounds such as those of the windscreen wipers have an even more advanced function, which is especially important to historical films: the world of the film is mixed with auditory elements that can activate the viewer's embodied memories of everyday experiences, including media consumption. The familiar sound facilitates empathy not just in the movie character but in the memory process itself. Auditory impressions such as the regular sound of the windshield wipers relate to filmic figurations that link the world of

---

37   Sobchack, *The Address of the Eye* 56.

the film with the viewer's unconscious embodied memories. I refer to these audiovisual stimulus structures as 'reminiscence triggers.'[38] This particular film experience is enriched by a 'warm familiarity'[39] and tends to be accompanied by positive emotional reactions. In this manner reminiscence triggers help to overcome feelings of strangeness and difference in regard to the world of the film. Audiovisually mediated impressions such as the protagonist's driving in the rain have the potential to generate resonances in the mind of the viewer, or, in Nietzsche's words, to trigger a "resonance of related sensations and moods."[40] The resonances activated here refer to primal experiences such as interpersonal contact, basic sensory impressions, or simple everyday experiences. Again, there is a double perception: the regular sound of the windshield wipers may subconsciously remind us of how our own thoughts once wandered off during a long drive while the music evokes exactly the same reminiscence in this particular moment of film experience. But the function of this reminiscence trigger goes far beyond that: while in the mode of remembering embodied experiences, we are confronted with a figurative historical world which immediately opens up in the mind of the film's protagonist. Through reminiscence triggers, the embodied experience of the historical is combined with a narrative strategy of 'mise-en-histoire,' the process of contextualizing and historicizing.[41] This is also expressed in the present film sequence: in a voiceover, Ari identifies the cause of the fragmented memory for the first time: the war in Lebanon. In the intersection of these levels, the film primarily addresses the processing of traumatic experiences, uncertain memories, and their relationship to concrete historical events. The use of reminiscence triggers, evocative music, and contextualizing voiceover adds a layer of reflection to the 'sonic histosphere.' I will examine this in the following section.

---

38   Greiner, "Sonic Histospheres." https://film-history.org/approaches/sonic-histospheres

39   Hugo Münsterberg uses the phrase "a certain warm feeling of familiarity" in his theoretical considerations about the effect of texts in product advertising. Although he did not have film in mind, he anticipates a crucial strategy for the emotional involvement of the viewer. Münsterberg, *Grundzüge der Psychotechnik* 423.

40   Nietzsche's metaphor of 'Miterklingen' describes the rapid succession and steady stream of moods to which feelings and memories are linked. Nietzsche, *Menschliches, Allzumenschliches* 28.

41   Greiner, *Histospheres*.

Self-Referential Structures and Reflection

In some recent historical films, the soundtrack fosters a specific mode of reception that I refer to as 'reflective listening.' Fundamentally, reflective listening is similar to what Michel Chion calls 'semantic listening'[42] in that it arouses spectators' interest in decoding the film sound as if it were a signal. However, reflective listening goes further: it creates connections and associations and develops interpretations. In order to specify more precisely which soundtrack techniques are required to achieve this, I will show how it not only molds the 'sonic histosphere' in individual sequences, but is also capable of creating connections and references that cut across sequences and go beyond linear production of meaning.

In *Waltz with Bashir*, Ari stops at the roadside close to the beach to reflect on the traumatizing events he recalled while driving in the rain. When he gets out of the car and stands on the promenade the texture of the music becomes thicker. The harmony of the sustained bass tones is significantly expanded on and embellished by a repetitive melody on solo violin. The enigmatic playing of the violin, which stands out far more prominently than the rest of the music, clearly delineates the sequence from the film's plot and assigns it a meta-level function. Memories of specific events emerge piecemeal out of the symbolic, imaginary visions. The urgent music creates a sense of unease and makes the spectator want to learn more about the events of the Lebanon War. This piece, Max Richter's "The Haunted Ocean," is used repeatedly from that point on. In memory and dream sequences throughout the film, it connects the filmic present to subjective fragments of memory. Not only the piece of music but the whole sequence is used repeatedly during Ari's conversation with two other friends, at first only partially, then in its full length. The repetition gives spectators the opportunity to reflect while simultaneously laying bare the film's use of repetition. The sequences are framed by information from the people Ari interviews and the memories evoked by this information. Through this process, the background of the enigmatic images is gradually revealed: for example, the fact that Ari himself fired the flares that immerse the scene in a surreal yellow light while the Christian Phalange militia were carrying out the massacre. The information given by Ari's former war comrades is compared with fragments of memory and assembled into a narrative. The repetitive structure of the piece of music, to which additional elements

---

42   Chion, *Audio-Vision* 28.

such as a solo violin are gradually added, reflects this process of decoding and reassembling.

Multiple sequences in *Waltz with Bashir* can be reciprocally linked through the repeated use of a piece of music like the haunted ocean theme and thus make reference to the constructed nature of the filmic illusion. On this basis, a space for reflection is then created in which the sequences are compared with and related to each other. Another example shows how the repeated use of a piece of music can also be used to question the veracity of memories. While Ari's friend Ori (speaking off-screen) describes a memory experiment that is visualized on-screen, Johann Sebastian Bach's Harpsichord Concerto No. 5 in F minor plays. In the experiment, the test subjects were shown photos from their childhood, one of which (a visit to an amusement park) was a fake. But most of the subjects nonetheless regarded the picture as real and with a little prompting could remember visiting the amusement park too. The soothing classical music—in combination with electrical sound effects and the stalls and visitors that are added to the image one after the other—creates the impression of an experimental setup. This effect is also significant in the second sequence where the piece is used. In another memory sequence, when a boy in an orchard fires an RPG at an Israeli troop transport, Bach plays once again. The sequence unfolds in slow motion, giving the spectator space to reflect. Only when the Israeli soldiers shoot down the boy in a hail of gunfire does the representation of time return to normal. The repeated use of Bach and the manipulation of time make the situation in the orchard seem like an experimental setup too, bringing the reliability of apparent memories into question. It marks and connects the protagonist's enigmatic fragments of memory as a mind map and shows how memories of concrete events are distilled from the flow of imaginary thoughts. Hence, the reflective linking of different sequences by means of film music can be either unifying or deconstructive in terms of the depiction of historical events. While the use of reminiscence triggers enhances the closeness of the viewer to the subject of the film by activating embodied memories, the mode of reflective listening enables a reflective reading, which requires a certain distance from the film.

Conclusion

Film music enables historical experience through film experience. Against the methodological background of Vivian Sobchack's phenomenology of film experience, this assumption leads to the following results: while seeing/hearing is an act performed by both the film and the viewer, historical films build a space-time structure that models a historical world and opens it up to embodied experience. In the 'histosphere,' the spectator's perceptions oscillate between a supposedly objective external view of a historical world and the subjective experiences of the film and its characters in this world. Film music—inseparably merged with the film images—is crucial for this double perception by determining the mood of film sequences. It elicits emotional reactions to historical processes, events, and situations. As I showed in the analysis of selected sequences of *Waltz with Bashir*, film music is able to create specific atmospheres to evoke both a physical and emotional resonance in the viewer. The resulting mood shapes the viewer's understanding and experience of the depicted past. Moreover, by involving the viewer in reenacted historical events and making them physically experienceable, the film can potentially trigger embodied memories and project them onto the historical content. In doing so, the world of the film is mixed with auditory elements that refer to everyday experiences, such as media consumption. In an experiential mode of viewing/hearing, these 'reminiscence triggers' connect the world of the film to the viewer's own embodied memories and historical references. The same goes for a specific mode of reception that I refer to as 'reflective listening.' Using the example of the repeated use of a piece of music in *Waltz with Bashir*, I have shown that the viewer understands the soundtrack as a signal which creates connections and associations. Hence, reminiscence triggers and reflective listening extend the cinematic experience of a historical world by a 'mise-en-histoire;' a strategy of contextualizing and historicizing. It is precisely this organic combination of embodied experience, mood, semiotics, and signification that makes music in historical film such a powerful agent for the creation of meaning.

Bibliography (last accessed 16 April 2020)

Altman, Rick, ed. *Sound Theory, Sound Practice*. New York: Routledge, 1992.
Ankersmit, Frank. *Die historische Erfahrung*. Berlin: Matthes and Seitz, 2012.
Balázs, Béla. *Der Geist des Films*. Frankfurt: Suhrkamp, 2001 (1930).
Balázs, Béla. *Der Film: Werden und Wesen einer neuen Kunst*. Wien: Globus, 1961.
Butzmann, Frieder, and Jean Martin. *Filmgeräusch: Wahrnehmungsfelder eines Mediums*. Hofheim: Wolke, 2012.

Chion, Michel. *La voix au cinema*. Paris: Cahiers du cinema/Éditions de l'Étoile, 1982.

Chion, Michel. *Le son au cinema*. Paris: Cahiers du cinema/Éditions de l'Étoile, 1985.

Chion, Michel. *Audio-Vision: Sound on Screen*. New York: Columbia Univ. Press, 1994.

Flückiger, Barbara. *Sound Design: Die virtuelle Klangwelt des Films*. Marburg: Schüren, 2012.

Greiner, Rasmus. *Histospheres: Zur Theorie und Praxis des Geschichtsfilms*. Berlin: Bertz and Fischer, 2020.

Hasebrink, Felix. "Das gezeichnete Gedächtnis: Erinnerung, Trauma und Animation in Waltz with Bashir." *FFK Journal* (2017): 17–32. http://www.ffk-journal.de/?journal=ffk-journal&page=article&op=view&path%5B%5D=3

Huizinga, Johan. *Verzamelde werken: 2. Nederland*. Haarlem: Tjeenk Willink, 1950.

Kamensky, Volko, and Julian Rohrhuber, eds. *Ton: Texte zur Akustik im Dokumentarfilm*. Berlin: Vorwerk 8, 2013.

Kappelhoff, Hermann, and Jan-Hendrik Bakels. "Das Zuschauergefühl: Möglichkeiten qualitativer Medienanalyse." *Zeitschrift für Medienwissenschaft* 5, 2 (2011): 78–96. DOI: 10.25969/mediarep/2623

Kreuziger-Herr, Annette, and Rüdiger Jantzen. "Mittelalter in Hollywoods Filmmusik: Miklós Rózsa, Ivanhoe und die Suche nach dem Authentischen." *Geschichte – Musik – Film*. Ed. Christoph Henzel. Würzburg: Königshausen and Neumann, 2010. 31–58.

Langkjær, Birger. "Der hörende Zuschauer: Über Musik, Perzeption und Gefühle in der audiovisuellen Fiktion." *montage AV* 9, 1 (2000): 97–124. DOI: 10.25969/mediarep/70

Meyer, Stephen C. *Epic Sound: Music in Postwar Hollywood Biblical Films*. Bloomington: Indiana Univ. Press, 2015.

Münsterberg, Hugo. *Grundzüge der Psychotechnik*. Leipzig: Barth, 1914.

Nietzsche, Friedrich. *Menschliches, Allzumenschliches: Ein Buch für freie Geister*. Frankfurt am Main: Insel, 2000 (1878).

Paul, Gerhard, and Ralph Schock, eds. *Der Sound des Jahrhunderts: Geräusche, Töne, Stimmen 1889 bis heute*. Bonn: BpB, 2013.

Ricoeur, Paul. *Zeit und Erzählung: Band I: Zeit und historische Erzählung*. München: Fink, 2007.

Sobchack, Vivian. *The Address of the Eye: A Phenomenology of Film Experience*. Princeton: Princeton Univ. Press, 1992.

Tollebeek, Jo, and Tom Verschaffel. *De vreugden van Houssaye: Apologie van de historische interesse*. Amsterdam: Wereldbibliotheek, 1992.

Online Sources (last accessed 16 April 2020)

Greiner, Rasmus. "Sonic Histospheres: Sound Design and History." *Research in Film and History* (2018). https://film-history.org/approaches/sonic-histospheres
Pauleit, Winfried, Rasmus Greiner and Mattias Frey. "Audio History of Film." *Research in Film and History* (2018). https://film-history.org/approaches/1418

Audiovisual Sources

Folman, Ari (Director). *Waltz with Bashir* (2008).
LeRoy, Mervyn, and Anthony Mann (Directors). *Quo Vadis* (1951).

"I've never understood the passion for Schubert's sentimental Viennese shit"—Using Metadata to Capture the Contexts of Film Music

Elias Berner (University of Music and Performing Arts Vienna)

Theoretical Background and the Issue of Digital Methods

In her 2001 publication *Hearing Film: Tracking Identification in Contemporary Hollywood Cinema*, Anahid Kassabian called for a "major shift in the studies of film," one which would consider music the main factor in identification processes in film.[1] These processes can, of course, just be read as part of an interaction with the political and social context of a given film and its topics. She understands film music as a semiotic system that—contrary to language—does not transmit meaning explicitly but transmits ideology in a codified manner.[2] Music in film emotionally binds its audience to certain messages, which are then experienced on a personal or private level while their political-ideological content is concealed. Part of Kassabian's approach to the analysis of film music is to reveal this content. In a 2016 article, Lauren Anderson criticized Kassabian, among other scholars with a similar approach, for relying heavily on generalized "figures of the audience," upon whom the music imposes a certain effect, while neglecting the highly differentiated and individual reactions that viewers and listeners tend to have while watching a film.[3] Crucial to Anderson's critique is the complaint that scholars like Kassabian divide the audience into two groups, one able to decode music correctly based on its members' 'knowledge' about a certain piece of music and another group

---

1   Kassabian, *Hearing Film* 2.
2   Ibid. 26. Kassabian refers to one of the main developers of social semiotics, Theo van Leeuwen, who described how non-emotional meaning is experienced emotionally, for instance in the case of advertisements.
3   Anderson, "Beyond Figures of the Audience" 39.

that—without the necessary insights into the music and its history—remains at the mercy of the abovementioned effects.[4] Anderson makes a valid point when she argues that this division relies on a very narrow understanding of musical 'knowledge.' For instance, Jeff Smith makes use of a composer's biographical information to interpret intertextual meaning—but this is information that most viewers probably don't have.[5] But in Kassabian's understanding of film music as social code, the biographical information alone would not be of interest without being socially and politically contextualized in reference to the topics and meanings projected onto the film. And even then, a composer's biography, or more precisely the various narratives in which it is told, is just one among many references that can be decoded into intertextual meaning. From the perspective of media and film music history, far more interesting is the information (to avoid the term 'knowledge') about how a certain piece of music, a melody, a rhythm, a musical style, or even simply a characteristic sound or timbre has been used in other films and other audiovisual media contexts. Neither 'the audience' nor a scholar is able to 'know' in which media contexts he or she has heard a certain piece of music or style before. Nevertheless, there is probably nothing wrong in assuming that these 'media experiences' with music and its characteristic conventions influence the perception of film music in a given scene and thus have to be acknowledged in an analysis. The decisive factor here is not whether a particular piece or style was actually heard by a specific member of the audience in all these contexts but whether a particular convention can be identified from its use in these different media contexts.

The broad question I would like to raise here is: To what extent can digitalization, the relatively easy accessibility of films on online platforms, countless movie databases with filmographic information etc., help us trace the multilayered ways in which, for instance, a certain piece of music is used in film and media history? In the *Telling Sounds* project we are developing research software for capturing and visualizing the interaction of music and its contexts across different audio and audiovisual documents and across different points in time through the use of metadata. The precise question considered in this article is how metadata must be designed in order to enable an examination of the portrayal of Nazi war criminals in relation to classical music in feature films. In other words: how can metadata be used to capture the

---

4   Ibid. 35.
5   Ibid. 26.

contexts of film music? Thus, these metadata cannot concern only the music or other filmographic information available on film databases but must be drawn from an analysis.

Scene Analysis

Our starting point will be an analysis of a scene from the HBO/BBC TV-production *Conspiracy*, which depicts the 1942 Wannsee Conference, where the systematic extermination of the European Jews was reportedly planned and organized. We will consider the film's last scene, when the Adagio of Schubert's Quintet C major D 956 is diegetically played on a record player.[6]

The conference is over, most of the participants have already left and the staff is beginning to clean up. Eichmann, who organized the conference, puts on a record which was given to him in a previous scene by Heydrich, who commented: "This will tear your heart out!"[7] When the music starts the camera shows a medium close-up shot of Eichmann lighting a cigarette next to the phonograph. This shot is cut by another medium close-up: an elderly butler in front of a piano, filmed from the back. Apparently moved by the music, he stops what he is doing. The camera cuts back to Eichmann. After he exhales the smoke, he asks the butler: "Does it tear your heart out?" In the cross-cut the butler answers: "Beautiful, sir!" Now Eichmann begins to shake his head gently before stating: "I've never understood the passion for Schubert's sentimental Viennese shit!" He then turns around and walks through the rooms of the villa, which is shown in a long shot. With several cuts and shot changes the camera follows Eichmann on his way to the exit. The A part of the Adagio (in E major) is still playing, and the dynamics and polyphonic structure of the music slightly intensifies. After Eichmann leaves the building and enters his car, the volume of the music is lowered and a voiceover begins to inform the audience of Heydrich's crimes and his assassination in 1942, after which Eichmann felt the duty to finalize the plans made at the conference. The film cuts to Heydrich as he gets on a plane to leave Berlin for Prague. During a closing cadence in the music, its volume is raised back to its initial level and the staff is again shown cleaning up the villa. As the dominant B major chord is modulated to B minor, which in conjunction with a crescendo creates a climatic

---

6   Pierson, *Conspiracy*: 01:36:20–01:47:18.
7   Ibid.: 01:31:02.

effect, the scenes of the cleanup are intersected with black and white still images of the various participants of the conference with text descriptions of how each of them ended up after the war. Importantly, the photo stills—stylized to look like historical photographs—show the actors, not the historical people who were portrayed. With the last chord of the A part of the Adagio, a long shot of the now tidied-up conference room is shown and the butler to whom Eichmann had talked is switching off the lights. The end credits are accompanied by the B part.

Figure 1: The Analysis described with Metadata.

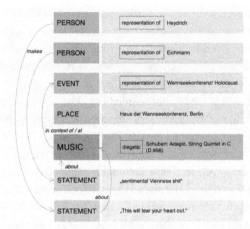

In the vertical perspective (in terms of the relation of the visual with the auditive) the music aligns itself with the 19th-century-style architecture of the villa's interior. The interaction of the images with the music in the horizontal perspective reveals how this final sequence is structured through Schubert's music. The beginning cut sequence between the medium close-ups of Eichmann and the butler follows the question-and-answer form of the motif played by the violin in the first measure. The rest of the A part of the Adagio relies on harmonic variations of this motif. Because of the structuring force of the music, all the characters in the sequence, even Eichmann, seem somehow controlled by the music. All the more irritating and surprising is Eichmann's cynical and pejorative comment in this context. Prior to the comment, the way he lights and then smokes his cigarette while the first bars of the Adagio play could easily lead one to interpret that he is enjoying the music. But the music's mood and style as well as Eichmann's vulgar comment must be read in the context of what had happened previously—in the narrative of the film—and afterwards, in historical reality. The music's melancholic mood may remind the audience of the terrible tragedy that followed. This aspect—the declaration of a contemporary perspective on the event—is absent in the staging, not to say in the intended reconstruction, of the conference up until this point in the film. The music creates a contrast with both the businesslike style of the conference, where the logistics of mass murder are debated, and the dry, documentary style of the film as a whole. Thus, the music can be interpreted as a statement made by the filmmakers at the conclusion of the film and as an attempt to depart from their (up until this point) 'objective' and neutral point of view on the event. Eichmann's comment on the music is less surprising when we consider his image beyond the scope of this movie. Based on Hanna Arendt's—controversial—concept of the 'banality of evil,' which she used to explain Eichmann's actions while observing his trial in Jerusalem in the 1960s, Eichmann is often characterized as an 'emotionless' petit-bourgeois bureaucrat perpetrator (without much intrinsic ideological, that is, antisemitic, motivation).[8] In the context of *Conspiracy*, these characteristics also serve to differentiate Eichmann from Heydrich, while at the same time describing their relationship: as already mentioned above, Heydrich in a previous scene enthusiastically recommends the record to Eichmann, whose later reaction to the music suggests a certain amount of aggression towards his superior Heydrich (which the obsequious Eichmann would never dare to express in the latter's presence), probably born out of his sense of inferiority in the face of Heydrich's upper-class art music ancestry. Heydrich's well documented affiliation with the upper class is symbolized not only by his love for the music of Schubert, but also by the building where the conference takes place—a 19th-century villa chosen by Heydrich, where he plans to live after the war. These two very different characterizations of Nazi war criminals are mediated through their contrary comments on partly diegetic classical music. The questions to ask are: To what extent do these characterizations appear as stereotypes in other films? Can they be found in similar configurations and is similar music used with either of these two perpetrator types? In order to

---

8   Arendt, *Eichmann in Jerusalem*. This view, of course, is subject of an ongoing debate. Cf. *inter alia* Lozowick, *Hitler's Bureaucrats*.

describe such a configuration with metadata, the following tags can be annotated in their respective categories and related to each other.

Single tags can be used for queries in online movie databases. As a first step I want to start with the tag 'PERSON' Heydrich and Eichmann to find out in which other films they appear and possibly examine if they are somehow related in these films to classical music in general, to Schubert more specifically, and even precisely, to the Adagio.

Heydrich and Classical Music in Film

Heydrich is a rather prominent character in feature films, TV series and documentaries about the holocaust. IMDb lists 31 productions where his name appears in the plotline. Most of the feature films deal with Heydrich's assassination in 1942. The oldest are the American films *Hitler's Mad Men* and *Hangmen Also Die*. For the latter Hanns Eisler wrote an original score, which he also referred to in *Komposition für den Film*, written together with Theodor W. Adorno and published in 1947. His scoring of Heydrich's death is described as a model of how to musically depict the barbarism of national socialism and calls for the avoidance of any heroism in the music:

> "Heydrich is a hangman, which makes the musical formulation a political issue; a German fascist could try to transform this criminal into a hero by means of sad, heroic music. [...] The music must bring the point harshly across. The dramatic solution: an association with the death of a rat. A brightly strident, almost elegant sequence, in a very high register, an expression of the colloquial German saying: wheezing [lit. whistling] from the last hole."[9]

Adorno and Eisler's concern about the effects of "sad heroic music" may be historically contextualized by considering the way Heydrich's death and subsequent funeral was staged by National Socialist propaganda in a German

---

9   "Heydrich ist der Henker, das macht die Formulierung der Musik zu einem Politikum: ein deutscher Faschist könnte durch traurige heroische Musik den Verbrecher in einen Helden zu verwandeln trachten. [...] Die Musik muss Bedeutungsakzente durch Rohheit setzen. Die dramaturgische Lösung wird angezeigt durch die Assoziation: Tod einer Ratte. Brilliant kreischende Sequenz, fast elegant, sehr hoch gesetzt, eine Auslegung der Redensart: aus dem letzten Loch pfeifend." (To 'whistle through the last hole' means to be on one's last legs.) Adorno and Eisler, *Komposition für den Film* 32.

newsreel. The newsreel shows a montage: the transfer of Heydrich's coffin from Prague to Berlin and the saluting Hitler in front of thousands of spectators to the (non-diegetic) sound of "Siegfried's Funeral March" from Wagner's *Götterdämmerung*.[10]

However, in postwar films things went a bit differently than Adorno and Eisler had postulated. Probably because of Heydrich's biographical background—he was the elder son of opera singer and composer Richard Bruno Heydrich, and it is said that he was an ambitious violin player—he was, in films after the end of the 2nd World War, portrayed as lover of (German) 'classical music.' In the earlier postwar productions Wagner was predominantly used for this purpose, as for example in the German *Canaris* from 1954. Also, more than 20 years later in the 1978 American TV Series *Holocaust*, Heydrich can be seen sipping a glass of red wine and listening to a record of "Siegfried's Funeral March" while he relaxes in his office after the 1938 Kristallnacht. The enjoyment of 'classical music' by Nazi war criminals while they are committing atrocities would become a *topos* in many films about the Holocaust from the seventies onwards. Concentration camp, deportation, and gas chamber scenes play a special role in this context. In the aforementioned *Holocaust* TV series, in the 1980s film *Playing for Time* (about the Auschwitz female camp orchestra), in the 1988 British TV film *Escape from Sobibor*, and even in *The Grey Zone* from 2001, scenes of this kind make diegetic use of very popular pieces of music by Johann Strauss or W. A. Mozart. In their decidedly happy mood—which is intended to contrast harshly with the camps and which may be interpreted as an ironic comment on the music's status—they differ markedly from the music that is associated with Heydrich, which generally has a darker and sterner character. It marks not only his educated upper-class background but at the same time characterizes him as a highly intelligent genius-like psychopath.[11] In more recent films such as *Lidice* (2011), *Operation Anthropoid* (2016), and *The Man with the Iron Heart* (2018), Heydrich can be seen (and heard) as a performer of mostly baroque violin pieces by G. F. Händel and J. S. Bach. Of course, each of these examples may be subjected to an in-depth analysis. It is however sufficient for the purposes of this paper to show that Heydrich is generally portrayed in film as a lover of classical

---

10   *Die Deutsche Wochenschau Nr. 615.* https://youtu.be/o9P17nUoGoQ
11   On the cliched use of classical, especially German classical music in Hollywood film to characterize psychopath villains: Hentschel, "Der Tod ist ein Meister aus Deutschland;" Yang, "Für Elise circa 2000" 6.

music. Heydrich's love of Schubert in *Conspiracy*, which I also interpret as a demarcation from Eichmann, fits a long-lasting convention of Heydrich portrayals in film. Nonetheless, Schubert does not appear in any previous or later films in connection with Heydrich. There are two questions we must ask next in order to further contextualize the configuration observed in the scene in *Conspiracy*. First, how is Eichmann portrayed in other films and what role does music play in them? Second, how does Schubert's music in general appear in films about the Holocaust, and how—if at all— is the Adagio of D 956 used in particular?

Eichmann

Films about Eichmann are predominantly set in the postwar period and either tell the story of how the Mossad kidnapped and arrested Eichmann in Buenos Aires in 1960, or they deal with his later public trial in Jerusalem, which was itself an historic media event. On the visual level, of course, these films mirror Eichmann's appearance during the trial: a middle-aged man wearing horn-rimmed glasses and somehow fitting the image of an unfeeling bureaucrat. Nevertheless, in depictions of past events in these films as well as in other films that do not exclusively focus on Eichmann (like *Conspiracy*), he can be seen depicted as a still-young SS officer. In comparison to Heydrich, his characterization in various films is a bit more diverse and demands a bit more analysis.

Like Heydrich, Eichmann also appears in the popular TV Series *Holocaust*, and it is worth taking a look (and listen) to the way he is introduced at the end of the first episode with the help of diegetic music:[12] One of the main (fictional) characters of the series, the young SS careerist Erik Dorf goes to Vienna with his wife and children to visit Eichmann, for whom he would work in the future. They meet in the Vienna Prater. The place (as well as Eichmann) is established with a detail shot of a turning carousel, which then zooms out into a long shot and cuts to a table talk between Eichmann and Dorf and his family. Eichmann kindly invites the children for lemonade and, later, a ride on the carousel because, of course, he wants the wife and children to leave the table in order to discuss 'business' privately with Dorf. However, when we

---

12   Chomsky, *Holocaust*: 01:14:49–01:19:19.

see the rotating carousel a version of the "Loreleilied" is played on a mechanical street organ. Its sound is slightly distorted and its individual note pitches quite unstable, which creates a kind of 'dirty' and menacing effect. This effect is even clearer when put in context with the previous scene: The Jewish Weiss family has to leave their apartment in Berlin. Mother and daughter sing the "Loreleilied" together while the son looks for his grandparents and finds them lying dead in their bed, holding hands. They committed suicide to escape the fate that awaits them. The calm singing voices of mother and daughter in the background emphasize this moment of peace and sorrow. With the hard cut from the dead grandparents in Berlin to the rotating carousel in Vienna, the song's melody continues but is played much faster, with a drastically different timbre that significantly changes its character. The mechanical street organ version seems like a caricature and mockery of the previous vocal duet. It sets the stage for Eichmann, whose appearance, in contrast to the image of the dead grandparents, is bizarre and perhaps even clownish, albeit not in a comedic, but a horrific manner. The audibly mechanical playing style of the street organ version may also hint at the industrial character of the so-called 'final solution,' for whose logistics Eichmann is held responsible. As in *Conspiracy*, Eichmann is set in opposition to (19th-century) bourgeois culture, which in *Holocaust* is repeatedly associated with the family Weiss, often via diegetic music. But Eichmann's bizarre 'clownish'—yet somehow tricky—brand of evil also differs from the more straightforward and sophisticated 'evil' depiction of Heydrich shaped by the dark tone of "Siegfried's Funeral." Thus, a contrast between the two famous war criminals can also be found in *Holocaust*, although unlike *Conspiracy* it does not culminate in one scene via a verbal comment on music. Moreover, the characterization of Eichmann in *Conspiracy* is quite different. Looking at other films with depictions of Eichmann proves that in comparison with the conventions of Heydrich's characterization, the use of pieces of 'classical music' in connection with Eichmann is much less homogenous. This may mirror the aforementioned discourse that resulted from Eichmann's appearance and his strategy of defending himself 'as someone who was just following orders' in his 1961 trial. Part of this debate is how to interpret Eichmann's emotionless behavior during the trial when he was confronted with his crimes by means of survivor testimonies and filmed material. Another BBC docudrama, *The Eichmann Show* (2015), which tells the story of the team that filmed the trial, shows precisely these moments by using the original footage of the trial while a fragment of the second movement from Henryk Górecki's Symphony No. 3 *Sorrowful Songs* is non-diegetically played. The music stitches together a montage of footage showing survivor Rivka Yose-lewska in the witness stand, the attorney who interrogates her, Eichmann in the dock (which is a glass box), the horrified reactions of the audience in black and white, short reenactments of some of those moments, filmed from different angles and in color; and most importantly, the reactions of the filmmakers in the control room, among whom one of the camera operators, himself a camp survivor, collapses.[13] Alongside the music on the soundtrack the original recording of Yoselewska's translator can be heard describing executions: she witnessed not only the shooting of her father but of her own infant child, who was torn from her arms. The history of the music's reception, in which it is heavily associated with the Holocaust,[14] the main theme of the lyrics—a mother's loss of her child—and the overall mood of the music all heavily connect it with the perspective of the victim and suggest empathy. This is supported by the synchronization of the narrated traumatic experience with the musical form. Yoselewska's report starts to become personal just as the introduction of strings and harps in the first ten measures is followed by a lower C-sharp minor chord played by the whole orchestra and lasting for several measures. The chord marks precisely the moment the camera operator starts to feel unwell, and on the visual level the original footage of Eichmann is shown for the first time in this sequence. The subsequent entry of the female solo part is synchronized with the moment the witness reveals that she had her baby with her. Eventually, the close-ups of a deadpan Eichmann become more frequent. These seem to be motivated by the audible instructions of the director in the control room, who unsuccessfully tries to detect some sign of emotion in Eichmann's facial expression. Contrast is here created by the impassivity of Eichmann, in contrast to which the sorrowful mood of the non-diegetic music is set; the music seems to express the emotions of the other people involved in the multilayered montage. Due to this contrast, Eichmann's actual 'reaction' may well be apprehended in the same manner as the "Viennese sentimental shit" comment spoken by his fictionalized character in *Conspiracy*.

Decidedly contrary to the bureaucrat image is the characterization of Eichmann in the 2009 feature film *Eichmann*, which makes frequent use of musical compositions. The film stages the interrogation of Eichmann by Avner Less prior to the trial. During the interrogation, Less can prove that

---

13   Williams, *The Eichmann Show*: 00:52:20–00:55:27.
14   Cf. Moore, "Is the Unspeakable Singable?"

Eichmann is lying when he says that he was just following the orders of Himmler and Hitler. The interrogation is interrupted by dramatized flashbacks showing young Eichmann in an SS uniform and without glasses during the war. In the first of these flashbacks, a piece of music is used in manner more reminiscent of the usual characterization of Heydrich. The flashback is triggered by Eichmann's monologue during the interrogation. However, it seemingly only takes place on the visual level. While the off-screen older Eichmann ponders, "and thinking of my role, which seems now so long ago in the past and almost unimportant since it did not succeed, I often ponder the lessons of history."[15] The young, handsome Eichmann is shown on the way to his office. He passes subordinates in the corridor who greet him with the Hitler salute. On the non-diegetic level, the action is accompanied by Bach's *Johannes Passion*. Before Eichmann is shown in his office, historical black-and-white photographs of prisoners on deportation trains and in concentration camps are intercut. In Eichmann's office, the camera follows his actions as he moves his middle finger along the desk to check for dust, while offscreen Eichmann 'comments' that "if five million are leaving through the smoke stacks, the particles come down somewhere."[16] With the first note of the choir after the instrumental intro, Eichmann is shown in profile with a large painting of Hitler in the background. In addition to the musical *fortissimo*, the volume of the music is now also increased significantly. After further intercuts of historic footage, Eichmann is then shown at work at his desk. Files are handed to him by an attractive young secretary. One could argue that the work of a bureaucrat is visually demonstrated, which may fit the cliché of the 'desk criminal.' However, the non-diegetic music shapes the on-screen action as heroic and powerful. This—in addition to his offscreen commentary—implies that Eichmann is anything but penitent regarding his deeds. On the contrary, in the context of Bach's reputation as a genius, the flashback suggests that Eichmann considers the organization of the Holocaust to be his work of art, if not to say 'creation.' A godlike position, which represents Eichmann's narrative perspective, is made particularly evident when the choir comes in during the profile shot of Eichmann standing in front of the painting of Hitler. As the sequence progresses, the polyphonic structure of the music is associated with the meticulous logistics involved in organizing mass murder. Unlike in *Conspiracy*, Eichmann does not comment

---

15   Young, *Eichmann*: 00:23:51.
16   Ibid.: 00:25:35.

on the music, but the music comments on him, displays his perspective and hence does not create a contrast. Although all the examples mentioned here would, according to a popular understanding, be classified under the term 'classical music,' they seem anything but interchangeable. This is equally due to their musical form and their cultural significance, which construct specific meaning in each film context, as I have shown in this analysis. Even if the sequence of cuts and Eichmann's derogatory commentary were adapted to *Johannes Passion*, it could not fulfill the same function in the final scene of *Conspiracy*. The second movement of Górecki's Symphony might fit that scene a bit better, but the far more modern style of the music and the polish lyrics would make it an extremely unlikely candidate for a recommendation by Heydrich, at least according to the cliché displayed in other films. Schubert's Adagio could probably not express trauma in the same way as Górecki's Symphony in *The Eichmann Show's* multilayered montage of witness statements during the trial. But because of the constant repetition of the main motif and the minor modulation, which could be synchronized with the cameraman's visible discomfort, and its melancholy expression, Schubert's Adagio would not be completely out of place. The polyphonic structure and expressive style of the *Johannes Passion* would instead intensify the close-ups of Eichmann in this scene, possibly suggesting that he is holding back his emotions. In any case, the mood of both Schubert's Adagio and the second movement of Górecki's Symphony in the flashback in *The Eichmann Show* would be completely inappropriate for the sequence in *Eichmann* because instead of conveying Eichmann's pride in his work it would instead bring across a feeling of sadness or even remorse, which cannot be linked to Eichmann's narrative perspective. In order to better understand the specific effect of Schubert's Adagio in the original example, its use in other Holocaust-related films will be examined.

Schubert and the Adagio from the C major Quintet in Holocaust Films

An IMDb query allows one to search for all films with soundtracks containing music by Schubert, or only for those films with Schubert's music that are also associated with the keyword "Holocaust." Without looking at individual films in detail, we can assert that Schubert's music (mostly either the so-called *Unfinished* Symphony in B minor or the *Ave Maria*) was used extensively in

American and British films from 1935 on, many of which dealt with the (then ongoing) 2nd World War and the National Socialists. In Germany and Austria, it was mainly used in films before the release of Willi Forst's 1933 Schubert biopic *Leise flehen meine Lieder*, then sporadically in the 1930s, seeming to disappear completely during the war in the 1940s before reappearing in 1953 with the release of the biopic *Franz Schubert*, directed by Walter Kolm-Veltée, an immigrant who went on to found the film academy of the University of Music and Performing Arts Vienna. However, these tendencies should be historically contextualized. Recently, musicologist Lily E. Hirsch wrote an article on the reception of Schubert by the Jüdischer Kulturbund in the 1930s in National Socialist Germany.[17] The disenfranchised minority considered him to be a 'Jewish-friendly' (or at least decidedly non-antisemitic) composer and projected their own marginalized position onto both the melancholy expressed in much of Schubert's music and his clichéd biography of the poor, unhappy, and lonely artist. At the same time, although Schubert was of course included in National Socialist cultural propaganda, his status was much less stable than that of, say, Wagner, Beethoven, or the Austrian Bruckner. For instance, German musicologist Richard Eichenauer wrote (as early) as 1932, that the main difference between the music of Schubert and Beethoven is the former's ceaseless oscillations between major and minor harmonies, which Eichenauer interpreted as a "harmonic weakness" originating in Schubert's supposed lack of "pure" German descent.[18] This may be read as a process of 'othering:' characteristics that are commonly gendered as female are ascribed to Schubert. Such a feminine differentiation of Schubert from Beethoven can be seen far beyond the boundaries of Nazi-era German musicology. An interpretation of Schubert as feminine and thus a deviation from Beethoven can already be found in the 19th-century essays of Robert Schumann.[19] This trend persisted in influential works by Adorno, Dahlhaus and McClary in in the second half of the 20th century, as Scott Burnham pointed out.[20] But how is all this reflected in the filmic use of this music?

Beethoven's music has been continuously used since the earliest holocaust-related films: *The Diary of Anne Frank* (1959) and *Judgement at Nuremberg* (1961), later on in *Band of Brothers* (2001, produced by Steven Spielberg).

---

17   Hirsch, "The Berlin 'Jüdischer Kulturbund' and the 'After-Life' of Franz Schubert" 469–507.
18   Eichenauer, *Musik und Rasse* 214–16.
19   Messing, *Schubert in the European Imagination* 3–4.
20   Burnham, *Beethoven Hero* 155.

Schubert's music was often heard in British and American blockbuster war movies during—and shortly after—the war, but since the 1990s his music has been used in several TV series and European art house films with (generally) more limited budgets. However, in *Taking Sides*, a film dealing with Wilhelm Furtwängler's denazification, the Adagio of the Quintet is used and also functions as 'the other' in contrast to Beethoven's music, which dominates the soundtrack. A brief analysis of the scene in *Taking Sides* in which the Quintet appears—in regard to its narrative and dramaturgical position—may reveal a connection to the Holocaust and, if not to Eichmann himself, than to the stereotype of a narrow-minded, bureaucratic, heartless Nazi perpetrator.

In the scene, the Adagio is performed in a ruined church in occupied, or rather, liberated Berlin in the year 1946.[21] Among the audience members are David Wills, a German-Jewish immigrant who has served in the US Army, and Emmi Straube, the daughter of a German resistance fighter involved in the attempted assassination of Hitler by Stauffenberg in 1944. The two are on their first date. Both work for Lt. Steve Arnold, a former insurance dealer who also fought against Germany in the war and now has the task of searching for evidence of Furtwängler's involvement with National Socialist politics. After the music plays for a few bars, it turns out that Wilhelm Furtwängler, who is currently not allowed to work as a conductor, is also sitting in the audience and listening to the music—deeply moved, of course. The music in this 'new' context has multiple layers of meaning, most of which can be connected to our initial example of Eichmann and the Wannsee Conference. The first layer, the connection of Schubert with the Holocaust and Jewish identity, which we have already contextualized historically, operates via the character of David Wills, who chooses the Schubert concert for his first date with Emmi, as we learn in the previous scene. Directly beforehand, we see the only scene of the film in which David confronts the Holocaust and the loss of his parents and other relatives: he stumbles through the ruins of a former synagogue and places a stone on the podium. That scene is accompanied by various noises, the sound aesthetic of which brings to mind Luigi Nono's *Ricorda cosa ti hanno fatto in Auschwitz*.

As a second layer, Schubert's music serves as a symbol of Wills and Straube's shared background: their 19th century German bourgeois education, hinted at elsewhere in the film through dialogue. The Adagio serves the function of opening or intensifying an additional side narrative: the

---

21   Szabó, *Taking Sides*: 00:45:21–00:47:24.

love story between the Jewish Wills and the German Straube, signifying reconciliation in the next generation. At the same time, in regard to the main plot, this scene marks a definite turning point; both Straube and Wills—and with them perhaps we the audience—are clearly 'taking sides;' Furtwängler's side against their boss Arnold's.

On the visual level, the Adagio is introduced with close-ups of women: First, Emmi Straube, still sitting in the office and touching her neck, flattered by David's invitation, then Emmi again, sitting next to David in the audience; then the female cellist on stage, who is roughly the same age as Emmi. This is even more remarkable considering that the film was up until this point completely dominated by male protagonists. On the one hand, this can be contextualized with the aforementioned *topos* of Schubert as a feminine variant of Beethoven. On the other hand, it is also a convention established in the scores of 1940s Hollywood melodramas that emotionalism and empathy expressed through music tends to be reserved for female characters as a demarcation from the rationally focused male protagonists.[22] As the music swells in the fourth measure, the camera zooms in to a close-up of Furtwängler. Close-ups of Furtwängler dominate the rest of the performance. Through this visual strategy, the diegetic music's mood can be related to Furtwängler's inner life. The whole scene mirrors the film's opening sequence, which shows Furtwängler actively conducting Beethoven's Symphony No. 5 in a church in wartime Berlin. In our mirrored scene, after the war, Beethoven has turned into Schubert, the church into ruins, and the active, powerful genius conductor into the passive, obviously sad and weak Furtwängler, who has been downgraded to a 'regular' audience member while nonetheless remaining just as obsessed with the music. Based on the already mentioned relationship between Beethoven and Schubert in music history and the visual strategy used, this transition can be interpreted as a form of 'othering' Furtwängler, showing his weak and gentle side, marking him as a victim. This becomes even clearer when we include the connection to the Holocaust described in our analysis of the 'first layer.' Through this scene—or more precisely, Schubert's music—a highly problematic shift of the status of victim takes place, shifted from the Jews mourned in the previous scene onto Furtwängler. Besides Jewishness and femininity, we can find a third layer of meaning, which concerns the historical background of the piece of music itself and also fits Furtwängler's status as victim. Understood as typical early 19th-century Biedermeier 'Hausmusik,' Schubert's music

---

22   Laing, *The Gendered Score*.

could also be interpreted as a shelter and, at the same time, outlet in times of massive surveillance and censorship in Metternich's police state. If we want to project the music's historical and political context onto Furtwängler's situation in this scene, the monitoring enemies are, of course, not so much the National Socialists, but the Allied troops, symbolized on the visual level by the spotlight held by an army soldier. This again references the opening scene: Furtwängler's performance gets interrupted by an Allied air raid announced by searchlights moving through the church's interior during the performance.

This enemy is personified in the character of Steve Arnold. Quite tellingly, he is excluded from this scene because he will not 'take the side' of Furtwängler. He would never go to a concert like this one. (He prefers Glenn Miller, whose music has a bodily effect on him.) Thus he—in contrast to David and Emmi—is unimpressed by Furtwängler and his musical achievements. Whenever the mystic power of music or Furtwängler's genius is mentioned by others, he reacts either cynically or even in a furiously pejorative manner. This stance towards music, or more precisely, 'art music,' reminds us of Eichmann's reaction to Schubert's music in *Conspiracy*. Looking at the analyses of the two scenes, we could go as far as interpreting that Steve Arnold in *Taking Sides* and Eichmann in *Conspiracy* are quite similarly characterized, with music playing a crucial role. A review of the film in the *New York Times* seems to support this interpretation:

> "'Hitler's bandleader,' he [Arnold] reviles him [Furtwängler] with the same kind of obscene language that Nazi officers in the Gestapo used to address Jews in less-than-human terms."[23]

Apart from a certain similarity between the characterizations of Eichmann and Arnold, 'Jewishness' and '19th-century bourgeoisie' (both of which play a role in the history of Schubert's reception) are relevant topics for analyzing the two scenes. The link to femininity as a strategy of 'othering' in *Taking Sides* is not, at first glance, traceable in *Conspiracy*. Projecting this strategy of 'othering' onto the characterization of Heydrich would lead to incorrect conclusions, which becomes clear when contextualized with Heydrich's musical characterizations in other films. Female characters are more or less completely absent in *Conspiracy*, along with any signs of empathy or emotionality, traits that are

---

23   Holden, "He Conducted the Orchestra for Hitler." https://www.nytimes.com/2003/0 9/05/movies/film-review-he-conducted-orchestra-for-hitler-now-he-s-making-nazi-hunter-s-day.html

often associated with, or even restricted to, femininity in film history. Thus, the appearance of the Adagio at the end of the movie can be interpreted as an attempt to compensate for this lack of 'feminine' expressions of empathy or emotionality in the rest of the film.

The correlation between the two scenes—of using the same piece of music in the same year—increases the significance of the interpretations made in each of the analyses. The abstracted metadata from the first analysis cannot —at least until now—in any way automatically establish connections to other scenes but can initially only provide the first clues for a search in the various databases. However, the connections to other film scenes established on the basis of these metadata should be documented using the tools of the Semantic Web and Linked Open Data in order to initiate follow-up analyses. The connections made in this way would enrich the significance of the respective analyses and help establish film music conventions in character construction.

Bibliography (last accessed 16 April 2020)

Adorno, Theodor W., and Hanns Eisler. *Komposition für den Film*. Frankfurt am Main: Suhrkamp, 2006 (1947).

Anderson, Lauren. "Beyond Figures of the Audience: Towards a Cultural Understanding of the Film Music Audience." *Music, Sound, and the Moving Image* 10, 1 (Spring 2016): 25–51. DOI: 10.3828/msmi.2016.2

Arendt, Hannah. *Eichmann in Jerusalem: Ein Bericht von der Banalität des Bösen*. München: Piper, 2011.

Burnham, Scott G. *Beethoven Hero*. Princeton: Princeton Univ. Press, 1995.

Eichenauer, Richard. *Musik und Rasse*. München: Lehmann, 1932.

Hentschel, Frank. "'Der Tod ist ein Meister aus Deutschland.' Nationalsozialismus als musikalisch vermittelter Subtext filmischer Gewaltdarstellungen." *Filmmusik: Musiktheorie* 27, 3 (2012): 266–277.

Hirsch, Lily. "The Berlin 'Jüdischer Kulturbund' and the 'After-Life' of Franz Schubert: Musical Appropriation and Identity Politics in Nazi Germany." *The Musical Quarterly* 90, 3–4 (Fall–Winter 2007): 469–507. DOI: 10.1093/musqtl/gdn021

Holden, Stephen. "FILM REVIEW; He Conducted the Orchestra for Hitler, and Now He's Making a Nazi Hunter's Day." *New York Times*, 5 September 2003. https://www.nytimes.com/2003/09/05/movies/film-review-he-con ducted-orchestra-for-hitler-now-he-s-making-nazi-hunter-s-day.html

Kassabian, Anahid. *Hearing Film: Tracking Identifications in Contemporary Hollywood Film Music*. New York: Routledge, 2009.

Laing, Heather. *The Gendered Score: Music in 1940s Melodrama and the Womans
Film*. New York, London: Routledge, 2016.

Lozowick, Yacoov. *Hitler's Bureaucrats: The Nazi Security Police and the Banality of
Evil*. E-Book: Continuum, 2010 (2000).

Messing, Scott. *Schubert in the European Imagination, Vol. 1: The Romantic and
Victorian Eras*. Rochester: Univ. of Rochester Press, 2006.

Moore, Alison. "Is the Unspeakable Singable? The Ethics of Holocaust Representation and the Reception of Górecki's Symphony no. 3." *Journal of
Multidisciplinary International Studies* 8, 1 (August 2011): 1–17. DOI: 10.513
0/portal.v8i1.1888

Yang, Mina. "Für Elise, circa 2000: Postmodern Readings of Beethoven in Popular Contexts." *Popular Music and Society* 29, 1 (February 2006): 1–15. DOI:
10.1080/03007760500142613

Online Sources (last accessed 16 April 2020)

International Movie Database. https://www.imdb.com/

"The Visual Center – Online Film Catalog." *Library Yad Vashem*. https://library.
yadvashem.org/index.html?language=en&mov=1

Audiovisual Sources (last accessed 16 April 2020)

Chomsky, Marvin (Director). *Holocaust*, Episode 4 (1978).

Die Deutsche Wochenschau Nr. 615 (18.06.1942). (= "Reinhard Heydrich Funeral."
YouTube. https://youtu.be/09P17nUoGoQ)

Ellis, Sean (Director). *Anthropoid* (2016).

Forst, Willi (Director). *Leise flehen meine Lieder* (1933).

Gold, Jack (Director). *Escape from Sobibor* (1987).

Jimenez, Cédric (Director). *The Man with the Iron Heart* (2018).

Kramer, Stanley (Director). *Judgment at Nuremberg* (1961).

Lang, Fritz (Director). *Hangmen Also Die* (1943).

Mann, Daniel (Director). *Playing for Time* (1980).

Nelson, Tim Blake (Director). *The Grey Zone* (2001).

Nikolaev, Petr (Director). *Lidice* (2011).

Pierson, Frank (Director). *Conspiracy* (2001).

Sirk, Douglas (Director). *Hitler's Mad Men* (1943).

Spielberg, Steven (Producer). *Band of Brothers* (2001).

Stevens, George (Director). *The Diary of Anne Frank* (1959).

Szabó, István (Director). *Taking Sides* (2001).

Williams, Paul Andrew (Director). *The Eichmann Show* (2015).

Young, Robert (Director). *Eichmann* (2007).

Connecting Research: The Interdisciplinary Potential of Digital Analysis in the Context of A. Kluge's Televisual Corpus

Birgit Haberpeuntner and Klaus Illmayer (University of Vienna and Austrian Academy of Science)

Introduction

As a lawyer, Alexander Kluge worked for the Frankfurt Institute for Social Research. As a filmmaker, he was one of the auteurs of New German Cinema and a driving force behind the *Oberhausener Manifest*.[1] As a prolific author, he wrote countless literary pieces, as well as theoretical and philosophical works, for instance his influential *Geschichte und Eigensinn*, which he co-authored together with the social philosopher Oskar Negt. Over the years, however, the lawyer, filmmaker and author added another encompassing segment to his oeuvre that has of yet received somewhat less attention in critical academic discourse: between 1988-2018, Kluge's production company dctp (Development Company for Television Program) produced about 3.500 episodes for television. And it is this segment of Kluge's work, i.e., the so-called *Kulturmagazine*, or Cultural Magazine Programs, that provide a particularly promising starting point for interdisciplinary digital analysis. In the following, we introduce the *Kulturmagazine* themselves in order to then outline current approaches in researching Kluge's TV production, as well as the reasons why digital analysis may be particularly relevant in this context. Finally, we aim at exploring the potentials as well as challenges of such digital analysis by means of a brief yet illustrative case study in order to conclude with a short prospect for future research.

---

1 Matthias Uecker argues that Kluge has often been referred to as "the intellectual and organizational spiritus rector of New German Cinema". Uecker, "Rohstoffe und Intermedialität" 82. (Translation by B.H.)

Kluge's *Kulturmagazine*: Current State of Research

Kluge's *Kulturmagazine* are of considerable (TV-)historical relevance.[2] From the beginnings of the dual broadcasting system, they were an integral part of Germany's television scene, yet they seemed like foreign objects in the midst of the stereotypical surroundings of commercial broadcasting stations.[3] Their status, however, was secured due to a peculiar stipulation that was part of the North Rhine-Westphalian media law: in the late 1980s, it was decided that commercial broadcasting stations had to offer fixed time slots to independent providers for cultural and investigative journalism, and that the provision of these segments was a prerequisite for commercial broadcasting stations to qualify as generalist channels. Kluge knew to apply for these slots, and he was awarded renewed licenses, over and over again, for 30 years. Due to the abovementioned stipulation, he enjoyed full editorial autonomy as an independent provider for television programs from 1988-2018.[4] Kluge founded his own production company, dctp,[5] in order to develop and produce three long-running formats for the commercial stations RTL and SAT.1: *10 vor 11* ran from 1988-2018; *News & Stories* from 1988-2017; and *Primetime: Spätausgabe* began airing somewhat later, in 1990, and ended in 2008.[6]

These three formats are collectively known as *Kulturmagazine*, and they mostly feature interviews but also more varied, almost TV-essayistic elements and episodes. As Tara Forrest puts it, these segments are constructed "out of a highly diverse collection of raw materials (including photographs, drawings, diagrams, clips from films and documentary footage)."[7] Thematically,

---

2   The *Kulturmagazine* ("Cultural Magazine Programs") have, for instance, been honored with several important awards, such as the Adolf-Grimme-Preis (1992, 1993, 2010) and the Hanns-Joachim-Friedrichs-Preis (2001).

3   Schulte and Siebers, "Vorwort" 7.

4   These time slots thus came with the added advantage that the commercial broadcasting stations' usual expectations with regard to ratings did not apply. Schulte and Siebers, "Vorwort" 7.

5   When it was founded in 1987, the production company was co-owned by the Japanese advertising agency *Dentsu* (37,5%), the newspaper *Spiegel* (12,5%), and the AKS (50%), a consortium of film directors, theaters, publishers and musical institutions. Lutze, "Projekt der Moderne" 18.

6   English translations of the *Magazine*-titles have been provided, for instance, by Elsaesser: he refers to them as *Ten to Eleven*, *News and Stories* (same in German and English), and *Primetime: Late Edition*. Elsaesser, "Stubborn Persistence" 22.

7   Forrest, "Raw Materials" 305.

the *Kulturmagazine* cover a head-spinning range: from 'fake interviews,'[8] to the natural sciences, brain research, space travel and biology; from the arts, music, opera, film and theater, to history, philosophy, sociology, and politics.[9] Apart from this encyclopedic thematic range, however, the *Kulturmagazine* at times also illustrate an intriguingly complex aesthetics, which points at potentialities of the television medium that had not yet been explored.[10] On the one hand, there is Kluge's particular style of leading interviews, which clearly deviates from journalistic standards: he would, for instance, allow the conversations to follow widely sprawling trajectories of association, or he would throw his interview partners off track by means of abrupt, digressive questions.[11] As Forrest explains in the introduction to her English-language reader on Kluge's works: "Kluge's intuitive mode of questioning seeks to animate the conversation partner by igniting the associative and imaginative capacities of his interview partner."[12] On the other hand, some episodes, or segments of episodes, developed into aesthetically complex experiments, such as audiovisual montage essays, combining different kinds of images, texts, and musical traditions. These more experimental segments and episodes tie in with Kluge's late essay films as well as with his literary works. Thus, these

---

8   In these 'fake interviews,' Kluge and his dialogue partners create, in a particularly entertaining way, an alternative reality between documentary material and fiction. While these episodes are often accompanied, or counteracted, by historical materials, his dialogue partners often take on fictional personalities, or 'regular' interview partners depart on fictional trajectories in order to "trade stories" with Kluge. Kluge in Lutze, "Projekt der Moderne" 24. Kluge explains, by reference to his conversations with Heiner Müller: "Up to 20% of these conversations with Heiner Müller are, in this sense, consciously fictional, meaning that we trade stories. He tells me mine, I tell him his, or we weave a topic together, of which we both know: it would not have existed like that historically, but it would have been lovely if it had." Ibid. (Translation by B.H.)

9   Schulte and Siebers, "Vorwort" 8.

10   Ibid., see also Lutze, "Projekt der Moderne" 29–30 or Schulte, "Television and Obstinacy" 319–20.

11   For more on Kluge's way of leading interviews, see Seeßlen, "Interview/Technik." Seeßleen quotes, among other things, an early newspaper article on the *Kulturmagazine*, in which his interview technique is described as follows: "The way in which this man leads his interviews is unique. Kluge's voice is quiet, but its inflection reveals a sense of curiosity. His technique contradicts everything a regular TV journalist would describe as his skill set: Kluge often poses his questions haltingly, he starts to ramble, leaping from one detail to the next. [...] He never gets to the point." Makowsky in Seeßlen, "Interview/Technik" 131. Which, to Seeßlen, *is* the point.

12   Forrest, "Editor's Introduction" 18–19.

Kulturmagazine constitute a reservoir of themes, aesthetic forms and experiments, motives, and figures of contemporary history—which return, often fictionalized, in Kluge's films and texts. At the same time, the TV programs not only cite each other but also and often include passages from Kluge's literary writings, which are thus newly contextualized and enhanced by means of a new, audiovisual mediality. These intermedial references and relations hold together what Thomas Elsaesser calls "the dada *Gesamtkunstwerk* that is [Kluge's] oeuvre."[13]

Kluge's vast and intermedial oeuvre offers itself up to academic research from all kinds of different disciplinary perspectives. During an early phase of critical reception, and roughly until 1990, engagement with Kluge's concept of the public, with his theoretical and philosophical works as well as his films was particularly prevalent; then, his TV projects began to attract attention. Since 2000, Kluge has made a reappearance as a literary figure, thus his books, and the intermedial relations between books, films and TV series moved to the forefront in academic engagement. Yet while Kluge's interdisciplinary work seems to generate diverse perspectives, there is still the challenge of productively and innovatively engaging with the immense scope of his oeuvre. In two international conferences dedicated to Kluge's work, which took place in Berlin (2012) and Liège (2013),[14] the magnitude of available materials was problematized, and it was concluded that computerized assessment methods and procedures would be relevant in the future to generate innovative forms of analysis. Such a digital approach was tested in an exemplary study of Kluge's literary works but has not yet been applied to his TV productions.[15]

Digital Analysis: Why, and How?

As of yet, research into Kluge's TV production is rather limited in scope and methodology; it may be diverse, but it is horizontal. What is more, analogous

---

13   Elsaesser, "Stubborn Persistence" 25.
14   Many of the contributions for these conferences have found their way into the first iteration of the *Alexander Kluge-Jahrbuch* (*Verteilte Nachrichten*, 2014), an annual publication dedicated to collecting new and innovative research into Alexander Kluge's work, which also includes primary texts written by Alexander Kluge, as well as reviews and bibliographies.
15   Martens, "Distant(ly) Reading Alexander Kluge's Distant Writing."

to Kluge's relevance within the framework of 'Autorenfilm,' New German Cinema or auteur film, his TV production is often understood as "auteur TV."[16] For that very reason, Kluge's work, or Kluge himself as the auteur, is usually at the center of critical attention. Digital analysis may assist in breaking with such prevalent patterns by allowing for the formulation of new research questions that have yet remained inexpressible while, at the same time, providing an empirical foundation for the hermeneutic tendencies of Kluge-research. The logic of author-driven engagement with Kluge's TV productions may be overcome, and instead of committing solely to topical or character-driven parameters, digital analysis may assist in providing an innovatively interlinked assessment of topics discussed, forms of expression and materials used (e.g., music, text citations, inter-titles), and of people interviewed. The generation of new research questions is, of course, dependent on the quality and quantity of the available information; but it is also, crucially, dependent on the way in which the data is connected. Digital analysis must thus aim at collecting quantitative and qualitative information in a comprehensive and innovatively structured way while allowing for interoperability with other projects.

In this manner, the material base may be widened significantly, and Kluge's TV production may be opened up for research from other disciplines. New research avenues may, for instance, be explored regarding a comprehensive investigation of historical patterns from various disciplinary as well as interdisciplinary angles. Key historical moments may be made traceable and analyzable in variable settings as they are translated not only into (documentary as well as fictionalized) audiovisual representations but also into films and literary works—and vice versa. Digital analysis may thus also open up aesthetic forms and processes to new and innovative research, and questions regarding inter-medial structures and relations may be reformulated and investigated in new and innovative ways. Digital analysis and the interconnectivity with other data sets may allow for future research into intermediality to reconstruct and analyze the processes of migration, media transfer, and metamorphosis that central historical themes and motives go through.

As for the question of 'how,' an important point to stress in advance is the fact that the digital approach that we aim at does not deal with the primary source material itself, i.e., the audiovisual material, but instead with metadata—and metadata needs to be aggregated. In some cases, basic information

---

16   Lämmle, *Televisuelle Intellektualität* 79.

may be gained from existing descriptions of the primary materials; nevertheless, this process almost always requires manual curation. The task of curating metadata is based on a data model that describes how and to what extent information is collected from the source materials. This data model, in turn, is created based on the main objectives and research questions of a project. For a digital approach to analyze the *Kulturmagazine*, it would seem to be a good starting point to begin by focusing on the people involved and the topics covered. Yet this first step already implies, as mentioned above, curation: to collect this basic data, descriptions must be sifted through, and—in case of missing or lacking description provided—the episodes themselves must be examined, and relevant information extracted on the fly.[17] Building upon this basic set of information, digital methods may then be applied in order to help understand the connections between single episodes or look at the development of certain elements and topics over time, thus providing insights into Kluge's aesthetics as well as his constant confrontation with and transformation of recurring contents. But it also provides us with the foundation for the implementation of more complex parameters that would allow for a more detailed and critical view of these diverse materials.

Going Interdisciplinary in the Digital Realm

One of the first and major tasks for projects in the field of digital humanities[18] is to develop a detailed understanding and a clear picture of the area of study and, therefore, of the kind of data that is produced. Because Alexander Kluge's oeuvre is as encompassing in its extent as it is disparate and widely disseminated through different types of media, this is not an easy task, especially because it is necessary to rely on a complex data model that allows for the interlinking of his materials. Keeping this in mind, it is absolutely feasible that, over time, more and more digital projects on Kluge's work are

---

17   Machine learning or automatic person recognition is often claimed to automatically extract such information, but in practice, it relies on an already trained corpus—which, in turn, also needs curation—and it does not provide for good data quality.

18   Providing a concise and conclusive definition of 'digital humanities' is a long-term discussion in the field itself, as is partly documented on the website https://whatisdigitalhumanities.com/. For a compact overview on the fields that digital humanities can cover, see Schreibman et al., *A New Companion to Digital Humanities*. Or, for more encompassing insights, see Gold et al., *Debates in the Digital Humanities*.

created, such as the one suggested by Martens for the analysis of his liter-ary works.[19] These should, ideally, be interconnectable so that a joint digital ecosystem is created. This ecosystem may, for instance, include written doc-uments that are transcribed and published as digital editions with encodings that highlight references to other projects. There may also be audiovisual ma-terials available on new and/or already existing online platforms, which may be watched and referenced down to single frames. In general, these consider-ations are crucial for every project that engages with the oeuvre of a producer of creative works.

However, digital projects are not only about collecting and interlinking but also about processing the materials and translating them to data.[20] Data, in this context, does not only mean digital copies of works but also, and mainly, contextual information *about* these works. This information may be scaled down to words or even letters, something that linguistic research is inter-ested in. For film studies, on the other hand, it may be relevant to analyze every frame of a movie by Alexander Kluge, which would provide us with in-formation about the inner logic of his aesthetics, e.g., the use of colors, over time. Television studies, on the other hand, may be interested in how the *Kul-turmagazine* changed the program scheduling of TV broadcasting stations in Germany.[21] Each such project would add valuable information for future re-search and provide new perspectives for approaching and analyzing the work of a prolific producer like Kluge. But how do we connect such existing and fu-ture data, and how do we connect it with the research results already available in publications? This question has recently and frequently been discussed in different digital humanities projects as more and more digital resources be-come available.[22] It also hints at the opportunity to improve interdisciplinary approaches as data from different sources and research perspectives are in-creasingly bound together. With regard to Kluge's *Kulturmagazine*, we would thus propose a digital platform that encourages the critical analysis of Kluge's

---

19 Martens, "Distant(ly) Reading Alexander Kluge's Distant Writing."

20 On the importance and consequences of this 'data turn' for scholarship, see Borgman, *Big data, Little data, No data* or Edmond, *Digital Technology and the Practices of Humanities Research*.

21 Other interesting digital methods are collected in Fickers et al., *Audiovisual Data in Dig-ital Humanities*.

22 Based on the mass of data that is currently available, the Europe-wide initiative Time Machine proposes to connect this data in a way that allows for us to navigate the past in a simulation that is created out of these connections, https://www.timemachine.eu/.

works with the help of methods from different fields, such as musicology, film, television, and media studies.

The focus of this platform's general approach to digital analysis stems, to a large part, from the field of digital television studies. In general, however, television studies is not as present in the digital humanities community as some might suspect,[23] which is probably due to a lack of available data, as most TV broadcasting is under copyright. Much of the materials are stored and hosted by the broadcasting companies themselves, so, at least in theory, there is a lot of data available. Also, private recordings must exist on a large scale. As an example, the Österreichische Mediathek, an Austrian archive for sound recordings and videos,[24] holds around 2 million assets of audiovisual heritage, but needs to limit the access to this material due to privacy and copyright issues. Connecting Kluge's *Kulturmagazine* to such a collection would provide valuable contextualization for discourse analysis. Yet, for the reasons outlined above, we do not see a lot of these materials available on digital research platforms.[25] In general, it is currently nearly impossible to build an open platform that offers direct access to audiovisual materials that were once broadcast on television. It is required to get permission from the rights holders, which is usually complicated with regard to television productions, as there are so many people and institutions involved. Yet digital researchers have found their own ways of dealing with this issue: as the difficulties of the current situation persist, the safest way is to link to broadcasting archives, where the audiovisual material may be available and access may be granted, and instead have only the metadata stored and analyzed in a research platform.

With regard to Kluge's *Kulturmagazine*, the circumstances are much more fortunate, as much of the audiovisual materials are available on the website of Kluge's production company, dctp, in the form of video streams.[26] This

---

23   While film studies are certainly present in digital humanities societies—e.g. the working group 'film and video' in the German- speaking digital humanities society, http://dig-hum.de/ag-film-und-video—the same cannot be said of television studies; there are also not many speakers from the field of television studies at digital humanities conferences.

24   *Österreichische Mediathek.* https://www.mediathek.at/

25   A rare exception would be the CLARIAH Media Suite, which was developed in the Netherlands, but this platform only allows access to the videos for research purposes, https://mediasuite.clariah.nl/.

26   *dctp: Das webTV der dctp.* https://www.dctp.tv/

website also serves as a good example, illustrating the difference between the collection and presentation of materials, and a representation of said materials in the form of metadata, the latter of which is necessary for a sustainable research process. One may be inclined to argue that to have the primary materials available on a website would be sufficient. Yet while this is certainly a first step, and it may help in our endeavor to the extent that we can reference it; it does not tell us a lot about the content or the aesthetics of these clips, especially not in a data-driven way. Without additional data collection, we cannot point to what is happening in these videos. What is more, even if there *are* descriptions, the vocabulary is not tailored to research. And even if it would be possible for us to intervene, for instance by encoding topic tags, difficulties would arise from the fact that dctp's aim is not research; their interests and perspectives are fundamentally different. And even research-tailored vocabularies may not be compatible with different research approaches.[27] Does this mean that we need to create a digital platform for every new approach? No, even though, at times, it may be the best available choice.

This leads us to a crucial aspect that digital research platforms need to be aware of: they must anticipate how their data may be used by others, and they must combine these anticipated scenarios with long-standing experience in how to model data and how to prepare a digital platform to enable connection points for other projects. Additionally, such a platform must be constructed in a way that allows for it to deal with different expectations and their effects on the created data. This is a big issue in the field of digital humanities, which may be summarized in one question: how do we establish interoperability between projects so that the data can be functionally and meaningfully connected?[28] Let us try to outline a possible answer in the context of our suggested project.

---

27   On the history and use of vocabularies—that can be also called taxonomies—and the incompatible development of vocabularies based on different research approaches, see Bay-Cheng et al., *Performance and Media*.

28   This is also an aim of 'linked (open) data,' an enhancement of the World Wide Web infrastructure, which not only works through simple links, but also adds semantic information to the references a link points to. For a brief introduction on how to establish meaningful connections, see Hooland et al., *Linked Data for Libraries, Archives and Museums*.

A Platform for the Digital Analysis of Kluge's TV Works

In order to digitally analyze the audiovisual materials that comprise Kluge's *Kulturmagazine*, a digital platform must be ready at hand. This may be a simple database, but in order to store data in a standardized way and to apply sophisticated digital methods that process this data, an ecosystem of tools must be created. There is a general agreement in the field of digital humanities to call such an ecosystem a digital research platform. Such a platform has to deliver on two fronts: first, it must harvest data, and, second, it must do so in a way that allows for this data to be analyzed. Both aspects need to be tailored to the underlying research questions.

Due to the rise of digital humanities in recent years, an increasing number of such platforms are available nowadays, but there is still no one-size-fits-it-all solution (and there probably never will be). Current projects experiment with techniques to connect single platforms on a more generalized level.[29] This is primarily done by applying standardized metadata schemata that data is mapped onto.[30] That way, agreements with regard to the interpretation of information are installed, which enables the sharing of knowledge between different research domains and platforms. This is particularly important for analyzing corpora from an interdisciplinary perspective, which is what we aim at with regard to Kluge's oeuvre. Additionally, an approach that is sensible to metadata sharing gives researchers enough space to express their individual findings while keeping the platform open for further inspection and analysis. A media studies scholar, for instance, may be interested in the audiovisual media practices that are constitutive of the aforementioned 'fake interviews.' Such an analysis, which may focus on camera angles and video editing, could then inform a musicologist, who is interested in how music and sounds are arranged, be it on a narrative, semiotic, or aesthetic level. Instead of letting these different approaches cross-pollinate, separate platforms are often created that only support the respective individual research focus. If both parties agree on the use of a shared metadata scheme, however, they can exchange information without disciplinary restrictions, with the added

---

29   One example is the Horizon 2020 funded project PARTHENOS, which aims at connecting data collections based on a shared ontology. *PARTHENOS Project.* http://www.parthenos-project.eu/

30   One of the most well-known metadata schemas is the Dublin Core Metadata Initiative, which defines a minimal set of often-used data fields, e.g. title and creator. *DCMI.* https://dublincore.org/

benefit of flexible integration of future projects, such as, in our example, the analysis of Kluge's films.

The application of an approach based on shared metadata schemata (or, to be more precise, on shared ontologies[31]) creates the possibility of developing platforms that are tailored to the scope and specific needs of particular research projects. Whereas researchers may rely on handy tools, such as spreadsheet editors, to organize data in an easy and concise way, such solutions are limited, especially when it comes to interlinking the entered information. To give an example, some people who are mentioned in episodes of Kluge's *Kulturmagazine* may have frequently occurring names, e.g. Maria Müller. It is more than likely that different people share this name. For the sake of certain kinds of analysis, e.g., a social network analysis, it is necessary for people to be individually and uniquely identified.[32] The general solution to such a problem is to apply unique identifiers to each person. If there are two different Maria Müllers mentioned in Kluge's televisual corpus, each is given a different identifier, e.g., MM1 and MM2. Such identifiers are necessary in order to create distinct information, which is required for definitive identification and interlinking.

Going one step further, the application of *shared* unique identifiers helps connect data between different data collections. 'MM1' and 'MM2' would only be a project-specific agreement; in another project, identifiers would certainly be handled differently, thus interlinking the identifiers of the two projects would not be easy. Yet if both projects agree to derive their identifiers from a dedicated identity platform, therefore having the same identifier for the same person, it is an easy task to connect such shared information. In order to do so, there are common authority files where a community collects minimal data to identify entities,[33] giving them a common unique identifier. Well-known authority files for people are GND and VIAF, for places GeoNames, and

---

31 On the relations between data models, metadata schemas, ontologies and generally on data in the digital humanities, see Flanders et al., *The Shape of Data in the Digital Humanities*. Although modeling of textual data is at the heart of this book, it provides generally valuable insights into the terminology and practices of data modelling.

32 This is called disambiguation and it is often connected to entity recognition, see as an example Foppiano et al., "entity-fishing: a DARIAH entity recognition and disambiguation service."

33 Entities are data sets that form the basic elements of a data model. Such entities are related to each other, forming an entity-relation-model. In digital humanities projects, entities are often persons, places, dates, or concepts.

for all sorts of different data, researchers may rely on Wikipedia (more precisely, Wikidata or DBpedia).[34] Using spreadsheets to apply mechanisms like unique identifiers may be possible, but the more complex a data model becomes, the more confusing the spreadsheet will get. Thus, it certainly makes sense to rely on platforms, even though their more complex structure requires technicians to take care of implementation and sustainability issues. The most obvious advantages of a platform, however, are, on the one hand, the obligation to create structured and standardized data,[35] which becomes particularly important as soon as more people cooperate on a project, and, on the other hand, the effect it has on data quality, which is a key factor for accurate analyses and the application of more sophisticated digital methods.

Kluge's oeuvre constitutes a prime 'candidate' for such a platform approach. As he uses different media types and formats, a simple index of parts of his works would not allow for the possibility of gathering and analyzing more complex information. Even if the *Kulturmagazine* are described in a very detailed and precise way, it is still crucial to allow for the connection of these descriptions with other, maybe future, data collections that may cover works of different formats or media. If the principle rules are not followed, however, a data silo is created that may be useful for a single project only, implementing barriers for the reusability of the data for other projects. The question is what an interoperable research platform might look like. Most importantly, it constitutes an interface that allows for easy data entry and for the modification of information that is extracted from the researched materials, e.g., the TV episodes in this case.[36] At the same time, the extracted data must be formatted and massaged in a strictly standardized way; the underlying rules must be

---

34   GND (Gemeinsame Normdatei) is the integrated authority file hosted by the German National Library, https://www.dnb.de/EN/Professionell/Standardisierung/GND/gnd_no de.html. VIAF is the Virtual International Authority File, https://viaf.org/. GeoNames is focused on locations, https://www.geonames.org/. Wikidata and DBpedia describe entities based on data models contrary to Wikipedia, which is focused on textual description; nevertheless, these three platforms are closely linked, https://www.wikidata.org/ and https://wiki.dbpedia.org/.

35   The opposite approach would be minimal computing, which questions common hardware and software considerations and argues for more simplicity. *Minimal Computing.* http://go-dh.github.io/mincomp/

36   An issue that is often underestimated is the importance of well-thought-out and balanced interfaces that support not only the contributors of data but also the consumers, see Whitelaw, "Generous Interfaces for Digital Cultural Collections."

derived from a data model that follows standardized agreements while also covering the particular specifications of Kluge's *Kulturmagazine*.

Moreover, it is necessary to contemplate and anticipate possible connections with other formats of Kluge's production, or even with the work of other artists. This modelling work necessitates the close collaboration of researchers on Kluge and digital humanities experts from the very beginning so that experiences from both perspectives can be taken into account. In general, the time, resources and expertise it takes to develop the data model for a research platform should not be underestimated. It takes time and plenty of discussion, and it is an iterative process. Without having this kind of expertise accompany the process from the very beginning, uninformed decisions at an early stage tend to have cascading effects, affecting the sustainability and reusability of a platform design. Take, for example, the idea of potentially (in a later phase of analysis) fostering research into sound and music in Kluge's work. If the initial data model is not capable of extending to a musicological perspective, such information cannot be interlinked or added. Either the enrichment of data is made impossible or, even more problematic, the setting of the platform does not allow for such additions, which has an adverse effect on the research project itself and hinders, in this example, cooperation with musicologists. In some respects, the agency of a digital research platform can manipulate the framework of the research project itself,[37] which must be kept in mind for the entire process of conceptualizing a digital project.

With regard to the objectives of the research project described in this paper, we consider the development of an ontology tailored to the oeuvre of Kluge as best practice.[38] An ontology describes, in a formalized way, the way in which the data model is built, and it defines the points of intersection with more generic ontologies like CIDOC CRM.[39] This also allows for adequate documentation so that other researchers get a clear picture of what kind of

---

37   More elaborate discussions on this topic may be found in Bartscherer et al., *Switching codes*. Interesting remarks on possible consequences are collected in Kim et al., *Disrupting the Digital Humanities*.

38   Recent initiatives do serve to illustrate this point, e.g. *The Swiss Art Research Infrastructure*, https://swissartresearch.net/ and *Data for History*, http://dataforhistory.org/. Such initiatives highlight the necessity to develop advanced digital research platforms that involve an interdisciplinary research community.

39   CIDOC CRM (Conceptual Reference Model) is oriented primarily on the GLAM (Galleries, Libraries, Archives, Museums) sector but is used more and more for all parts of cultural heritage and digital humanities production. *CIDOC CRM*. http://cidoc-crm.org /

data to expect and how to integrate their data with what is already there. A generic ontology acts as a broker onto which different research projects may be mapped. As we have mentioned above, it is no longer necessary to define entities, like people or places, over and over again, as there are well-proven conceptual definitions that may be adopted. For the generic parts, it is thus sufficient to take the definitions from a community-agreed ontology. Additional project-specific information, however, must be described specifically for the respective ontology of the project.

The adoption of well-proven conceptual definitions allows for conformity on a basic level, thus preparing data for automatic processing and interlinking. This strategy is called semantic modelling[40] as it focuses on sharing information instead of data structures. This also includes the integration of shared vocabularies, linked (open) data methods, and technology that releases data to the public via interfaces (e.g. API, semantic querying like SPARQL). Most of these requirements are collected in the acronym of the FAIR data principles, which stands for findable, accessible, interoperable, and reusable.[41] In detail, however, these principles are not only about technological ways to share data, but also about sharing conceptual issues that research projects working with digital platforms need to find answers to. The driving factor to apply the FAIR data principles is the guarantee of a research data life cycle. Data that is created and processed should also be prepared for reuse by others, and it should be preserved long-term in a way that it remains findable, reproducible, and processable in the future. This takes the pressure off the issue of sustainability with regard to the platforms as the data should be self-explanatory, and therefore agnostic, so that it can be reused in different technical frameworks. The only precondition is that standards and community guidelines must be applied as far as possible.

---

40   Semantic modelling aims at supporting the connection of data from different domains with the help of the semantic web, see Meroño-Peñuela, "Digital Humanities on the Semantic Web."

41   Wilkinson et al., "The FAIR Guiding Principles for Scientific Data Management and Stewardship." The current version of the FAIR data principles is available at: https://www.go-fair.org/fair-principles/

Case Study: An Opera Stenograph

As a case study, we have chosen a short but complex clip entitled *Fünf Stunden PARSIFAL in 90 Sekunden* (i.e., *Five hours of PARSIFAL in 90 seconds*), a video that reveals some of the abovementioned intermedial relations and complexities. Providing an exemplary analysis of the relevant parameters of this clip allows us to illustrate some of the potentials for future research as well as challenges of digital analysis in this context.

First, we offer some background information and a brief interpretational framework for this segment. This 90-second clip may be referred to as an "opera stenograph," as Christian Schulte calls it.[42] This opera stenograph is part of a particular project that has occupied Kluge since the 1980s, which has spread through all of his preferred forms of expression, i.e., his literary writings, his films, and his TV productions; Kluge himself refers to this project, at times, as an "imaginary guide to opera."[43] It is imaginary because it is not a guide to an existing repertoire of musical theater; instead, Kluge is more interested in possibilities, in missed chances and possible stories suitable to be opera-ized—yet not in a way that would reproduce the tragic finality that Kluge ascribes to 'traditional' opera, the quasi-teleological narrative progression[44] with overdeveloped and exalted passions and emotions. Instead, Kluge tries to infuse these stories, and the emotions that are somehow bound within them, with a new kind of historical experience.[45] Kluge's "imaginary opera guide" experiments are conceived of as literary as well as audiovisual counter-projects, as "operas of possibility;"[46] or, in other words, these counter-projects serve to create spaces in which music, or art as such, may become what Kluge conceives of as historical testimony.

There are many literary manifestations of this opera guide project. One of the most significant ones is called "Götterdämmerung in Wien" (i.e., "Twilight of the Gods in Vienna"), which aims at the deconstruction of Wagner's opera. Kluge tells the story of how, in March of 1945, Baldur von Schirach, Gauleiter of Vienna, ordered one last performance of *Götterdämmerung*. But then, the

---

42   Schulte, "Opern-Stenogramme" 49.

43   Kluge, "Erster imaginärer Opernführer."

44   Tara Forrest also points at the intrinsic connection between Kluge's challenge to historicist historiography and his challenge to the tragic finality of operatic narratives. Forrest, "Editor's Introduction" 16.

45   Schulte, "Opern-Stenogramme" 49.

46   Ibid.: "Möglichkeits-Opern." (Translation by B.H.)

opera house in Vienna was bombed and burned down, and the orchestra was dispersed in various shelters. They were connected only by field telephones. Nonetheless, they managed to rehearse and eventually record and film themselves playing fragments of *Götterdämmerung*. Fragments, because, as Kluge writes, they did not "constitute a unified sound [...], the noise of the final battle for Vienna could not be filtered out."[47] These fragments were found by Russian soldiers, and through a labyrinth of re-discoveries, they made their way to Paris, where they were played for Jean-Luc Godard. With this literary piece, Kluge's project is to deconstruct Wagner's music in order to turn it into historical testimony. Wagner can only be salvaged, Kluge seems to say, by letting him pass through deconstruction and historical emergency, which—as this text illustrates—necessarily leads to the interface between fact and fiction. Yet fact and fiction each remain abstract on their own; they must be constellated in order to create space for a mélange of subjective emotional and objective factual worlds.[48] Testimony can only happen in such a constellation. And Kluge describes his task of creating such testimony as one of calling upon "contemporary history, to document it, and to subjectively revive and magnetize these documents by means of music."[49]

Five hours of PARSIFAL in 90 seconds is part of this imaginary opera guide project. With this audiovisual opera stenograph, Kluge opens up a space of possibility by 'documenting' an opera production that never happened, namely a *Parsifal*-staging by Einar Schleef—years after the actor-director's death. While Schleef did indeed intend to stage *Parsifal*, his plan never came to fruition. Thus, what this video clip effectively does is arrange existing materials in such a way that they tell a story of possibilities at the interface of fact and fiction, of subjective emotional and objective factual worlds. All of these (re-)arranged materials are taken from two other *Kulturmagazine*, in which Kluge interviewed Schleef.[50] We see draft drawings of stage scenery, which Schleef did make, as he did plan on staging *Parsifal*. Yet most of the

47   Kluge, "Götterdämmerung" 67: "Die Orchesterfragmente ergaben keinen einheitlichen Klang [...], die Geräusche des Endkampfes um Wien waren nicht auszufiltern." (Translation by B.H.)

48   Schulte, "Opern-Stenogramme" 51.

49   Kluge, "Autor im Fernsehen" 22: "das heißt die Zeitgeschichte heranzuziehen, sie zu dokumentieren und diese Dokumente durch Musik wieder subjektiv zu bewegen und zu magnetisieren." (Translation by B.H.)

50   More precisely, the materials are taken from two episodes: "Endkampf in einer Ritterburg / Einar Schleef und die Gesangsmaschinen des Parsifal," *News and Stories*, SAT.1,

images that we see stem from a 1996 staging of Brecht's *Herr Puntila und sein Knecht Matti* (i.e., *Mr. Puntila and his Man Matti*), in which Schleef was the main protagonist, as well as the director.

Significance, then, is attributed by means of context, reference and aesthetic choice. In his deconstruction of Wagner, Kluge makes the actual *Puntila*-staging pretend to be a *Parsifal*-staging—which never happened. 'Credibility,' if you will, is attributed to this Wagner 'opera of possibility,' on the one hand, by the very particular montage of the *Puntila*-recording, which is edited to resemble the story of *Parsifal*, revolving around a huge round table. At the same time, the *Puntila*-recording is projected into the vertical plan of what may be interpreted as an opera house[51] but is actually a planetarium, which is recognizable as such due to the distinctive planetarium projector at the center of the image in combination with the characteristic dome of the building.[52] Around it, there is a dynamic starry sky, one of Kluge's favorite motives, to illustrate and problematize the notion of enclosedness from the outside: inside, there is an enclosed projection of stars, outside the limitless starry sky. This complex relation of enclosedness and openness also plays out with regard to time: the most significant aesthetic choice in this clip is clearly the time lapse, or, as Kluge calls it, "Zeittotale," a temporal long shot, which is 'responsible' for the eternal opera's being condensed to 90 seconds. However, the most significant strategy of 'fake-authenticating' the video as a *Parsifal*-staging is the musical track: Wagner's music remains largely unaltered in this video as we listen to a passage from the second act, the prelude to "Die Zeit ist da."[53] Against this background, it would thus be particularly interesting to trace the function of Wagner's music throughout Kluge's "imaginary opera guide" project in order to find out more about music's potential of subjectively reviving and magnetizing historical documents, as Kluge puts it.

Now, the question is how to make such relations traceable in digital analysis. Based on what we have outlined above with regard to the role of digital platforms for research, this case acts as a good example for outlining how such platforms may be connected in a beneficial way. For one, this 'opera stenograph' is adapted and reused by Kluge in various different ways

---

26.06.1995, and "Herr Puntila und seine Tochter Eva / Einar Schleef inszeniert Bert Brecht am Berliner Ensemble in ungewöhnlicher Weise," *10 vor 11*, RTL, 17.06.1996.

51   Schulte, "Opern-Stenogramme" 53.

52   Many thanks to Johann Lurf for pointing this out to us, and for even sending us images of Zeiss planetarium projectors for comparison.

53   Schulte, "Opern-Stenogramme" 53.

throughout the *Kulturmagazine* and other works; thus it would be interesting to find traces of this process of transformative reiteration. Information with regard to the context of the audiovisual materials, as compared to other manifestations, may provide additional assistance in understanding the way in which Kluge uses these materials within and between different media settings. With the help of shared ontologies and vocabularies, one could identify as many references to these materials as are available on different platforms and databases.[54]

A first step would still have to be the collection of basic metadata and the creation of an 'aesthetic vocabulary' specific to Kluge's TV works. As the clip illustrates, there is usually only a relatively limited repertoire of aesthetic techniques and procedures that Kluge makes use of, and at times Kluge himself, or secondary literature about Kluge, has assigned specific names or labels to describe these projects, techniques and procedures, such as Kluge's "Zeittotale," or the imaginary opera guide. Establishing such a limited vocabulary specific to Kluge's TV aesthetic would make it more feasible of a task to gather the relevant data from the episodes, and it would assist users in tracing certain particularities within the intermedial 'Kluge-universe.' References may be defined within this universe, e.g., to other *Kulturmagazine*, but also, by means of shared ontologies and vocabularies, with 'outside' data sets that would provide, say, metadata about Wagner's "Die Zeit ist da," or about Einar Schleef and his theater production.

If a musicology database were to provide information about the attributed effect of music, possibly in combination with further co-references on the usage of this music in objects of cultural heritage, like theater performances, it would be possible to juxtapose this information in a virtual research environment in order to get fresh insights about contexts and possible new ways of interpretation.[55] Tracing the use of recurring topics, projects, songs, people, motives, techniques, etc., is an advanced digital method that holds enormous potential for research, but it relies on the digital availability of the

---

54   This could assist in bringing together projects that are in different states of maintenance, such as the Kluge Digital Resource, https://kluge.freizo.org/, or clips and lectures by and about Alexander Kluge on the website of Christian Schulte's *Passagen*-project at the University of Vienna, https://passagen.univie.ac.at/.

55   The research project *Telling Sounds* has the potential of providing such insights if material on Kluge were to be processed on their research platform. https://www.mdw.ac.at/imi/tellingsounds/?l=en

data—and on a common agreement as to how to connect it. Shared ontologies, defined by a research community, represent a big step forward for such a digital research approach. That way, new interdisciplinary perspectives may be developed on tangible and intangible objects of cultural heritage, as well as their reuse, re-mixing and remediation—and for these processes in particular, Kluge's oeuvre constitutes an excellent starting point for further investigation. In this context, the aim of an advanced and forward-looking digital research project should be to illustrate relations and interconnections between people, ideas, etc., and to investigate cultural techniques that establish new contexts—even if it may take some time to create fruitful collaborative settings and gather all the necessary technological and conceptual puzzle pieces together in order to undertake such a challenge.

Prospect

In this paper, we have delved into the potentials and challenges of digital analysis in the context of an encompassing, diverse and intermedial oeuvre of works, with the main objective of fostering new forms of interdisciplinary research. In doing so, we have focused on Alexander Kluge's televisual corpus, i.e., the so-called *Kulturmagazine*, in the context of which an exhaustive, metadata-based survey of these audiovisual materials in the form of a digital platform would seem to be the most promising digital approach. Yet in order to make an intermedial oeuvre like Kluge's attractive, accessible, and researchable for scholars from a broad range of different fields, it is essential to provide for the interconnectivity of the gathered data from the outset. Reflecting on such a digital approach based on the FAIR data principles with regard to the *Kulturmagazine*, we have identified a set of parameters and guidelines, such as shared ontologies and vocabularies, the development of advanced research platforms and ecosystems, as well as the deliberate and anticipative planning of interdisciplinary interfaces. For the sake of effective and fruitful collaboration between disciplines as diverse as musicology, film, television and media studies, contemporary and cultural history, political or social studies, we offer these guidelines as a starting point for future collaboration, and we would urge prospective digital projects with similar interests to adopt and adapt these guidelines.

Bibliography (last accessed 16 April 2020)

Bartscherer, Thomas, and Roderick Coover, eds. *Switching Codes: Thinking Through Digital Technology in the Humanities and the Arts.* Chicago: Univ. of Chicago Press, 2011.

Bay-Cheng, Sarah, Jennifer Parker-Starbuck and David Z. Saltz. *Performance and Media: Taxonomies for a Changing Field.* Ann Arbor: Univ. of Michigan, 2015.

Borgman, Christine L. *Big Data, Little Data, No Data: Scholarship in the Networked World.* Cambridge, MA: MIT Press, 2015.

Edmond, Jennifer, ed. *Digital Technology and the Practices of Humanities Research.* Open Book Publishers, 2020. DOI: 10.11647/obp.0192

Elsaesser, Thomas. "The Stubborn Persistence of Alexander Kluge." *Alexander Kluge: Raw Materials for the Imagination.* Ed. Tara Forrest. Amsterdam: Amsterdam Univ. Press, 2012.

Fickers, Andreas, Pelle Snickars and Mark J. Williams, eds. *Audiovisual Data in Digital Humanities, Special Issue, VIEW Journal of European Television History and Culture* 7, 14 (2018).

Flanders, Julia, and Fotis Jannidis, eds. *The Shape of Data in the Digital Humanities: Modeling Texts and Text-based Resources.* London: Routledge, 2019.

Foppiano, Luca, and Laurent Romary. "entity-fishing: a DARIAH entity recognition and disambiguation service." *Digital Scholarship in the Humanities,* Tokyo, Japan (September 2018). https://hal.inria.fr/hal-01812100/

Forrest, Tara. "Editor's Introduction." *Alexander Kluge: Raw Materials for the Imagination.* Ed. Tara Forrest. Amsterdam: Amsterdam Univ. Press, 2012. 13–21.

Forrest, Tara. "Raw Materials for the Imagination: Kluge's Work for Television." *Alexander Kluge: Raw Materials for the Imagination.* Ed. Tara Forrest. Amsterdam: Amsterdam Univ. Press, 2012. 305–17.

Gold, Matthew K., and Lauren F. Klein, eds. *Debates in the Digital Humanities: 2016.* Minneapolis: Univ. of Minnesota Press, 2016. https://dhdebates.gc.cuny.edu/

Hooland, Seth Van, and Ruben Verborgh. *Linked Data for Libraries, Archives and Museums: How to Clean, Link and Publish Your Metadata.* London: Facet, 2015.

Kim, Dorothy, and Jesse Stommel, eds. *Disrupting the Digital Humanities.* punctum books, 2018. DOI: 10.21983/p3.0230.1.00

Kluge, Alexander. "Was ich als Autor im Fernsehen treibe." *Funk-Korrespondenz* 48, 3 (1993): 21–23.

Kluge, Alexander. "Götterdämmerung in Wien." *Chronik der Gefühle, Band 1: Basisgeschichten*. Frankfurt am Main: Suhrkamp, 2000. 66–73.

Kluge, Alexander. "Herzblut trifft Kunstblut: Erster imaginärer Opernführer." *Facts and Fakes: Fernseh-Nachschriften 2/3*. Eds. Christian Schulte and Reinald Gussmann. Berlin: Vorwerk 8, 2001.

Kluge, Alexander, and Christian Schulte. "The Opera Machine." Trans. Tayler Kent. *Difference and Orientation: An Alexander Kluge Reader*. Ed. Richard Langston. Ithaca, NY: Cornell Univ. Press, 2019. 305–17.

Lämmle, Kathrin. *Televisuelle Intellektualität: Möglichkeitsräume in Alexander Kluges Fernsehmagazinen*. Köln: Herbert von Halem, 2013.

Lutze, Peter C. "Alexander Kluge und das Projekt der Moderne." *Kluges Fernsehen: Alexander Kluges Fernsehmagazine*. Eds. Christian Schulte and Winfried Siebers. Frankfurt am Main: Suhrkamp, 2002. 11–38.

Martens, Gunther. "Distant(ly) Reading Alexander Kluge's Distant Writing." *Vermischte Nachrichten: Alexander Kluge-Jahrbuch 1*. Eds. Richard Langston, Gunther Martens, Vincent Pauval et al. Göttingen: V&R unipress, 2014.

Meroño-Peñuela, Albert. "Digital Humanities on the Semantic Web: Accessing Historical and Musical Linked Data." *Journal of Catalan Intellectual History* 1, 11 (2017): 144–49. DOI: 10.1515/jocih-2016-0013

Pomerantz, Jeffrey. *Metadata*. Cambridge, MA: MIT Press, 2015.

Schreibman, Susan, Raymond George Siemens and John Unsworth, eds. *A New Companion to Digital Humanities*. Chichester: Wiley-Blackwell, 2016.

Schulte, Christian. "Television and Obstinacy." Trans. Philip Thomson. *Alexander Kluge: Raw Materials for the Imagination*. Ed. Tara Forrest. Amsterdam: Amsterdam Univ. Press, 2012. 318–51.

Schulte, Christian. "Opern-Stenogramme." *Maske & Kothurn: Die Bauweise von Paradiesen – Für Alexander Kluge* 53, 1 (2007): 49–54.

Schulte, Christian, and Winfried Siebers. "Vorwort." *Kluges Fernsehen: Alexander Kluges Fernsehmagazine*. Eds. Christian Schulte and Winfried Siebers. Frankfurt am Main: Suhrkamp, 2002. 7–10.

Seeßlen, Georg. "Interview/Technik oder Archäologie des zukünftigen Wissens: Anmerkungen zu den TV-Interviews Alexander Kluges." *Kluges Fernsehen: Alexander Kluges Fernsehmagazine*. Eds. Christian Schulte and Winfried Siebers. Frankfurt am Main: Suhrkamp, 2002. 128–37.

Uecker, Matthias. "Rohstoffe und Intermedialität: Überlegungen zu Alexander Kluges Fernsehpraxis." *Kluges Fernsehen: Alexander Kluges Fernsehmagazine*. Eds. Christian Schulte and Winfried Siebers. Frankfurt am Main: Suhrkamp, 2002. 82–104.

Whitelaw, Mitchell. "Generous Interfaces for Digital Cultural Collections."
DHQ: Digital Humanities Quarterly 9, 1 (2015). http://www.digitalhumani
ties.org/dhq/vol/9/1/000205/000205.html

Wilkinson, Mark D., Michel Dumontier, Ijsbrand Jan Aalbersberg et al. "The
FAIR Guiding Principles for Scientific Data Management and Stewardship." *Sci Data* 3, 160018 (March 2016). DOI: 10.1038/sdata.2016.18

Online Sources (last accessed 16 April 2020)

AG Film und Video: Digital Humanities im deutschsprachigen Raum. http://dig-hu
m.de/ag-film-und-video

CIDOC CRM. http://cidoc-crm.org/

CLARIAH Media Suite. https://mediasuite.clariah.nl/

Data for History Consortium. http://dataforhistory.org/

DBpedia. https://wiki.dbpedia.org/

DCMI. https://dublincore.org/

Debates in the Digital Humanities. https://dhdebates.gc.cuny.edu/

DNB: The Integrated Authority File (GND). https://www.dnb.de/EN/Professione
ll/Standardisierung/GND/gnd_node.html

FAIR Principles – GO FAIR. https://www.go-fair.org/fair-principles/

GeoNames. https://www.geonames.org/

Kluge Digital Research. https://kluge.freizo.org/

Minimal Computing. http://go-dh.github.io/mincomp/

PARTHENOS Project. http://www.parthenos-project.eu/

SARI: Swiss Art Research Infrastructure. https://swissartresearch.net/

"Telling Sounds." *University of Music and Performing Arts Vienna*. https://www.
mdw.ac.at/imi/tellingsounds/?l=en

The Swiss Art Research Infrastructure. https://swissartresearch.net/

Time Machine Europe. https://www.timemachine.eu/

VIAF. https://viaf.org/

What Is Digital Humanities? https://whatisdigitalhumanities.com/

Wikidata. https://www.wikidata.org/wiki/Wikidata:Main_Page

Audiovisual Sources (last accessed 16 April 2020)

dctp: Das webTV der dctp. https://www.dctp.tv/
"Fünf Stunden PARSIFAL in 90 Sekunden." *dctp.* https://www.dctp.tv/filme/
    minutenfilm-einar-schleef
"Onlinearchiv." *Österreichische Mediathek.* https://www.mediathek.at/
Passagen-Videos. https://passagen.univie.ac.at/

Modelling in Digital Humanities: An Introduction to Methods and Practices of Knowledge Representation

Franziska Diehr (Prussian Cultural Heritage Foundation)

When talking about 'modelling,' it is not clear what exactly is being referred to. Several disciplines of the sciences, humanities and arts, and especially in the academic fields of philosophy, mathematics as well as computer and information studies are concerned with the question what 'modelling' is and if it serves a general, cross-disciplinary purpose. Models are doubtless used in all of the above fields, but to what extent? Do all pursue the same goal when they create models?

The field of digital humanities as an interdisciplinary movement is experimenting with the application of computational methods to (if not even forcing their incorporation with) the investigation of objects of humanistic inquiry. Which role do 'models' and the act of 'modelling' play in this regard?

McCarty demands that "we need to see it [modelling] as a form of craftsmanship set into the context of scholarship."[1] With this paper, I aim to contribute to the development of a practice of modelling for digital humanities while carefully considering what was discussed about the theory of models in various research areas. Although 'modelling' is often considered to be 'intuitive,' it is far from being an unformalizable process. I argue for 'modelling' to be understood as a scholarly method. Therefore, I investigate methods and practices as well as theoretical foundations of knowledge representation for application in digital humanities. In this paper, I compile practices that can be used to support the application of computational methods to objects which are inherently ambiguous, vague, and full of uncertainties.

---

1   McCarty, *Humanities Computing* 22.

Theories of Models as Representation of Knowledge

Following Mahr in his observation that 'models' have increasingly been the subject of investigation in various fields since the 1960s, their more general investigation (especially by Stachowiak in 1973) has also led to a broad interest in the process of 'modelling' and its applicability as an interdisciplinary method.[2]

Different formats are used to approach the questions around being a 'model' and the practical applicability of 'modelling.' In their white paper Flanders and Jannidis describe the discussions and outcomes of a workshop on knowledge organization and data modelling. In it they stress that in the context of digital humanities the understanding of 'modelling' is a more general one than data modelling in the sense of computer science: "[...] data modelling is the modelling of some segment of the world in such a way to make some aspects computable [...] the task at hand is to define and study the more general concept [of modelling]."[3]

The project "Modelling between Digital and Humanities: Thinking in Practice"[4] researched the term 'modelling' and how it is used in different domains. Its main outcomes are an extensive bibliography as well as publications dedicated to classifying the term 'modelling' in the context of digital humanities.

Methods and techniques regarding the modelling of specific questions are also subject to a broad scope of research papers in the digital humanities. Special issue no. 4 of the German open access journal *ZfdG* on modelling vagueness using graph technologies[5] gives a worthwhile example of how (graph-based) modelling is used for specific use cases in humanities research.

This paper focuses on the aspects of 'model' and 'modelling' that help in their practical usage. A comprehensive overview of (all) available definitions is not given, but an assemblage of certain approaches useful for the application of the method in the context of digital humanities is provided.

---

2   Mahr, "Information Science" 367.
3   Flanders and Jannidis, "Conference Report" 3.
4   Ciula, "Modelling Between Digital and Humanities."
5   Kuczera et al., "Die Modellierung des Zweifels."

Approaches to Defining 'Model' and 'Modelling'

While discussing different approaches to the definition of the concept 'modelling' in his book *Humanities Computing*, McCarty also presents a more general approach to 'modelling.' He describes it as an epistemological activity in which heuristic methods are used to construct and manipulate models.[6]

As mentioned before, Stachowiak researched the theory of models in a general sense. He characterizes a 'model' with three substantial characteristics: (1) 'Abbildungsmerkmal' (the mapping characteristic), which means that "models are representations of natural or artificial originals." (2) 'Verkürzungsmerkmal' (the reduction characteristic) explains that "models do not have all the attributes of the originals they represent." (3) 'Pragmatisches Merkmal' (the pragmatic feature) lays out that a model is the outcome of an intentional process. It can only represent things that are based on and influenced by the pragmatic view of the modelling subject.[7]

In his approach, Mahr focuses on a model's purpose and determines it with the following three aspects: (1) a model is a 'thing for itself:' it is an entity on its own like a picture, a text, a set of rules. (2) A model is 'about something:' it represents characteristics and/or experiences of an object by selecting, generalizing, and correlating them in a new form. (3) A model is 'for something:' it serves a specific purpose. When put into use, 'knowledge' can be gained from the model.[8] Or as Hughes explains it: "from the behavior of the model we can draw hypothetical conclusions about the world over and above the data we started with."[9] But can we trust our models? Mahr clarifies that a model does not claim to hold any truth, "but rather forms of demonstrability, possibility, and choice."[10]

Following Geertz, who also attributes to models 'aboutness' and 'purposefulness' (a model 'of' and model 'for'),[11] McCarty also distinguishes these two aspects: "[it is] either a representation of something for the purposes of study, or [it is] a design for realizing something new."[12]

---

6   McCarty, *Humanities Computing* 24.
7   Stachowiak, *Allgemeine Modelltheorie* 132–133.
8   Mahr, "Das Wissen im Modell" 11–12.
9   Hughes, "Models and Representation" 331.
10   Mahr, "Information Science" 365.
11   Geertz, *The Interpretation of Cultures* 93.
12   McCarty, *Humanities Computing* 24.

'Aboutness' and 'purposefulness' together make up the model's functionality as a 'tool for knowledge creation.' Simplifying Mahr's description,[13] a model incorporates the derivation of the initial object as well as the hypothesis which premised the model's build (Stachowiak's *Pragmatisches Merkmal*). Thus informed, the model offers new modes of observation, which fundamentally differ from those which are applicable (or not applicable) to the examination of the represented object itself.[14] The information extracted from this observation can result in the extension or creation of knowledge. Or as Hughes put it "[...] if we examine a theoretical model [...], we shall achieve some insight into the kind of representation that it provides."[15]

Taking those general reflections on the concept of 'model' into account, the following is focused on one particular aspect: the model's functionality of representing knowledge. Understanding what is meant by abstracting the original object and what implications Stachowiak's *Pragmatisches Merkmal* has on the model as a tool of knowledge creation is crucial when actually performing the act of 'modelling.'

Coming from the field of artificial intelligence, Davis et al. define the term 'knowledge representation' by identifying five characteristics: (1) "a knowledge representation is a surrogate, a substitute for the thing itself"—a model of something.[16] (2) A knowledge representation describes the domain the object lives in. It offers a set of "ontological commitments" explaining relevant aspects concerning the world of the object. (3) A knowledge representation is a "fragmentary theory of intelligent reasoning," meaning that the rules of logic are used to make sense of the excerpt of the world under study. (4) A knowledge representation is used for analysis with computational methods in a pragmatic way. (5) A knowledge representation is "a medium of human

---

13   Mahr, "Information Science" 376.
14   For example, when observing phenomena in the world of physics (e.g. quantum physics), there are no techniques applicable for the observation of the initial object because models are used to prove the existence of the object in the first place. Mahr uses the discovery of the Higgs particle to illustrate how knowledge is created by the use of models, while also explaining the interaction between the aboutness and purposefulness of a model.
15   Hughes, "Models and Representation" 329.
16   This understanding is comparable with the *Abbildungsmerkmal* defined by Stachowiak as well as the second aspect determined by Mahr—"a model of something."

expression," and in this regard also a way for human beings to express and discuss knowledge.[17]

An even more concrete approach is formulated by Silberschatz et al. when they specifically define the term 'data modelling' as applied in computer science: "A collection of conceptual tools for describing data, data relationships, data semantics, and consistency constraints."[18]

Reflecting on all presented perspectives on 'model' and 'knowledge representation,' a practical approach is needed that can be used as a guideline when creating computational models for digital humanities research. "Modelling makes the semantics of 'knowledge objects' explicit and transfers them into a data structure."[19] In this sense 'modelling' can be defined as the method used to construct a machine-readable model that represents objects in a pragmatic perspective. Constructing such a model entails being aware of this and therefore reflecting on the definitions and methods that are applied to the object and domain. Modelling is a process of building an ontological understanding. In this perspective, modelling can be seen as a hermeneutic method used to gain knowledge about something that is to be studied further using computational methods.[20]

The Practice of Modelling

Using this approach as a guideline, the following part of the paper illustrates the practical aspects of modelling.

Flanders and Jannidis observed two types of motivation for modelling in (the broader field of) digital humanities. On the one hand there is 'curation-driven modelling,' where authorities develop models and metadata schemes for the purpose of making information findable, accessible and usable.[21]

As libraries are information providers to the public and to scholars, they have pioneered curation-driven modelling. In contrast to museums and archives, libraries are far more advanced in the use of computational practices for representing knowledge about their collections. They work

17   Davis et al., "What is a Knowledge Representation?" 17.
18   Silberschatz, *Database System Concepts* 8.
19   Sowa, *Knowledge Representation* 132.
20   Diehr, "Modellierung von Entzifferungshypothesen."
21   Flanders and Jannidis, "Conference Report" 4–5.

constantly on the optimization of cataloguing practices and as well as the description of (non)bibliographical resources, such as authority files.

The curation of authority files became an especially important task which digital research relies on as well. Using persistent identifiers for the identification and disambiguation of entities like persons, organizations, places, and works has become an indispensable task for libraries. Arguing that the classification and identification of entities is also a task of knowledge representation, in this perspective curating authority files can be seen as a form of curation-driven modelling.

Another example of a library effort of curation-driven modelling is the METS/MODS standard.[22] While MODS is a schema for describing bibliographical items such as books and manuscripts, METS provides a mechanism to combine the structural features of the item with its digital facsimile. Using these standards in combination, libraries provide a useful service for research. Users do not have to visit the library in person in order to examine the contents and appearance of a book, for instance. Cross-institutional and long-term digitization efforts like the German 'VD 18'[23] made it possible for libraries to provide an enormous amount of their book collections as digital facsimiles with structured metadata.[24]

On the other hand, there is 'research-driven modelling,' where (individual) researchers develop models to study objects and domains that are subject to specific research questions. The outcome of this modelling process is either a project-specific adaptation of an existing standard, or a genuinely novel model, for instance a domain-specific ontology. As this paper focuses on research-driven modelling, the following lays out how to model research-driven knowledge representations.

As pointed out at the beginning of this paper, the act of modelling can be formalized. In doing so, a resilient description of the process is needed. In *Knowledge Organization and Data Modelling in the Humanities*, Flanders and Jannidis describe three steps of data modelling: (1) 'conceptual modelling' is concerned with "the identification and description of the entities and their

---

22   "MODS standard Version 3.7." https://www.loc.gov/standards/mods/; "METS standard Version 1.12." https://www.loc.gov/standards/mets/

23   *Verzeichnis Deutscher Drucke des 18. Jahrhunderts – VD18 (Index of German prints of the 18th century)* funded by Deutsche Forschungsgemeinschaft (DFG). https://gso.gbv.de/DB=1.65/

24   An example for a digital VD 18 collection, see "VD18 digital." https://gdz.sub.uni-goettingen.de/collection/vd18.digital

relationship in the 'universe of discourse'"—attributes and relations of object and domain are to be defined. This step can be viewed as the most challenging but also the most interesting part of the whole modelling process. (2) 'Logical data modelling' refers to the process of 'translating' the conceptual model into an actual data structure, a syntax like XML or "defining the tables of a database according the underlying relational model." (3) 'Physical data modelling' is the actual implementation as a data model in a digital environment that enables functionalities for data storage and querying as well as "optimization of the database for performance."[25] This paper focuses on the first two steps.

Requirement Analysis

The conceptual modelling step should be preceded by a definition of what is required of the model. By means of the requirements analysis, information is acquired that is needed for the construction of the model. This may seem like a trivial task, but is in fact an intensive phase of revisiting the object of inquiry and the specific views of the domain it 'lives' in as well as methods, traditions, and constraints which are brought into hypothesis building.[26] In this section, practices are presented that are useful for gaining the necessary information as well as structuring and analyzing it.

Before going into detail regarding the methods, I would like to present a set of prototypical questions that can be used as a starting point to gain information about the object and its domain in each of the presented methods as well as other possible formats of information acquisition:

Which attributes characterize the object? Which categories describe the objects regarding its theme/subject?
Which features of the object are crucial for answering the research question?
How can the nature of relation to other materials, actions, actors, places etc. be described? How can it be structured?
Which sources of knowledge are consulted? Where are they derived from?
Which methods were formerly applied to the object?
Where does the object 'live'? Is there a specific 'ecosystem' or domain?

---

25   Flanders and Jannidis, "Conference Report" 3.
26   Diehr, "Modelling Vagueness."

From which pragmatic perspective is the object described? Which (disciplinary) domain-specific perspectives are relevant?

The 'interdisciplinary workshop' is a practice that is especially useful if many
different perspectives on the object of inquiry are needed, for instance as a
kick-off for a research project or as an initial step into a new field of interest. In this scenario, a variety of experts from different domains share insights on how the object of inquiry is regarded in their field and how research
challenges are approached with respect to the field's tradition and current
practice. As a creative input session or trigger for a fruitful discussion, this
practice also risks information overload. If resources are available to manage the post-processing workload (such as extracting key issues from a video
recording), modelling will hugely benefit from this approach.

A common method of information acquisition described by Pickard[27] and
Reinhold is the 'expert interview.' The person (or team) in charge of the actual modelling interviews (several) domain experts using a prepared questionnaire. As well as the previous described practice, "expert interviews can
be used to gain a high degree of context knowledge, which is of crucial importance when modelling domain-specific knowledge."[28] But the challenge with
this method is that the interviewer already has to have deep insights into the
domain in order to be able to prepare and ask relevant questions.[29] Thus this
practice can be recommended if the modelling person (or team) and the in-
terviewees are both equally familiar with the field of research. Also, it is a
suitable information acquisition method if a focus on the research questions
is already set and other perspectives are ruled out.

This paper presents a new method that partially integrates procedures
from the expert interview. In comparison to the previously described methods, this method aims at much more detailed results. It is highly integrated
and also functions in dialogue with software development practices.

As the names suggests, the 'iterative questionnaire' integrates the questioning of experts in an ongoing process. On the basis of an initial examination of the object and its domain a draft is conceived. This is then presented
to a fixed group of domain experts, who work together in the upcoming phase
of questioning rounds. The first evaluation will show where weaknesses in the
questionnaire lie: How can object attributes be described even more clearly?

---

27   Pickard, *Research Methods in Information*.
28   Reinhold, "Das Experteninterview als zentrale Methode" 330.
29   Ibid.

Which relations to adjacent topics come to light? This is followed by a spec-ification of the question catalogue, in which certain questions will result in more refined answers, while others will allow associative thoughts.

While this phase is key to conceptual modelling, ideally the advanced questionnaire is also used to specify the functionalities of the software com-ponents: e.g. which field type is required to describe a specific object at-tribute, how to establish relations between objects, and so on.

This illustrates that requirement analysis is not an isolated task; it is ac-companied by the actual modelling process (Figure 1). After an initial phase of information aggregation, an iterative process of questioning, modelling, and evaluating will be initiated. The model will be finalized when evaluation finds no more irregularities. Because it is hard to communicate the progress of the modelling process to those who are not modelling themselves, the parallel development of a graphical user interface (GUI) is useful. Even a prototyped GUI with reduced functionality and a sparse design communicates the un-derlying model much better than any diagram of the model itself could (in most cases). This makes it much easier to display the modelling progress and make the results of the modelling comprehensible.

Figure 1: The iterative process of modelling.

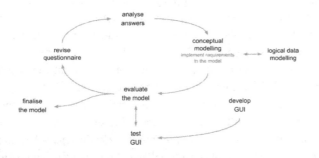

The 'iterative questionnaire' aims at gradually asking more precise and specific questions so that a high degree of accuracy is achieved at the end of the process. Compared with the previous methods, this one is more time consuming, but it also has key benefits: a high level of precision and accu-racy is reached and the developed model will be most fitting to the specific research needs. This method also contributes significantly to the hermeneutic process: Because experts work collaboratively on the questionnaire and discuss the subject regularly, knowledge transfer processes are activated. That helps to reflect on common practices and traditions of disciplinary views. In this perspective the method may lead to new insights on the research object, and it also may contribute to novel approaches to methods for studying it.[30]

Conceptual Modelling

The act of conceptual modelling can be described as a heuristic performance: from a pragmatic perspective, assumptions are made about things and how they work. But how were those assumptions made in the first place and how are they to be formalized into a model? In this section, I approach the methodology of conceptual modelling as a heuristic practice that is used to represent knowledge.

Conceptual modelling aims at developing an ontological understanding through the explicit description and definition of objects, their relationship to each other, and to their domain. By acquiring information on object and domain through the requirement analysis, a knowledge base was gained. In order to formulate a conceptual model that formalizes this knowledge into a workable and computable model, that which Sowa calls "ontological categories"[31] must firstly be defined. Defining those categories means performing an "intentional activity that has scope, granularity, and (perhaps multiple) levels of abstractions" as well as providing "explicit semantics."[32] This definition is particularly difficult when it comes to vague and uncertain information, regarding which Sowa points out: "any incompleteness, distortions, or restrictions in the framework of categories must inevitably limit the generality of every program and database that uses those categories."[33] That is why the process of conceptual modelling should be undertaken with an acute awareness of the pragmatic perspectives that are applied to the model.

In their presentation of *A Reference Framework for Conceptual Modelling*, Delcambre et al. refine the act of conceptual modelling even further, distinguishing between a 'conceptual model' as a product of modelling and 'conceptual model language' as the grammar used to formulate the model. In their argument a conceptual model refers to a domain-specific model or ontology and

---

30   Diehr, "Modelling Vagueness."
31   Sowa, *Knowledge Representation* 51.
32   Delcambre et al., "A Reference Framework" 30.
33   Sowa, *Knowledge Representation* 51.

the conceptual model language to a foundational ontology, a reference model used to specify more or less generic concepts.[34]

Conceptual modelling is a process of identification and categorization. Attributes of objects and relations between them and their domain are identified and formally described and categorized. In their paper *Toward a Methodology for Building Ontologies*, Uschold and King reflect on the modelling process—and specifically upon the act of categorization—when formulating a conceptual model (in this case an ontology).[35] Therefore they consult Lakoff's theory of categorization, in which he outlines three aspects that are used when categorizing reality:

> "(1) 'Basic-level categorization:' The idea that categories are not merely organized in a hierarchy from the most general to the most specific but are organized so that the categories that are cognitively basic are in the middle of a general-to-specific hierarchy. Generalization proceeds upward from the basic level and specialization proceeds downward.
>
> (2) 'Basic-level primacy:' The idea that basic-level categories are functionally and epistemologically primary with respect to the following factors: gestalt perception image formation, motor movement, knowledge organization, ease of cognitive processing (learning, recognition, memory etc.) and ease of linguistic expression.
>
> (3) 'Reference-point, or "metonymic" reasoning:' The idea that a part of a category (that is, a member or subcategory) can stand for the whole category in a certain reasoning process."[36]

It was Rosch who first introduced the concept of "basic-level categories or prototype theory."[37] As it is not pertinent to the case being made here, I do not want to go into much more detail; it should be sufficient to point out that a basic-level category can be understood as a prototype of a real thing, the first 'mental image' or concept that comes to mind when observing something. Lakoff illustrates this as follows:[38]

The attributes applied to the superordinate will be inherited by all following sub-categories and therefore be true for them. An attribute of a subordi-

---

34   Delcambre et al., "A Reference Framework" 31.
35   Uschold and King, *Towards a Methodology for Building Ontologies*.
36   Lakoff, *Women, Fire and Dangerous Things* 13.
37   Rosch et al., "Basic Objects in Natural Categories."
38   Lakoff, *Women, Fire and Dangerous Things* 46.

SUPERORDI-NATE	ANIMAL	FURNITURE
BASIC LEVEL	DOG	CHAIR
SUBORDI-NATE	RETRIEVER	ROCKER

nate is a specified attribute of a superordinate (like a chair for 'seating' as a specification of furniture which 'support human activities') or a novel feature that is not applicable to any of its superordinates (a rocking chair that 'swings back and forth').

For the practice of conceptual modelling this can be used as a blueprint: The subordinate could be used to describe an instance of a category, e.g. 'Ludwig Wittgenstein.' Depending on the domain (which specifies what is of main interest), the basic-level category could be 'philosopher' or 'logician,' and the superordinate 'person.' The next step is to assign attributes and relations to the basic level and superordinate, using inheritance to build an ontological understanding that makes more and more specific statements the further down the hierarchy it proceeds. In this regard, 'instances' can be understood as the data onto which the model is to be applied.

When designing a model that comprises such an ontological understanding of the domain, there is always a danger of incorporating too many attributes and/or categories into the model. As the model should be designed to answer hypotheses which were made prior to the modelling, it should be limited to "minimal ontological commitment;" Gruber explains further that

> "[...] an ontology should make as few claims as possible about the world being modeled, allowing the parties committed to the ontology freedom to specialize and instantiate the ontology as needed. [...And it should define] only those terms that are essential to the communication of knowledge consistent with that theory."[39]

Following Gruber's advice in practice can cause discussions about the model's comprehensiveness: experts may anticipate theories and further questions that could be applied onto the model in future. But bearing in mind Stachowiak's *Pragmatisches Merkmal*, a model is designed at a specific time for a specific reason from a certain perspective. Future research may have other

---

39   Gruber, "Toward Principles for the Design of Ontologies" 3.

methods at hand or, in the meantime, new or extended knowledge could have been gained, outdating the model's use. Thus, there is no need to overextend the current model with assumptions of possible applications.

Using Reference Models and Standards for Logical Data Modelling

In order to evaluate if the semantics were defined with the required care, Delcambre et al. advise mapping the constructed model to another (referential or standardized) model.[40] This step can be also understood as a part of logical data modelling in which the conceptual model is transferred into a machine-readable syntax. In the following sections, I illustrate how the model to be constructed can be aligned with existing models (e.g. in the form of metadata standards or reference ontologies) and how this can be used to transfer it into a machine-readable data model.

While also providing semantics for the description of objects and their domains, metadata standards[41] often come written in a machine-readable syntax, such as XML or RDF. The reuse of existing metadata standards does not only provide meaningful concepts and a vocabulary for the alignment of the constructed model but can also aid with logical data modelling. Using the same syntax as the referential metadata standard makes its application comfortable. However, another syntax can obviously always be used, as data can be converted into other data formats that may be more fitting to the model.[42]

To illustrate this, I use the project-specific application of the guideline of the Text Encoding Initiative (TEI)[43] for the development of the text corpus of the project *Text Database and Dictionary of Classic Mayan*[44] as an example.

---

40   Delcambre et al., "A Reference Framework" 34.
41   Durrell, *Data Administration*: "Metadata are structured, coded data that describe the characteristics of information-carrying entities for the purpose of identifying, researching, evaluating and managing the entities described."
42   The right syntax to formulate the model is based on the structure of the conceptual model. If the structure is shown to be quite simple, there is no need to reach for an elaborate syntax: the rule of thumb can be 'form follows function.'
43   *TEI: Text Encoding Initiative.* https://tei-c.org/
44   The project *Text Database and Dictionary of Classic Mayan* is funded by North Rhine-Westphalian Academy of Sciences, Humanities and the Arts (Project No. I.B.17). Its goal since 2014 is the compilation of a dictionary for the script and language of Classic Mayan by creating a machine-readable corpus of all known inscriptions and codices. The author was part of the team from 2014–2018 and was responsible for the con-

The TEI Guidelines are a de facto standard for text-based research, particularly for editorial scholarship.[45] A huge community is applying those guidelines and also constantly improving them. The TEI does not insist on using XML as syntax for applying the guidelines, but many TEI-related frameworks and transformation routines rely on XML as the syntax of choice. The TEI guidelines provide semantics for describing a variety of characteristics of the textual material, for instance elements like <p> (paragraph) and <l> (line) can be used to describe the structure of a text. There are also elements to describe the condition of the text carrier like <damage> as well as editorial interventions with elements like <supplied> and <note>.

Figure 2: Excerpt of a TEI document from the corpus of the Text Database and Dictionary of Classic Mayan showing the encoding of a hieroglyphic text using the TEI Guidelines and the XML syntax.

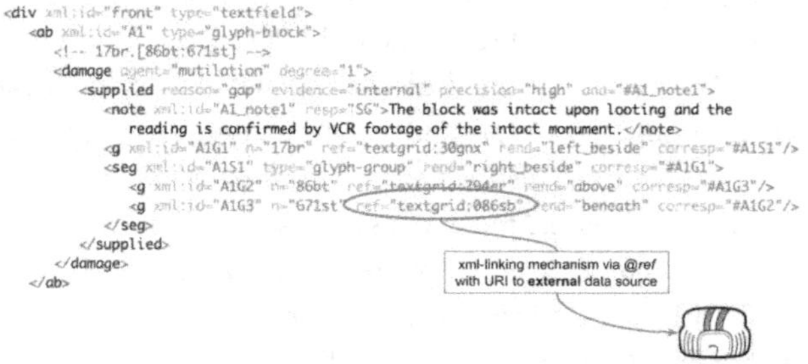

XML as a syntax consists of elements and attributes which specify the elements: e.g. <supplied> is specified by @reason="gap," @evidence="internal." The attribute @ana contains a reference to a XML identifier, which is used as a mechanism for linking elements in a document or even across documents (which is referred to as 'stand-off markup').[46] In Figure 2 the value of @ana in

ceptual development of the virtual research environment, including the realization of metadata schemas and ontologies. For more information see *Textdatenbank und Wörterbuch des Klassischen Maya.* https://mayawoerterbuch.de/

45   Along with the TEI, there are several initiatives specifying the guideline for special domains such as *EpiDoc* (subset of the TEI for epigraphic purposes). https://sourcefor ge.net/p/epidoc/wiki/Home/; *CBML Comic Book Markup Language.* http://dcl.slis.indiana. edu/cbml/; *MEI: Music Encoding Initiative.* https://music-encoding.org/

46   "20.4 Stand-off Markup." https://www.tei-c.org/release/doc/tei-p5-doc/en/html/NH.ht ml#NHSO

the <supplied>-element refers to a <note> with @xml:id="A1_note," in which the editor explains why it was possible to reconstruct a damaged glyph.

XML also provides a further linking mechanism using @ref, which also allows linking to an external data source. A particularity of the text corpus of Classic Maya is that it does not contain transcripted text.[47] Due to ongoing classification and deciphering tasks, it is not possible to provide transliterations for the hieroglyphic text. Instead, Uniform Resource Identifiers (URI)[48] are used to refer to the description of the used sign variant, which is stored in another database using another metadata schema (an ontology written in RDF).

This example illustrates how existing vocabularies and standards can assist with logical data modelling. Authorities curating data (like libraries) as well as research-driven communities (such as the Text Encoding Initiative) have developed a great amount of useful vocabularies, which can be useful when developing a project-specific data model. The challenging task may be to find the suitable ones, as available resources collecting those vocabularies (like Linked Open Vocabularies)[49] still lack comprehensiveness.

Challenges of Modelling Humanities Data—An Example

A modelling process needs sensible attention and a high degree of awareness. In the humanities we deal with complex knowledge. We deal with interpretations based on prior processes that generated knowledge at a certain time by pre-informed subjects. This is utterly different from how computational methods work, because algorithms are limited to exact assertions. McCarty states that "programmatic explicitness and precision is radically inadequate for representing the full range of knowledge."[50] Modelling means to be aware of what can be ignored and why. A model can only represent what it is built for, and further methods applied to the model depend on that. This is especially important when dealing with vague and uncertain information.

Since 'knowledge' about objects can be questioned or interpreted differently, it can be necessary to represent the various levels of knowledge in the

47   For further information on the encoding strategy of the text corpus of Classic Mayan
      see Sikora, "Interlinked."
48   "Uniform Resource Identifier (URI)." https://tools.ietf.org/html/rfc3986
49   Linked Open Vocabularies. https://lov.linkeddata.es/dataset/lov
50   McCarty, Humanities Computing 25.

model in order to counteract distortions and to limit the knowledge base precisely in the sense of the defined ontological categories.[51]

To illustrate the complexity that has to be dealt with in digital humanities projects, I again use an example from the project *Text Database and Dictionary of Classic Mayan*.

Classic Mayan is an as-of-yet not fully deciphered script of the Maya culture, which inhabited pre-Columbian Yucatán. Due to the nature of the hieroglyphs, one sign can have multiple readings. These readings depend on the co-text the sign is used in, but can also be influenced by other factors, such as the type of text carrier it is written on, its temporal or spatial usage etc. Additionally, there are contradicting hypotheses on the deciphering of signs due to different approaches to decoding as well as the availability of material. The project's goal is to linguistically analyze the texts with respect to all reasonable hypotheses. A need arose for a way of formally assessing the level of confidence of the reading proposals. For that, a system was modelled that combines ontological modelling[52] and propositional logic (Figure 3).

Figure 3: Modelling of the criteria-based system for the qualitative assessment of reading proposals of the Text Database and Dictionary of Classic Mayan.

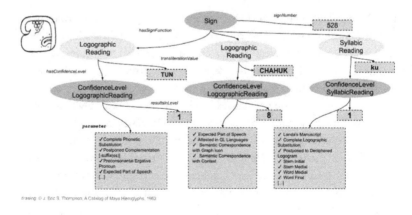

drawing: © J. Eric S. Thompson, A Catalog of Maya Hieroglyphs, 1962

---

51   Diehr, "Modelling Vagueness" 37.
52   *Text Database and Dictionary of Classic Mayan*. https://classicmayan.org/

Based on rules of logic, the system assesses a qualitative level of confidence.[53] This helps with the linguistic analysis and ultimately contributes to the ongoing deciphering of the script.

The approach of the *Text Database and Dictionary of Classic Mayan* project also illustrates the possibilities that emerge when different data models are combined. It can also serve as a prototypical example for other applications. It is a concept of separate but interlinked ontological-based data models (Figure 4).

Each model fulfills a different purpose: encoding the text corpus, linguistically annotating and analyzing text, classifying linguistic signs, referencing bibliographical resources, and documenting text carriers. Together they form a system that provides rich functionalities that enable epigraphers and linguists to decipher the Classic Mayan script.[54]

This case may illustrate a specific case for the purpose of deciphering an ancient script, but it also serves as an example of dealing with diverse and complex materials and sources. Instead of documenting texts and their carriers, a model can be imagined, one that is used for researching complex entanglements of music and media history, describing and relating audiovisual documents as well as source materials.

Conclusion

This paper laid out theoretical foundations and practical approaches to modelling (complex) knowledge for the purpose of research and analysis with the help of computational methods. As has been argued, modelling is regarded

---

53 Diehr, "Modelling Vagueness" 40.

54 The TEI/XML document forms the central part. Its encoding is enriched by multiple other resources to support specific functions and workflows for annotation, documentation and analysis: a Sign Catalogue for the classification of signs and graphs as well as their variants; an ontology for the documentation of the text carriers (both of them aligned with CIDOC CRM and written in RDF and supported by further knowledge organization systems, which are modelled in SKOS/RDF); the tool ALMAH for linguistic annotation and analysis; a project bibliography (for which Zotero is used); documentation and organization of archival material (which is managed by the DARIAH-DE service ConedaKOR). Bringing all those information sources together provides a holistic research environment for analyzing and deciphering the script of Classic Mayan.

Figure 4: The virtual research environment of the project Text Database and Dictionary of Classic Mayan uses multiple models and information sources.

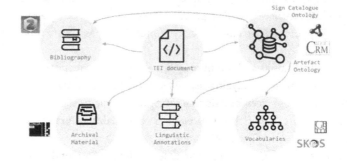

as a hermeneutic method that builds an ontological understanding of the object of inquiry and the domain perspective(s) it has been regarded with. Or as Ciula and Eide put it: "In digital humanities we do not only create models as fixed structures of knowledge, but also as a way to investigate a series of temporary states in a process of coming to know."[55]

As illustrated, special attention should be paid to the modelling of vague and uncertain information. Unwanted bias built into the model can cause false observations. In contrast, the careful modelling of phenomena, the vagueness and uncertainties of which are anticipated, may enable one to see things from new and different perspectives and to draw new conclusions.

The flexibility of computational models makes it possible to create and/or reuse models and combine them to fit specific needs. In doing so, holistic research environments can be developed. Nevertheless, the development of specialized models to address specific needs is recommended. A 'one model fits all' solution will not satisfy highly specialized research tasks and specific research interests.

As an interdisciplinary movement, digital humanities bridges the gap between computer science and traditional humanities studies. Particularly in the field of knowledge representation and the theory and practice of modelling, digital humanities should play a major role in training in the skills that

---

55   Ciula and Eide, "Reflections on Cultural Heritage" 37.

are needed for (not just) computer-aided but, first and foremost, data-driven approaches to humanistic research. The skill set should be grounded on a theory that comprises aspects of philosophy and logic, knowledge representation and engineering, as well as information and computer science.

In their survey Delcambre et al. asked experts from different fields about their ideas on (conceptual) modelling. Their participants particularly stressed the necessity of human involvement in the modelling process and thereby strongly emphasized a cognitive presence when creating knowledge. Nowadays, more and more tasks are being solved by artificial intelligence and machine learning algorithms, which are often referred to as 'black boxes' because the internal learning processes of the machines are not transparent to us. Nevertheless, they perform tasks quickly and produce satisfactory results. Those are profound arguments in favor of making use of such methods. When applying them to humanities research, we should carefully take into account the extent to which human intelligence and the processes of knowledge creation are needed when modelling. In this perspective, digital humanities may contribute to the discourse on digital ethics, critically examining the application of artificial intelligence for sensitive tasks of research as well as for general usage by humanity.

Bibliography (last accessed 16 April 2020)

Ciula, Arianna, et al. "Modelling Between Digital and Humanities: Thinking in Practice." *Digital Humanities 2016: Conference Abstracts – DH 2016*, Krakow, Poland (July 2016): 762–763.

Ciula, Arianna, and Øyvind Eide. "Reflections on Cultural Heritage and Digital Humanities: Modelling in Practice and Theory." *Proceedings of the First International Conference on Digital Access to Textual Cultural Heritage*, Madrid, Spain (May 2014): 35–41. DOI: 10.1145/2595188.2595207

Davis, Randall, et al. "What is a Knowledge Representation?" *AI Magazine* 14, 1 (Spring 1993): 17–33. DOI: 10.1609/aimag.v14i1.1029

Delcambre, Lois M. L., et al. "A Reference Framework for Conceptual Modelling." *Proceedings of the 37th International Conference on Conceptual Modelling – ER 2018*, Xi'an, China (October 2018): 27–42.

Diehr, Franziska, et al. "Modelling Vagueness – A Criteria-Based System for the Qualitative Assessment of Reading Proposals for the Deciphering of Classic Mayan Hieroglyphs." *Proceedings of the Workshop on Computational*

Methods in the Humanities 2018 – COMHUM, Lausanne, Switzerland (June 2018): 33–45.

Diehr, Franziska, Sven Gronemeyer et al. "Modellierung von Entzifferungs-hypothesen in einem digitalen Zeichenkatalog für die Maya-Schrift." *Zeitschrift für Digitale Geisteswissenschaft*, special issue 4 (January 2019). DOI: 10.17175/sb004_002

Durrell, William R. *Data Administration: A Practical Guide to Data Administration*. New York: McGraw-Hill, 1985.

Flanders, Julia, and Fotis Jannidis. "Conference Report." *Knowledge Organization and Data Modelling in the Humanities*, Brown Univ. Providence, USA (March 2012): 1–38. URN: urn:nbn:de:bvb:20-opus-111270

Geertz, Clifford. *The Interpretation of Cultures: Selected Essays*. London: Fontana, 1993 (1973).

Gruber, Thomas R. "Toward Principles for the Design of Ontologies Used for Knowledge Sharing?" *International Journal of Human-Computer Studies* 43, 5–6 (November 1995): 907–28. DOI: 10.1006/ijhc.1995.1081

Hughes, R. I. G. "Models and Representation." *Philosophy of Science* 64 (December 1997): 325–336. DOI: 10.1086/392611

Kuczera, Andreas, Thorsten Wübbena and Thomas Kollatz. "Die Modellierung des Zweifels: Schlüsselideen und -konzepte zur graphbasierten Modellierung von Unsicherheiten." *Zeitschrift für digitale Geisteswissenschaften*, special issue 4 (January 2019). DOI: 10.17175/sb004_013

Lakoff, George. *Women, Fire and Dangerous Things: What Categories Reveal about the Mind*. Chicago: Univ. of Chicago Press, 2008 (1987).

Mahr, Bernd. "Das Wissen im Modell." *KIT-Report* 150 (2004): 1–21.

Mahr, Bernd. "Information Science and the Logic of Models." *Software and Systems Modelling* 8, 3 (May 2009): 365–83. DOI: 10.1007/s10270-009-0119-2

McCarty, Willard. *Humanities Computing*. Hampshire: Palgrave Macmillan, 2005.

Pickard, Alison. *Research Methods in Information*. London: Facet, 2007.

Reinhold, Anke. "Das Experteninterview als zentrale Methode der Wissensmodellierung in den Digital Humanities." *Information-Wissenschaft & Praxis* 66, 5–6 (October 2015): 327–33. DOI: 10.1515/iwp-2015-0057

Rosch, Eleanor, et al. "Basic Objects in Natural Categories." *Cognitive psychology* 8, 3 (July 1976): 382–439. DOI: 10.1016/0010-0285(76)90013-X

Sikora, Uwe, et al. "'Interlinked!:' Schriftzeugnisse der Klassischen Mayakultur im Spannungsfeld zwischen Standoff- und Inline-Markup in TEI-XML." *DHd 2019 Digital Humanities: Multimedial & Multimodal: Konferenzabs-*

tracts, Frankfurt, Germany (March 2019): 143–47. DOI: 10.5281/zenodo.25 96095

Silberschatz, Abraham, et al. *Database System Concepts*. [Place of publication not identified]: McGraw-Hill Education, 2019.

Sowa, John F. *Knowledge Representation: Logical, Philosophical and Computational Foundations*. London: Brooks Cole, 2000.

Stachowiak, Herbert. *Allgemeine Modelltheorie*. Wien, New York: Springer, 1973.

Uschold, Mike, and Martin King. *Towards a Methodology for Building Ontologies*. Edinburgh: Univ. of Edinburgh Press, 1995.

Online Sources (last accessed 16 April 2020)

CBML Comic Book Markup Language. http://dcl.slis.indiana.edu/cbml/

CIDOC CRM. http://cidoc-crm.org/

CLARIAH-DE. https://www.clariah.de

EpiDoc: Epigraphic Documents in TEI/XML. https://sourceforge.net/p/epidoc/w iki/Home/

Linked Open Vocabularies. https://lov.linkeddata.es/dataset/lov

"Linking, Segmentation, and Alignment. Stand-off Markup". *TEI: Text Encoding Initiative*. https://www.tei-c.org/release/doc/tei-p5-doc/en/html/SA.h tml#SASO

MEI: Music Encoding Initiative. https://music-encoding.org/

"METS standard Version 1.12." *Library of Congress*. https://www.loc.gov/stand ards/mets/

"MODS standard Version 3.7." *Library of Congress*. https://www.loc.gov/stand ards/mods/

"Ontology of the Sign Catalogue for Classic Mayan." *Text Database and Dictionary of Classic Mayan*. https://classicmayan.org/documentations/catalogu e.html

Text Database and Dictionary of Classic Mayan. https://classicmayan.org/

Textdatenbank und Wörterbuch des Klassischen Maya. https://mayawoerterbuch. de/

"Text Encoding Initiative: P5 Guidelines." *TEI: Text Encoding Initiative*. https:// tei-c.org/guidelines/p5/

"20.4 Stand-off Markup." *TEI: Text Encoding Initiative*. https://www.tei-c.org/ release/doc/tei-p5-doc/en/html/NH.html#NHSO

"Uniform Resource Identifier (URI): Generic Syntax." *IETF Tools*. https://tools.
   ietf.org/html/rfc3986

"VD18 digital." *SUB: Göttinger Digitalisierungszentrum*. https://gdz.sub.uni-goe
   ttingen.de/collection/vd18.digital

Verzeichnis Deutscher Drucke des 18. Jahrhunderts – VD18. https://gso.gbv.de/DB
   =1.65/

Playing with a Web of Music: Connecting and Enriching Online Music Repositories[1]

David M. Weigl and Werner Goebl (University of Music and Performing Arts Vienna)

Towards Richer Online Music Public-Domain Archives

Classical music represents both a treasured cultural heritage and a living, contemporary tradition, perpetuated and continuously reinterpreted through practice, performance, scholarly analysis, and listening enjoyment. Music libraries and archives assemble, preserve, and organize classical music resources for retrieval, but currently underserve the more dynamic aspects of our interactions with this repertoire. Enriching these interactions is important in order to engage, broaden, and diversify the classical music audience, thus sustaining this tradition.[2]

The EU Horizons 2020-funded TROMPA project[3]—Towards Richer Online Music Public-domain Archives—is addressing this challenge by combining music information retrieval (MIR) technologies and crowd-sourcing approaches to publish, interlink, contextualize, and augment public-domain classical music resources.[4] Building on large existing music repositories, TROMPA provides services for the discovery, enhancement, and contribution of musical scores, recordings, analyses, and interpretations, applying

---

1   This publication incorporates and expands on text from "Interweaving and enriching digital music collections for scholarship, performance, and enjoyment" by authors David M. Weigl, Werner Goebl, Tim Crawford, Aggelos Gkiokas, Nicolas F. Gutierrez, Alastair Porter, Patricia Santos, Casper Karreman, Ingmar Vroomen, Cynthia C. S. Liem, Álvaro Sarasúa and Marcel van Tilburg, presented at the *6th International Conference on Digital Libraries for Musicology* (2019). DOI: 10.1145/3358664.3358666
2   Melenhorst and Liem, "Put the Concert Attendee in the Spotlight."
3   *Trompa*. https://trompamusic.eu
4   Weigl and Goebl, "Interweaving and Enriching Digital Music Collections."

open, standard web and MIR technologies to ensure reusable, reproducible, reinterpretable, scalable, and sustainable access to the data produced.

Within the project, we are building an infrastructure around publicly licensed music resources on the Web, adhering to FAIR principles of making data Findable, Accessible, Interoperable, and Reusable.[5] Digital encodings of musical scores play a central part, both as resources of primary interest and as structural frameworks for interlinking multimodal musical representations.

In this chapter, we provide an overview of the TROMPA project. Then, in section 2, we situate its origins within the heritage of three multi-institutional predecessor projects focusing on technologically enriched classical music concert experiences, digital music scholarship, and semantic Web technologies. We present several major Web repositories of publicly licensed music content in Section 3 before describing TROMPA's data infrastructure for interconnecting and enriching such repositories in Section 4. Section 5 describes five user types targeted by specialized Web applications under development as part of the project, as well as considerations pertaining to privacy and data ownership arising when users enrich and generate new music resources through their interactions with these applications. Section 6 introduces the Music Encoding Initiative and its XML schema underlying the dynamic digital scores forming the basis of TROMPA's user-facing applications. Finally, we characterize the Companion for Long-term Analyses of Rehearsal Attempts (CLARA), a TROMPA Web application serving the needs of instrumental players engaged in music practice, in Section 7; we then offer conclusions and future perspectives in Section 8.

Background

TROMPA builds on a number of previous wide-ranging, multi-institutional research projects around the interlinking and enrichment of music resources in a variety of use cases.

---

5   Wilkinson, "The FAIR Guiding Principles for Scientific Data Management and Stewardship."

Performances as Highly Enriched aNd Interactive Concert eXperiences (PHENICX)

PHENICX was an international collaborative research project funded under the European Union's Seventh Framework Programme. Motivated by notions that technological developments in the current digital age could offer new opportunities to make symphonic classical music more accessible to broader audiences, the project had two main focus areas.[6] Research was performed both into improving the audiovisual analysis techniques necessary for enabling multimodal enrichment, and into finding ways to make such enrichments engaging and useful for the intended broader audiences.

Though producing impactful demonstrations of technologically enriched concert experiences,[7] scalability was limited in part by the expensiveness of processes required to generate clean and well-structured input data (e.g., digital score encodings, score-aligned performance recordings) assembled under the supervision of human experts. In TROMPA, we are addressing this limitation through crowd-sourcing components that more scalably incorporate human insight into enrichment activities, while placing greater emphasis on the use of standardized Web technologies and FAIR data practices facilitating reuse of the data we generate beyond the confines of the project.

Transforming Musicology

This wide-ranging UK-based AHRC-funded project included a focus on semantic linking of musical resources and workflows, demonstrating how scholars might take fuller advantage of the possibilities for presentation, analysis and discovery inherent in a Web of digital resources organized as Linked Data.

Methods for capturing scholarly practice in terms of workflow were studied as an exercise in the semantic approach by analyzing and comparing the steps needed to achieve useful results in a number of music(ologic)al

---

6   Gómez, "PHENICX;" Liem, "Innovating the Classical Music Experience in the PHENICX Project."

7   E.g.: Arzt, "Artificial Intelligence in the Concertgebouw;" Gasser, "Classical Music on the Web-User Interfaces and Data Representations;" Melenhorst et al., "A Tablet App to Enrich the Live and Post-Live Experience of Classical Concerts;" Sarasúa Berodia, "Mapping by Observation."

tasks.[8] Other work in the SLICKMEM and SLOBR projects immediately preceding Transforming Musicology investigated the problems of aligning multiple datasets compiled with inconsistent formats or standards.[9] Subsequent follow-up projects have focused on the application of tools and workflows assembled under Transforming Musicology toward multimedia scholarly publishing and access to music digital libraries.[10]

Fusing Audio and Semantic Technologies for Intelligent Music Production and Consumption (FAST)

FAST was a multi-institutional UK EPSRC-funded project at the intersection of audio processing technologies, studio science, and the Semantic Web. The project defined Digital Music Objects (DMOs), flexible constructs consisting of recorded music essence coupled with rich, semantic, linked metadata with applications throughout the music value chain, from production through to distribution and consumption.[11] DMOs retain provenance traces of their activities throughout this chain, with implications for music digital libraries.[12]

Though not sharing TROMPA's focus on public-domain classical music, the notion of the DMO is particularly informative in an environment focusing on the interlinking of music metadata, provenance-tracked contributions by human and machine agents, and reuse and reinterpretation within different usage contexts.

Music Collections on the Web

A wealth of music resources is available digitally on the Web, composed of various types of music information, including scans of music score sheets, music encodings, audiovisual performance recordings, and metadata describing each of these resources and documenting extra-musical facets such as bib-

---

8   Nurmikko-Fuller, "A Linked Research Network that is Transforming Musicology."

9   Weigl and Lewis, "On Providing Semantic Alignment and Unified Access to Music Library Metadata."

10   Lewis, "Publishing Musicology Using Multimedia Digital Libraries;" Page, "MELD: A Linked Data Framework."

11   Sandler, "Semantic Web Technology for New Experiences."

12   De Roure, "Music and Science."

liographical information—works, composers, performers; composition, arrangement, publication, and performance events; and so on.

Though such resources and descriptions are publicly available in numerous Web-accessible repositories, each repository typically presents only subsets of both repertoire and information modality. The prospect of combining and inter-referencing, for instance, various editions of a musical score, performance recordings by various interpreters, alongside musicological commentary by various scholars, offers exciting possibilities for unified music exploration and analysis; but this prospect is hindered by the typically disparate nature of music repositories on the Web.

One of the largest and most notable collections, the International Music Score Library Project (IMSLP), also known as the Petrucci Music Library,[13] contains over 475,000 scores by more than 17,500 composers. All scores included in IMSLP belong to the public domain in either Canada or the US. The IMSLP is an important source for musicians and scholars seeking printed editions of classical music pieces, often offering multiple versions of the same composition. IMSLP also contains Creative Commons-licensed recordings uploaded by users, and links to commercial recordings provided by music labels, which paid subscribers can listen to.

Another important public-domain classical music score repository is the Choral Public Domain Library (CPDL),[14] which holds over 32,000 choral and vocal works by at least 3,200 composers. Both IMSLP and CPDL are important repositories as sources for different technologies and use cases in the TROMPA project.

The main resource for public-domain structured (and machine-readable) music metadata is MusicBrainz,[15] an 'open music encyclopedia' maintained by a global community of users. Although aimed broadly at music of all genres, MusicBrainz contains an impressive number of classical works, composers and performers. The MusicBrainz data model includes many features that uniquely suit classical music, including distinctly identifying compositions and movements, annotating compositions with catalogue numbers, and relating recordings to people who participated in them—e.g., performing orchestra, any soloists, the conductor—as well as specific information about composers and works performed. Data quality and quantity vary on initial

13   *IMSLP Petrucci Music Library.* https://imslp.org
14   *Choral Public Domain Library.* https://www.cpdl.org/wiki
15   *MusicBrainz.* https://musicbrainz.org

contribution, but community members can correct, adjust or complement the data. MusicBrainz' structured data model and use of unique identifiers have made it an authority for music identification.

The biggest non-commercial collections of audio recordings can be found in specialized music archives and libraries. They are often part of national libraries, like the British Library Sound Archive[16] or the Deutsches Musikarchiv.[17] Such collections are generally not publicly accessible outside of their source institution, remaining effectively 'invisible' (no audio playback; no display of artwork or record covers) and not searchable without specialist access.

Muziekweb,[18] based in Rotterdam, does provide publicly accessible collection of music data. It offers access to over 600,000 CDs and 300,000 LPs, described using international library standards, which it is matching to domain-relevant repositories, including MusicBrainz, Wikidata, sheet music archives, and streaming services. The archive, including digitized audio data that can be used for audio analysis and high-quality metadata, makes Muziekweb a relevant authority for classical music in the TROMPA project.

Each of these repositories provides useful information, but their interconnection is limited. Users of these platforms (and many others available on the Web) are often unaware that the other platforms exist. Most repositories use their own vocabulary and description standards, and typically do not integrate complementary information available across collections. Breaking through these 'silos' of music information by interconnecting music resources across repositories is a key motivation for the TROMPA project.

A Data Infrastructure for Interconnecting and Enriching Music Collections

Integrating and ingesting different datasets into a single combined repository ('data warehousing') is a complex problem, involving the alignment and translation of potentially different representations and data schemas.[19] However, the motivation of TROMPA is not to supplant established Web music repositories by copying entity descriptions and media representations into

---

16   "Sounds." https://sounds.bl.uk
17   "German Music Archive." https://www.dnb.de/EN/Ueber-uns/DMA/dma_node.html
18   *Muziekweb*. https://www.muziekweb.eu
19   Weigl and Kudeki, "Combine or Connect."

a centralized database and unified schema, but rather to describe them by reference, using URIs to address, interlink, and contribute layers of enriched descriptors and content to resources hosted in situ at their native (TROMPA-external) Web locations.

Schema.org,[20] a formalized vocabulary for describing Web resources, provides a core data model for this purpose of virtual integration across music repositories. This is augmented by other widely used, standardized vocabularies, including the Dublin Core Metadata Initiative's[21] vocabulary for encoding bibliographic relationships, the Simple Knowledge Organisation System's (SKOS)[22] vocabulary for mapping relations (providing the 'glue' for interconnecting entities across repositories), and the Web Annotation vocabulary[23] and PROV ontology[24] for capturing and tracking the provenance of contributions to enrich these resources by TROMPA users (Section 5) and by automated music information retrieval processes. Further established vocabularies are adapted for specialized applications, such as for the alignment of musical scores and performance recordings (Section 7).

Graph databases are ideally suited to support such flexible, mutably specified interconnection of Web-based resources. TROMPA has opted to adopt a Neo4j property graph database for this purpose. This database, exposed for query via a GraphQL endpoint, forms the core of the TROMPA Contributor Environment (CE), a data infrastructure that also comprises a number of component APIs for multimodal query, display and annotation of music resources, and automated assessment of scores and performances. Querying via the standard SPARQL[25] query language for Linked Data is not supported; while this would allow maximally flexible semantic queries over the CE graph, it is prone to performance issues at scale[26] and does not trivially support the automated processing of newly arriving data driving TROMPA's enrichment processes. However, each node in the graph can be accessed via a persistent URI through an HTTP wrapper interface, providing a JSON-LD[27] represen-

---

20   *Schema.org.* https://schema.org
21   *Dublin CoreTM Meta Data Initiative.* https://dublincore.org/specifications/dublin-core/dc mi-terms/
22   *SKOS Simple Knowledge Organization System.* http://www.w3.org/2004/02/skos/core.ht ml
23   *Web Annotation Vocabulary.* https://www.w3.org/TR/annotation-vocab/
24   *PROV-O: The PROV Ontology.* http://www.w3.org/TR/prov-o/
25   *SPARQL 1.1 Query Language.* https://www.w3.org/TR/sparql11-query/
26   Fields, "A Case Study in Pragmatism."
27   *JSON-LD 1.1.* https://www.w3.org/TR/json-ld/

tation of the respective entity and its associated properties and values, thus interweaving the CE graph with the wider Web of Linked Open Data.

Figure 1 illustrates several enrichment processes coordinated by the CE upon resources in TROMPA-external music repositories. A PDF score is ingested into the CE by reference to its URI. Automated processes validated and improved by human insight through crowd-based activities are triggered in order to arrive at a machine-readable digital music encoding, which is aligned with recordings of performances of the work enabling rich interactions and analyses serving TROMPA users.

Figure 1: The TROMPA Contributor Environment (CE) interlinks and coordinates enrichment activities upon repositories of publicly licensed music resources on the Web.

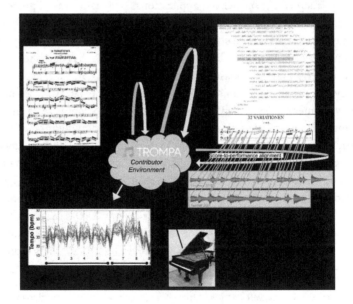

Five Types of User Contributing to One Web of Data

TROMPA explicitly targets five user types—music scholars, instrumental players, choir singers, orchestras, music enthusiasts—through Web applications providing specialized views of the graph described above, designed to fulfill information needs and usage requirements identified in user studies conducted throughout the project. Beyond consuming music content, each user produces information associated with resources described by the CE through their interactions with these applications, such as: scholarly annotations, rehearsal marks, score encodings, recordings of rehearsal renditions or the subjective ratings of such recordings.

Users may wish to retain private access to the resulting data; to share only selectively with specified other users; or, to maintain private drafts until a contribution is ready for publication. To support such behaviors, and to yield greater control to users over their data in a principled manner, TROMPA's Contributor Environment is affiliated with a secondary, decentralized layer of Personal Online Datastores (PODs; Figure 2) that also act as identity providers for TROMPA applications.[28]

Figure 2: Data generated by users in their interactions with TROMPA applications is stored in personal online datastores (PODs). Each user retains fine control of access to their data, allowing them to retain private drafts, share with selected other users or the public, or publish their contributions to the TROMPA Contributor Environment (CE) under an open license.

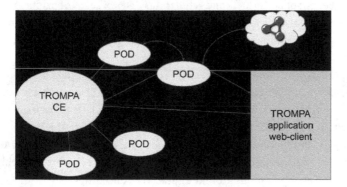

Contributions generated by a user's interactions with such applications are stored in the user's POD, referenced by a URI which can be requested

---

28   Mansour, "A Demonstration of the Solid Platform for Social Web Applications."

through an HTTP interface. An access control layer allows the user to selectively share or retain private access to each generated data item, or to open it to the public. PODs may be hosted with any POD provider on the Web, including options for self-hosting by users with the required technological expertise; as such, user-generated contributions hosted in this way are not tied into the TROMPA infrastructure, and remain open for reuse in other contexts and within other applications.

Users may further choose to publish their contributions under an open license, at which point the relevant data is ingested into the CE's graph, and thus made discoverable by other TROMPA users. Each type of user stands to benefit from improvements to this graph: contributions published to the CE by one type of user stand to provide holistic benefits to other users across all use cases—e.g., scholars and enthusiasts stand to benefit from access to recorded renditions by instrumental players and choral singers, who in turn stand to benefit from access to scholarly insight and subjective listener ratings of their performances.

Music Encodings as a Basis for Dynamic Semantic Music Notation

Digital music scores form a core information modality around which many of TROMPA's applications are built. Beyond providing graphical music notation for the benefit of performers and scholars (as PDFs of scans of printed musical scores might also provide), the musical meaning conveyed by the notation must also be machine-readable to support the rich interactivity offered by TROMPA's user-facing applications.

The Music Encoding Initiative's (MEI) XML schema offers a suitable encoding format.[29] Music encodings adhering to the MEI schema are versatile music information Web resources comprehensively capturing musical meaning within a finely addressable XML structure. Paired with the Verovio[30] engraver, which reflects the hierarchy and identifiers of the source MEI document into its generated SVG output, this supports the creation of richly interactive Web applications around digital score encodings.[31]

---

29   Crawford, "Review: Music Encoding Initiative."

30   *Verovio.* https://www.verovio.org

31   Pugin, "Interaction Perspectives for Music Notation Applications."

Typical MEI workflows involve initial scholarly or editorial activities to generate an encoding, followed by its subsequent publication and use. Further iterations may derive new encodings from precedents; but the suitability of MEI to interactive applications also offers more dynamic alternatives in which the encoding provides a framework connecting data that is generated and consumed simultaneously in real time. Exemplars include compositions which self-modify according to external contextual parameters such as the weather at the time of performance,[32] or compositions assembled by user-imposed external semantics, such as a performer's explicit choices and implicit performative success at playing musical triggers within a composition.[33]

When captured, these external semantic signals (interlinked with the MEI structure) themselves encode the evolution of a dynamic score during a particular performance. They have value beyond the immediate performance context; when archived, they allow different performances to be revisited and compared.[34]

MELD (Music Encoding and Linked Data),[35] a semantic framework and set of open-source client libraries for the creation of dynamic digital scores, offers a route to the implementation of such ideas. MELD was developed during the FAST project as a means of instantiating Digital Music Objects,[36] and applied toward multimedia publication of music scholarship in work related to the Transforming Musicology project.[37] In TROMPA, we are extending MELD with facilities for general-purpose and user-customizable score annotation, automated and highly granular (note-level) score-to-performance alignment, and with new capabilities for performance feature visualization.

TROMPA applies this tooling to provide musicians with applications that capitalize on the affordance for dynamic interactions with digital scores, providing fruitful ground to incorporate reflection and introspection into the music rehearsal process.

---

32   Arkfeld, "'Fortitude Flanked with Melody.'"
33   Kallionpää, "Composing and Realising a Game-Like Performance."
34   Benford, "Designing the Audience Journey through Repeated Experiences."
35   Weigl and Page, "A Framework for Distributed Semantic Annotation."
36   Sandler, "Semantic Web Technology for New Experiences."
37   Lewis, "Publishing Musicology Using Multimedia Digital Libraries;" Page, "MELD: A Linked Data Framework."

A Performance Companion for Instrumental Players

Performance companions target instrumental players and ensembles with applications to support them in their daily rehearsal regime, enriching rehearsal and teaching situations through immediate feedback on one's own and others' performances.[38]

TROMPA's CLARA (Companion for Long-term Analyses of Rehearsal Attempts)[39] is a MELD application that provides performers with a digital score that tracks their performance, aligning a performed MIDI stream with the score encoding such that temporal positions along the performance timeline are associated with corresponding notes according to their digital identifiers within the score. This alignment is accomplished in two modes, both using variations of hidden Markov model (HMM)-based score following systems for symbolic (MIDI) instrumental performances:[40] a real-time mode enabling interactions such as automated page turning and highlighting of notes in the score as they are played; and offline alignment performed within a few seconds immediately after each rehearsal attempt is completed, capable of more robust alignment by virtue of post-hoc access to the entire performance, and providing for more complex interaction mechanisms allowing the performer to revisit and review their rehearsal rendition by simultaneously navigating the score, and, via the aligned performance timeline, the corresponding MIDI stream.

The alignment of score and rehearsal encodings further enables visualizations to be created of visualizations of particular performance features—such as tempo curves—connected to score positions, providing the performer with immediate feedback regarding corresponding stylistic and technical aspects of their rehearsal rendition (Figure 3). To make this feedback as intuitive as possible, in this analytical viewing mode the score is rendered as a single, fully expanded system, with feature visualizations displayed above such that each unit of score-time, and the corresponding part of the visualization share a position on the X-axis. This achieves a continuous correspondence of graphical progression across the screen (corresponding to score-time), and temporal

---

38   Arzt, "Towards a Complete Classical Music Companion;" Goebl, "Unobtrusive Practice Tools for Pianists."

39   "Clara Schumann 200." https://iwk.mdw.ac.at/trompa-clara

40   Cancino-Chacón, "The ACCompanion v0.1;" Nakamura, "Performance Error Detection and Post-Processing."

progression through a rehearsal rendition (corresponding to the timeline of a recorded performance).

Figure 3: CLARA interface visualizing tempo curves for six renditions of Beethoven's 32 Variations in C minor (WoO 80). The colored tempo curve corresponds to the currently selected rendition; coloration of tempo curve and notes indicates current playback position; note hue corresponds to performance dynamics (MIDI velocity).

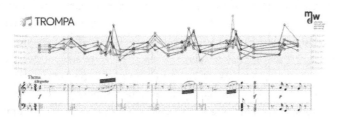

The notion of score position in this case is operationalized using the X-position of all note elements associated with a particular performance timeline instant during the alignment process. The corresponding score time is calculated by averaging the qstamps (score-based timestamps in terms of the number of quarter notes from the beginning of the encoding) obtained from the Verovio toolkit for the note elements aligned to the timeline instant. The tempo curve visualizes the change in score time per change in performed time, with Y-positions reflecting the difference in average qstamp associated with each timeline instant and its immediately preceding neighbor (q) divided by the difference in seconds between the performed instant's timeline position and that of its immediately preceding neighbor (t), multiplied by 60 to arrive at an approximate measure of beats (in fact, quarter notes) per minute for a given timeline instant. Visualizations of other feature types (e.g., dynamics, performance errors determined during the alignment stage) are currently under development.

Like Verovio's score engraving, CLARA feature visualizations are also generated as semantically structured SVGs, supporting in-browser interactions such as highlighting corresponding regions of the visualization during playback, and tapping on regions of the visualization to spool to the appropriate playback position. Beyond interactive review of a single rehearsal rendition, this enables systematic comparison of multiple renditions, allowing users to tap on the different tempo curves to listen in to the corresponding section played in different rehearsal attempts.

Rendition timelines are gathered for a particular comparison view according to their URI's inclusion within a Linked Data Platform (LDP)[41] container, itself a simple Linked Data structure stored in the user's POD (Personal Online Datastore; Section 5). A selected rendition can be shared with another user by adding a reference to the rendition's URI into a corresponding LDP container on the other user's POD; the same rendition can be included in many containers (potentially owned by many different users), and one user may manage a number of different containers, each potentially including renditions by different users. Further, CLARA supports the creation of Web Annotations targeting specified score regions and selected corresponding renditions. These annotations are themselves Linked Data structures with their own URIs, meaning they too can be shared between different users.

Through these mechanisms, we foresee performers tracking their own rehearsal progress; comparing their playing with selected peers; communicating with their teachers through annotations and by comparison with reference renditions; and incorporating notable pianists' renditions into their comparisons.

The rehearsal companion provides a powerful tool for reviewing one's rehearsal progress by allowing rehearsal attempts to be captured, gathered, and compared with fine granularity, providing insights into the evolution of the stylistic and performative aspects of one's renditions of a piece over time. Consider, for instance, the case of a pianist practicing a new piece (say, Beethoven's *Appassionata*). She selects a score on her tablet computer. As she practices, her performance is streamed to an alignment process coordinated by the CE, which generates metadata to synchronize her performance timeline with the digital score. After she has finished playing her rehearsal rendition, a note-level tempo curve visualization is immediately available for her inspection. She can now compare her tempo curves with those extracted from her favorite recording of the piece on YouTube or Spotify, performed by, for instance, Claudio Arrau. While listening to Arrau's performance, she jots down a personal note about a particular section of the *Appassionata*. She publishes her comment to TROMPA's CE as a Web Annotation that targets both the relevant section of the digital score and the corresponding timespan of Arrau's performance.

---

41   *Linked Data Platform 1.0.* https://www.w3.org/TR/ldp/

Apart from instrumental players, this data, expressed in interoperable fashion using Web standards, becomes available for reuse by others—providing scholars with empirical data on performance practice (e.g., to determine a typical tempo profile of the *Appassionata* as rehearsed in the 'wild'), or music enthusiasts with a landscape of renditions to listen into and explore.

Conclusion

In this paper, we have presented an overview of TROMPA, an international project aiming to interconnect and enrich public-domain music repositories on the Web, rooting the project's ambitions in its predecessor projects around music semantic technologies, enriched concert experiences, and digital musicology scholarship; describing exemplar collections of publicly licensed music content to convey the richly varied resources available in openly accessible, but disparate, repositories on the web; then outlining the data infrastructure we are assembling to interconnect these repositories within a knowledge graph, ever-expanding through publicly licensed user contributions.

We have detailed CLARA, the Companion for Long-term Analyses of Rehearsal Attempts, a TROMPA application enabling musicians to track, analyze, and share insights on the evolution of rehearsal renditions. We have presented this as an exemplar application available to instrumental performers, as one of five user types (alongside music scholars, choir singers, orchestras, and music enthusiasts) explicitly targeted by applications making use of and adding to the knowledge graph managed within TROMPA's Contributor Environment. Beyond these use cases, we provide for future project-external reinterpretation, recontextualization, and reuse beyond any application currently anticipated by the project through its emphasis on publicly licensed content, standardized Web technologies, and FAIR data practices.

Together, we envision these technologies and their user base to function as a social machine[42] continuously playing with and expanding an interconnected Web of music information, a process in which "the people do the creative work and the machine does the administration"[43]—and, in our case, the music information processing. We are faced, however, with a cold-start problem; in order to be attractive to new users, we require MEI encodings for mu-

---

42   Hendler, "From the Semantic Web to Social Machines."
43   Berners-Lee, *Weaving the Web* 172.

sicians to rehearse, and recorded rehearsal renditions to seed comparisons. Within TROMPA we are addressing this issue through crowd-sourcing techniques and by recruiting participants at partner institutions.[44] We will require coordination with the wider community of digital musicology scholars, music encoding specialists, music information researchers and practitioners, and performers with an affinity for the digital in order to fully achieve our vision of a shared, dynamic, and richly interactive repertoire of publicly licensed scores, performance recordings, and other associated music information resources.

Acknowledgements

This project has received funding from the European Union's Horizon 2020 research and innovation program H2020-EU.3.6.3.1., supporting the study of European heritage, memory, identity, integration, and cultural interaction and translation, including its representations in cultural and scientific collections, archives and museums, to better inform and understand the present by richer interpretations of the past under grant agreement No. 770376. We gratefully acknowledge the collaboration of all our colleagues in the TROMPA consortium.

Bibliography (last accessed 16 April 2020)

Arkfeld, Joseph, and Raffaele Viglianti. "'Fortitude Flanked with Melody:' Setting Emily Dickinson's Poetic Fragments to Music via a Digital Dynamic Score." *Proceedings of the Music Encoding Conference*, Maryland, USA (May 2018).

Arzt, Andreas, et al. "Towards a Complete Classical Music Companion." *Proceedings of the 20th European Conference on Artificial Intelligence – ECAI 2012*, Montpellier, France (August 2012). DOI: 10.3233/978-1-61499-098-7-67

Arzt, Andreas, et al. "Artificial Intelligence in the Concertgebouw." *Twenty-Fourth International Joint Conference on Artificial Intelligence*, Buenos Aires, Argentina (July 2015): 2424–30.

---

44   MEI encodings generated by TROMPA project activities are available at https://github.com/trompamusic-encodings

Benford, Steve, et al. "Designing the Audience Journey through Repeated Experiences." *Proceedings of the 2018 CHI Conference on Human Factors in Computing Systems*, Montréal, Canada (April 2018): 1–12. DOI: 10.1145/3173574.3174142

Berners-Lee, T., and Mark Fischetti. *Weaving the Web: The Original Design and Ultimate Destiny of the World Wide Web*. New York: Harper Collins, 1999.

Cancino-Chacón, Carlos, et al. "The ACCompanion v0.1: An Expressive Accompaniment System." *Late Breaking/Demo Session, 18th International Society for Music Information Retrieval*, Paris, France (2018).

Crawford, Tim, and Richard Lewis. "Review: Music Encoding Initiative." *Journal of the American Musicological Society* 69, 1 (Spring 2016): 273–85. DOI: 10.1525/jams.2016.69.1.273

De Roure, David, et al. "Music and Science: Parallels in Production." *Proceedings of the 2nd International Workshop on Digital Libraries for Musicology*, Knoxville TN, USA (June 2015): 17–20. DOI: 10.1145/2785527.2785530

Fields, Ben, Penelope Phippen and Brad Cohen. "A Case Study in Pragmatism: Exploring the Practical Failure Modes of Linked Data as Applied to Classical Music Catalogues." *Proceedings of the 2nd International Workshop on Digital Libraries for Musicology*, Knoxville TN, USA (June 2015): 21–24. DOI: 10.1145/2785527.2785531

Gasser, Martin, et al. "Classical Music on the Web-User Interfaces and Data Representations." *Proceedings of the 16th International Society for Music Information Retrieval Conference*, Malaga, Spain (October 2015): 571–77.

Goebl, Werner, and Gerhard Widmer. "Unobtrusive Practice Tools for Pianists." *Proceedings of the 9th International Conference on Music Perception and Cognition – ICMPC9*, Bologna, Italy (August 2006): 1–5.

Gómez, Emilia, et al. "PHENICX: Performances as Highly Enriched aNd Interactive Concert eXperiences." *Proceedings of SMC Sound and Music Computing Conference*, Stockholm, Sweden (July–August 2013): 681–88.

Hendler, Jim, and Tim Berners-Lee. "From the Semantic Web to Social Machines: A Research Challenge for AI on the World Wide Web." *Artificial intelligence* 174, 2 (February 2010): 156–61. DOI: 10.1016/j.artint.2009.11.010

Kallionpää, Maria, et al. "Composing and Realising a Game-Like Performance for Disklavier and Electronics." *Proceedings of New Interfaces for Musical Expression – NIME'17*, Copenhagen, Denmark (May 2017): 464–69.

Lewis, David, et al. "Publishing Musicology Using Multimedia Digital Libraries: Creating Interactive Articles Through a Framework for Linked

Data and MEI." *Proceedings of the 5th International Conference on Digital Libraries for Musicology*, Paris, France (September 2018): 21–25. DOI: 10.1145/3273024.3273038

Liem, Cynthia C. S., et al. "Innovating the Classical Music Experience in the PHENICX Project: Use Cases and Initial User Feedback." *1st International Workshop on Interactive Content Consumption (WSICC) at EuroITV*, Como, Italy (June 2013).

Mansour, Essam, et al. "A Demonstration of the Solid Platform for Social Web Applications." *Proceedings of the 25th International Conference Companion on World Wide Web*, Montréal, Canada (April 2016): 223–226. DOI: 10.1145/2872518.2890529

Melenhorst, Mark S., et al. "A Tablet App to Enrich the Live and Post-Live Experience of Classical Concerts." *CEUR Workshop Proceedings, no. 1516, 2015. Third International Workshop on Interactive Content Consumption – ACM TVX'15*, Brussels, Belgium (June 2015).

Melenhorst, Mark S., and Cynthia C. S. Liem. "Put the Concert Attendee in the Spotlight: A User-Centered Design and Development Approach for Classical Concert Applications." *Proceedings of the 16th International Society for Music Information Retrieval Conference*, Malaga, Spain (October 2015): 800–06.

Nakamura, Eita, Kazuyoshi Yoshii and Haruhiro Katayose. "Performance Error Detection and Post-Processing for Fast and Accurate Symbolic Music Alignment." *Proceedings of the 18th International Society for Music Information Retrieval Conference*, Suzhou, China (October 2017): 347–53.

Nurmikko-Fuller, Terhi, and Kevin R. Page. "A Linked Research Network that is Transforming Musicology." *WHiSe @ ESWC*, Anissaras, Greece (May 2016): 73–78.

Page, Kevin R., David Lewis and David M. Weigl. "MELD: A Linked Data Framework for Multimedia Access to Music Digital Libraries." *2019 ACM/IEEE Joint Conference on Digital Libraries – JCDL, IEEE*, Milan, Italy (June 2019): 434–35. DOI: 10.1109/JCDL.2019.00106

Pugin, Laurent. "Interaction Perspectives for Music Notation Applications." *Proceedings of the 1st International Workshop on Semantic Applications for Audio and Music*, Monterey CA, USA (October 2018): 54–58. DOI: 10.1145/3243907.3243911

Sandler, Mark, et al. "Semantic Web Technology for New Experiences Throughout the Music Production-Consumption Chain." *2019 International Workshop on Multilayer Music Representation and Processing – MMRP, IEEE*, Milan, Italy (January 2019). DOI: 10.1109/MMRP.2019.00017

Sarasúa Berodia, Álvaro, Julián Urbano and Emilia Gómez. "Mapping by Observation: Building a User-tailored Music Conducting System from Spontaneous Movements." *Frontiers in Digital Humanities* 6 (February 2019). DOI: 10.3389/fdigh.2019.00003

Weigl, David M., and Kevin R. Page. "A Framework for Distributed Semantic Annotation of Musical Score: 'Take it to the Bridge!'" *Proceedings of the 18th International Society for Music Information Retrieval Conference*, Suzhou, China (October 2017): 221–28.

Weigl, David M., David Lewis et al. "On Providing Semantic Alignment and Unified Access to Music Library Metadata." *International Journal on Digital Libraries* 20, 1 (August 2019): 25–47. DOI: 10.1007/s00799-017-0223-9

Weigl, David M., Deren E. Kudeki et al. "Combine or Connect: Practical Experiences Querying Library Linked Data." *Proceedings of the Association for Information Science and Technology* 56, 1 (October 2019): 296–305. DOI: 10. 1002/pra2.24

Weigl, David M., Werner Goebl et al. "Interweaving and Enriching Digital Music Collections for Scholarship, Performance, and Enjoyment." *Proceedings of the 6th International Conference on Digital Libraries for Musicology*, The Hague, Netherlands (November 2019): 84–88. DOI: 10.1145/3358664.33586 66

Wilkinson, Mark D., et al. "The FAIR Guiding Principles for Scientific Data Management and Stewardship." *Scientific data* 3 (March 2016). DOI: 10.103 8/sdata.2016.18

Online Sources (last accessed 16 April 2020)

Choral Public Domain Library. https://www.cpdl.org/wiki

"Clara Schumann 200." *MDW*. https://iwk.mdw.ac.at/trompa-clara

Dublin Core™ Meta Data Initiative. https://dublincore.org/specifications/dublin-core/dcmi-terms/

"German Music Archive." *Deutsche Nationalbibliothek*. https://www.dnb.de/EN/Ueber-uns/DMA/dma_node.html

IMSLP Petrucci Music Library. https://imslp.org

JSON-LD 1.1. https://www.w3.org/TR/json-ld/

Linked Data Platform 1.0. https://www.w3.org/TR/ldp/

MusicBrainz. https://musicbrainz.org

Muziekweb de muziekbibliotheek van Nederland. https://www.muziekweb.eu
PROV-O: The PROV Ontology. http://www.w3.org/TR/prov-o/
Schema.org. https://schema.org
SKOS Simple Knowledge Organization System. http://www.w3.org/2004/02/skos
  /core.html
"Sounds." *British Library.* https://sounds.bl.uk
SPARQL 1.1 Query Language. https://www.w3.org/TR/sparql11-query/
Trompa. https://trompamusic.eu
Verovio: A Music Notation Engraving Library. https://www.verovio.org
Web Annotation Vocabulary. https://www.w3.org/TR/annotation-vocab/

A Few Notes on the Auditive Layer of the Film ★

Johann Lurf (Artist and filmmaker)

When I was asked to write about my film★for this publication, I immediately thought of sharing my considerations regarding the auditive level of the film. But first of all, I would like to give an overview of the work to readers who are unfamiliar with ★.

In 2009, as I watched the film *Stromboli* by Rossellini (1950) during a lecture in Harun Farocki's film class at the Academy of Fine Arts in Vienna, one moment struck me particularly. It was a shot of the clear starry night sky, which appeared to be more like a painting than a photographic reproduction, but in the context of the film the image could easily be accepted as realistic. I wondered how other films depict the starry night sky, so I started to research this image in cinema. My initial expectation was that most scenes of starry skies would be taken from stock footage, imagery that can be bought for use in film and reused over and over again, but instead I found that most starry night sky shots in films are unique. My second assumption was that I could determine on the basis of the constellations if the scene shows a view from the Southern or the Northern Hemisphere, thus revealing the shooting location and maybe even the time of the year, as we see a different sector of the starry sky in different seasons. But I was wrong again. Most starry skies in feature film history actually show an entirely made-up formation of stars—or should I say random white dots on a dark background.

In the context of a narrative film, an obviously constructed starscape is usually accepted by the audience and understood as given or even real. So I focused more on the methods of the filmmakers, on how they show clear starry skies and which audio elements are used in the soundtrack when we see stars, and how this has changed over the decades.

My 2017 film ★ compiles a large number of these scenes in chronological order of their first appearance. The film does not alter the image, duration, or speed of the scene and keeps the soundtrack intact, enabling us to travel through perceptions of space and clear night skies in cinema over the course of more than a century. The length of each scene is the same as it was in the film it was taken from. To enable comparison of the shots with each other, no object other than stars is shown; when something else enters the frame, the sequence ends and we jump to the next scene.

With this method, the soundtrack proves to be especially revealing, although the segments rarely consist of complete scenes. We hear mostly fragments of dialogue, sentences, or even words, and only parts of musical arrangements and sound effects. Despite the limited time we have to listen to these sound snippets in ★, we can apprehend a lot from the acoustic information provided. Voices can reveal within a split second the emotional state, the approximate age and gender, as well as the intention of the speaker, even in a language unfamiliar to the listener. Languages, dialects, and intonation changes a great deal from decade to decade. We can hear, in the 1930s for example, how choruses sing to the starry skies, expressing the wish for mankind to unite, while in the 1950s more sinister voices convey invisible threats coming from outside. Both decades are strongly influenced by the politics of their times and carry a male, authoritarian tone. The '60s become more playful, especially in the use of music, as the influence of contemporary and pop music increases. Nonetheless, we hear that orchestral arrangements remain predominant in film music. While working on this project, it surprised me that it took until the 1980s for more colloquial language to appears in films, after many years of methodical or formally pronounced dialogue.

I decided not to subtitle my searched-footage-film so that we can experience the excerpts as intended by the filmmakers who created them, and not by the foreign-language audience. Apart from that, the subtitles would draw attention away from the images and sounds and toward the language, or even toward the content of the language or translation. Adding subtitles would result in a reading exercise instead of a sensual experience; the absence of text allows us to focus on the complexity of the sound. The film's title, ★, was chosen to avoid selecting a main language for the film, as the starry skies are universal, and the concept is not bound to any geographical region. In spoken language, I call the film 'Starfilm' in English and 'Sternfilm' in German, but any language may use its own words to name the film.

Viewers are at times overwhelmed by the amount of starry skies but gain a broad insight into how this filmic element is used and the strong emotional effects it has on us. The film gives us an overview, and we gain a better understanding of space in cinema. Each viewer brings her or his personal experience, knowledge, and state of mind to the theater, which results in a vast variety of perceptions. After the screening of my film at the opening of the *Music–Media–History* conference in March 2019, I was able to learn more about the perspective of musicologists on my film as well as methods of analyzing moving images and sounds. I see★as artistic research, but there are elements in it which relate to academic inquiry, especially the field of media history.

After working on the film for some time, I understood that this chronological compilation also show-cases the history of sound in cinema. It starts with the silent film era and then proceeds to the early 1930s, when synchronous sound was added to the moving images, revolutionizing cinema with optical soundtracks—in mono, of course. Soon after, we hear a notable excerpt from Disney's 1940 film *Fantasia*, which uses an early stereo format called Fantasound, which was only used for this film. Since 1955, 6-track magnetic sound has been used in large format 70mm film, which improved the sound quality in cinema significantly, while adding a spatial dimension through the use of multiple speakers behind the screen and a separate surround channel around the audience. The introduction of subwoofers in theaters only began in 1974. Since then, low frequencies have become part of the soundscape of cinemas and are an essential characteristic of many films. Dolby refined multichannel analogue optical sound in cinema over the course of many years before introducing the first digital soundtrack in 1992. The number of audio channels in cinemas has since multiplied but the basics remain constant: the center speaker behind the screen reproduces voices, and music is mostly played from the speakers on the side and rear walls. To remain as close as possible to the original perception of the audience in their respective decade, I incorporated the sound channel layouts of each scene as faithfully as possible in my film. The experience of this film became a journey through the technological developments in cinema. This led to a unique screening at the Cinemateket Copenhagen in 2018, when the Danish Film Institute asked an experienced silent film piano player to provide accompaniment for the silent film excerpts at the beginning of★. The difference in the impression created by these first few minutes was astounding, and the music smoothly blended the scenes together.

Given the chronological framework of this project, the question of how to end the film came up, and I realized that it would be most appropriate for the project to expand in the future. I started to show the film when it reached a duration of 90 minutes, as this is often considered a standard length for a feature film. Since then, I add scenes every year from contemporary films as well as newly found excerpts from the past and arrange them according to the timeline. This expands the film not only from its end, but also fills in gaps in the history of cinema as my research continues. I cannot foresee what will happen, but I am very curious about the future scenes that will find their way into in the next edition of my film and the themes they will bring with them—I can't wait to find out!

Related Link (last accessed 16 April 2020)

http://johannlurf.net/de/

Afterword

John Corner (University of Leeds)

I have benefited greatly from reading this collection of essays variously exploring, in relation to specific projects, how the new possibilities of digital humanities research can enhance cultural historiography. The inquiry into the production, forms, and consequences of cultural practice—here, practices concerning the positioning and functions of music with film—is clearly entering a new phase of both expanded and intensified endeavor. I am struck by the way in which the chapters show both a highly detailed specificity in pursuing their analyses of particular contexts and works and, at the same time, a broader connection both to more general cultural patterns and to interdisciplinary perspectives for investigating these. This is not, of course, a straight contrast between the specific and the general since, as many writers here bring out well, expanded historical 'surveillance' and searchability at the general level brings out more sharply interconnections, parallels and precedents at the level of specific examples. So the increased informational range of the broad 'map' leads to enhanced engagement with points upon it or, to put it temporally, with moments within the historical flows which it charts.

In this short note of comment, I want to reflect upon what I have read, indicating whilst doing so some of the directions towards which it points future research. I shall carry out the task by the use of five subheadings, although I am aware that the presence of strong interconnections rather than separation in respect of much of this work means that some of what I say might be seen to belong under more than one heading.

Maps

'Mapping' is one of the key activities made possible by the application of digital technology and associated research methods. It provides the researcher with a much greater range of data than before, including from sources that might previously not have been included but whose availability in digital forms (such as on websites and within television archives, for instance) now enables access and analysis. This massively expanded overview allows the (continuous) ordering of material into chronologies, classifications, and patterns, permitting research both to 'read inwards' and to 'read outwards.' 'Reading inwards,' as I have already suggested, involves using data resources to identify and assess the significance of elements and combinations in artefacts and production settings that only become fully apparent when put within a more extensive body of accessible material and its surrounding contexts and timeframes. 'Reading outwards' involves taking the products of localized analysis and adding them to the broader informational repository, where they can form part of the data used in tracing more general patterns and trends, data which will be subsequently used in the conducting of further acts of local analysis.

Forms

All of the research collected here variously concerns media forms, mostly the location of music within the audiovisual contexts of films in what is often a varied and dense context of intermediality. In part, therefore, it attempts to develop further our understanding of the varieties of aesthetic organization not only of musical examples themselves but of their location and framing within broader schemes of sound design developed in relation to the broader aesthetic and social purposes at work in filmmaking. It identifies the significant figures and tropes at work, patterns of conventional meaning and association, as part of its close scrutiny of formal structures and style. What horizontal and vertical relations are established? In what ways does repetition feature? Such analysis is carried out by reference to the expansive comparative materials which research can now assemble so that the aesthetic vocabularies become more visible in the character and function of their local application (another example of the movement between 'reading outwards' and 'reading inwards' noted above). At points, issues of generic transformation are raised as work initially developed for one medium is made active within the terms of another. Indeed, the use of preexisting music as soundtrack or the use of music played within a film (via recording or diegetic performance) necessarily involves new kinds of fusion, incorporating but also modifying and expanding through its intermediality the core musical aesthetic itself. There is also suggestive consideration, warranting further inquiry, of the distinctive 'music of the voice,' the modes of speech, particularly nondramatic recorded speech, which are a powerful part both of the aesthetics of sound and our shifting historical sense of social and individual identities. The factors at work here, in forms, meanings and feelings, were decisively shaped and expanded by radio talk, reworked by television and are now being further changed by web usage.

Histories

Much of the work is concerned with aspects of history, both the history of forms and expressive patterns and also the historical knowledge and feelings which specific forms and usages at work in the films seem variously to signify and bring to consciousness. Apprehensions of the historical thus appear in many of the chapters. They are framed both in terms of academic inquiry, what the data and previous research tells us about specific people, events, and the deployment of artistic works across a chronology but also, more obliquely, in terms of the imaginative response, the 'sense of the historical,' which listeners and viewers might generate from given films. This sense can be seen as in part phenomenological in that it is a product of particular encounters within the structure of an aesthetic experience (see below) rather than an analytic practice. As a form of historical imaginary, it can be organized for experiencing around a particular historical event, a place, a specific person (e.g. composer), or be more generally commemorative (e.g. a 'period') in character. Such organization will bring information to bear but, with its mythic richness and resonance, this information will not simply convert into 'knowledge' but also be an important contributor to the mood in which sounds are heard and therefore in which the broader audiovisual pattern is interpreted, often via schemata and frames of which the interpreter is unaware.

Audiovisual Experience

I have noted how many of the studies connect with the kinds of audiovisual experience, and their yield of information and feeling, that given strategies of sound design encourage. This is where questions of consequences are raised,

both for the appreciation of films and music and for the ways in which the productions, however modestly, combine with other factors in the construction
of political and social perspectives, often embedded in perceptions of history,
and subject themselves to almost constant revision and change. Of course, the
subjectivities which people bring to their viewing and listening are diverse,
resourced from what are sometimes very different bodies of knowledge and
previous experience. Speculating too freely about what is 'taken' from what
is seen and heard can be hazardous, although close textual analysis continues to offer a guide to the kind of routes and destinations which listeners
and viewers are offered. Although it is rightly out of the frame for many of
the research priorities at work here, subsequent developments might expand
into limited kinds of empirical viewer study in order to plot more precisely
the range of pleasures and understandings that specific works generate. This
would almost certainly inform more refined analytic accounts both of active
aesthetics and of the significance of thematic variations.

Protocols of Analysis

This is a rather clumsy phrase but it covers the wide range of thoughtful attempts here to examine the best procedures and sequences of investigation
to pursue, along with some of the risks, analytic and ethical, to which certain routes may expose themselves. At stages, research is often necessarily
strongly quantitative in character, requiring a tight statistical discipline. At
other stages, it is qualitative in ways that draw on a range of approaches from
musicology, film and new media studies as well as on historical scholarship,
including that which places an emphasis on forms of narrative. The idea of
interdisciplinarity is relevant here of course. This has been widely used as a
descriptor of research ambitions in media, communication and cultural studies but demonstrating it in practice, in relation to particular analytic tasks,
has often proved a challenge. What elements are to be taken from what disciplinary sources and how are they to be combined to produce not only co-
herence but improved understanding? Such questions make for a tough investigative agenda but many of the chapters show the potential for this to be
productive if there is a clear sense of research priorities and a proper recognition of the way in which the scope of argument relates not only to the quality
of analysis but also to the strength of available evidence.

I will conclude by noting, first of all, how my own longstanding involvement in media research—including media history, the analysis of production practices, media forms, and audience studies—has informed my appreciation of the work assembled here. More specifically, an interest in the use of music within documentary film and television brings me very close to many of its key themes.[1]

Continued dialogue across the relevant disciplines, aided by conferencing and journal activities, will be important in engaging further with questions of approach, questions which are bound to involve dispute as well as agreement. This is a necessary part of interdisciplinarity, which is best seen as *dynamic*, involving continuous exchange and modification of its terms, rather than as *static*, a somehow *already achieved* integration. Comparative studies, possibly extending to investigate the responses of 'ordinary' media users, will help further to identify the strengths and limitations of particular conceptualizations. We can all readily agree that the broadest access to relevant data by the international research community will help both in the assessment and impact of published work and in the development of new projects. We can also agree that the forms taken by published work need to go beyond conventional academic writing, however useful that may continue to be, and to connect with the full possibilities of the digital culture upon which much investigation is now based.

---

1   My first attempt at looking at the general relationships and variations involved here was in the article "Sounds Real: Music and Documentary." *Popular Music* 21, 3 (2002): 357–66. I developed this further in relation to diverse examples in Chapter 8 "Music and the Aesthetics of the Recorded World" of Holly Rogers's, ed. *Music and Sound in Documentary Film*. London: Routledge, 2014. My most recent involvement in related questions was as coeditor with Geoffrey Cox of the collection *Soundings: Documentary Film and the Listening Experience*. Huddersfield: Huddersfield Univ. Press, 2018. This collection, exploring a range both of conventional and experimental applications of music and sound, including aspects of sound design, is free to download at https://unipress. hud.ac.uk/plugins/books/17/ (last accessed 16 April 2020)

List of Contributors

Elias Berner studied musicology at the University of Vienna. He is currently part of the Telling Sounds research project at the University of Music and Performing Arts in Vienna. He was awarded a Junior Fellowship (2015–2017) at the IFK (Internationales Forschungszentrum Kulturwissenschaft) for his PhD Project "Memory, Provocation, Consolation: Music in Films about the Shoah."

John Corner is Visiting Professor in Media and Communication at the University of Leeds and Professor Emeritus of the University of Liverpool. Since the 1970s he has published widely on media history, documentary, political communication, and cultural analysis in international journals and in books. His monographs include "Television Form and Public Address" (1995), "The Art of Record" (1996), "Critical Ideas in Television Studies" (1999), and "Theorising Media" (2014).

Franziska Diehr studied museology (BA) and information science (MA) in Berlin. She graduated in 2013 with a thesis on ontology-based data modelling for the description of scientific collections. Since then she has been working as a research associate in several humanities projects, where she designs digital applications and developes project-specific data models. Ms. Diehr is currently part of the Temporal Communities: Doing Literature in a Global Perspective cluster at Freie Universität Berlin, Germany. Her research focuses on knowledge representation, especially with respect to the challenges of dealing with vague and uncertain information and the application of graph technologies in the digital humanities.

Werner Goebl is Associate Professor for Music Acoustics and Performance Science at the Department of Music Acoustics-Wiener Klangstil (IWK) at the University of Music and Performing Arts, Vienna. His current research projects include motion and eye gaze analysis in musical ensemble interaction (funded by the Togetherness in Music Ensembles Austrian Science Fund FWF), piano action acoustics and ergonomics (funded by the Austrian Research Promotion Agency FFG), and music informatics and digital approaches to cultural heritage, funded by the European Commission (TROMPA—Towards Richer Online Music Public-domain Archives).

Rasmus Greiner is Researcher (Senior Lecturer) in film studies at Bremen University, Germany. He is currently leading Audio-visual Histospheres, a three-year BMBF-funded research project. He is founder and general editor of the open access journal "Research in Film and History." His areas of research comprise audiovisual production of history, global film culture, war movies, genre studies, and film aesthetics.

Birgit Haberpeuntner is a teaching and research assistant at the Theater, Film and Media Studies Department at University of Vienna, and currently works as a freelance translator. From 2015–2017, she was a Junior Fellow at the International Research Center for Cultural Studies. Before that, Haberpeuntner studied English and American Studies, Translation Studies, and Theater, Film, and Media Studies at the University of Vienna, at Concordia University in Montreal and Columbia University in New York. Her research focuses on media/cultural theory, postcolonial studies, Walter Benjamin, and critical theory.

Hanns-Werner Heister. Publications on the methodology of musicology; on the aesthetics, sociology, history, and anthropology of music (in particular music and human perception, the origins of language and art); on political and popular music, new music, jazz; on the music and musical culture of Nazism; on the resistance movement and exile; on the aesthetics and history of music theater; media/technology and institutions of music culture; music analysis; music and other arts, psychoanalysis, play, math, cybernetics, fuzzy logic; and on gardening. "The Concert. Theory of a Cultural Form," 2 vols. (1983), "Jazz" (1983), "Of the Universal New. Analyses of Engaged Music: Dessau, Eisler, Ginastera, Hartmann" (2006), "In/Finity. Encountering György Ligeti" (2008), "Background Sound Art" (2009), "Heinz Gellrich – Times, Paths, Signs" (2014).

Klaus Illmayer is researcher at the Austrian Centre for Digital Humanities and Cultural Heritage (ACDH-CH) at the Austrian Academy of Sciences. He is involved with the SSHOC (Social Sciences and Humanities Open Cloud) project, part of the European Union's Horizon 2020 project. He received a PhD in Theatre, Film, and Media Studies from the University of Vienna. His research focuses on the intersection of digital humanities (DH) and theater studies, the application of semantic Web technologies in DH, and the development of research infrastructures.

Julia Jaklin is currently writing her master's thesis at the University of Vienna in the field of musicology. Since December 2018 she has been part of the Telling Sounds project at the University of Music and Performing Arts, Vienna (mdw). She also studies computer science at Vienna University of Technology (TU Wien). Her fields of research are digital musicology and cultural studies in musicology with a focus on music and identity.

Johann Lurf was educated at the Academy of Fine Arts in Vienna. He is known as an experimental filmmaker who cannot easily be subsumed under one style or category. His works examine various modes of vision and motion, but his more formally oriented films are always accompanied by strong narratives that, however subtly, examine society, codes, norms, perception, and the history and development of cinema itself. Dabbling in short and feature-length films, analog and digital formats, mixing found footage with his own, Lurf has made a wide variety of cinematic works, many of which have been featured in film festivals and cultural institutions, notably the Sundance Film Festival, the Anthology Film Archives and LACMA.

Winfried Pauleit is Professor of Film Studies and head of the ZeMKI research Lab Film, Media Art and Popular Culture at the University of Bremen. He is currently task leader of the EU Horizon 2020 project Visual History of the Holocaust: Rethinking Curation in the Digital Age (2019–2022). He is academic director of the annual International Bremen Film Conference and coeditor of its annual book series. He is also the editor of two peer-reviewed open access journals: "Research in Film and History" (founded in 2018) and "Nach dem Film" (founded in 1999). His publications include: "Sonic Icons. Prominent Moments of Cinematic Self-Reflexivity." In: Research in Film and History (New Approaches, 2018); https://film-history.org/approaches/sonic-icons.

Matej Santi studied violin and musicology. After graduating with a degree in violin pedagogy from the University of Music and Performing Arts in Vienna, he taught violin and was active as a musician. He then obtained his PhD in musicology at the same institution, concentrating on central European history and cultural studies. He is a music history lecturer at the University of Music and Performing Arts, Vienna. Since 2017 he has been part of the Telling Sounds project as a postdoctoral researcher. His publications deal with topics ranging from the 17th to the 21st centuries.

Christian Schwarzenegger is a researcher and lecturer (Akademischer Rat) at the Department of Media, Knowledge and Communication at the University of Augsburg, Germany. During the 2020/21 winter term he is Visiting Professor at the Department of Communication Studies at the University of Salzburg, Austria. His research interests include mediatization and the impact of digital transformation with an emphasis on everyday life and participation in digital society, as well as historical communication research and media memory studies.

Derek B. Scott is Professor of Critical Musicology at the University of Leeds and researches music and cultural history. His books include "Sounds of the Metropolis: The 19th-Century Popular Music Revolution in London, New York, Paris, and Vienna" (2008) and "The Ashgate Research Companion to Popular Musicology" (2009). The research for his most recent book, "German Operetta on Broadway and in New York, 1900–1940" (2019), was funded by the European Research Council.

Cornelia Szabó-Knotik is Associate Professor of Musicology at the University of Music and Performing Arts Vienna, retired. Her main interests lie in the field of media studies and contemporary music history, focusing on the aesthetic content as well as the social and cultural importance of music and on the implications of digitalization and audiovisual media for constructing the history of music today, specifically in the context of the ongoing Telling Sounds research project.

David Morrison Weigl is an interdisciplinary researcher in cultural and social informatics, with a focus on music informatics and Linked Data and semantic Web applications. After completing his doctoral studies at the School of Information Studies, McGill University, and at Montreal's Centre for Interdisciplinary Research in Music Media and Technology (CIRMMT), he conducted postdoctoral research at the Oxford e-Research Centre, University of Oxford, where he investigated the application of novel digital technologies and workflows in music industry and music scholarship contexts. There, he contributed as lead developer on Music Encoding and Linked Data (MELD), a semantic framework supporting distributed semantic digital music notation.

At the Dept. of Music Acoustics-Wiener Klangstil, University of Music and Performing Arts Vienna (mdw), he has extended his work in this direction to the interlinking and enrichment of publicly licensed music resources on the Web as Data Officer of the EU Horizon 2020 TROMPA project, Towards Richer Online Music Public-domain Archives.

Emile Wennekes is Chair Professor of Musicology: Music and Media at the University of Utrecht. From 2006–2011 he was the first Head of School of the Media and Culture Studies department. In 2017, his chair was modified from Musicology: Post-1800 Music History into Musicology: Music and Media, now also officially embracing his main field of research. Wennekes has published on a broad range of subjects which include a biography of the conductor Bernard Haitink (co-published with historian Prof. Dr. Jan Bank), the reception of the music of Bach, Liszt, Mahler and Mozart, music within Second Life, conductor films, Vitaphone shorts, and contemporary music in the Netherlands.